Bobby Robson

The Ultimate Patriot

BOB HARRIS

Bobby Robson

The Ultimate Patriot

BOB HARRIS

First published as a hardback by deCoubertin Books Ltd in 2020.

First Edition

deCoubertin Books, 49 Jamaica Street, Baltic Triangle, Liverpool, L1 0AH.

www.decoubertin.co.uk

ISBN: 978-1-9162784-1-7

A CIP catalogue record for this book is available from the British Library.

Cover design by Leslie Priestley.

Typeset by Thomas Regan | Milkyone Creative.

*Bobby loved children and they reciprocated,
so I would like to dedicate this book to my grandchildren,
the twins Sean and Lydia, alongside Lucy and Oscar.*

FOREWORD

BY GARY LINEKER

I HAVE NO DOUBT THAT WITHOUT THE INFLUENCE of Bobby Robson I would not have had the life I have enjoyed.

He was special to me from the moment he first welcomed me into the England squad in 1984. I remember it well. There were a few injuries and I received a phone call from my club manager Gordon Milne at Leicester City who told me to grab a toothbrush, pick up my boots from the ground and drive to Wrexham to join the squad to play Wales two days later.

I admit I was as nervous as a kitten when I pulled into the hotel car park and was even more so when I stepped into the foyer to be surrounded by England players. Then the manager appeared, put an arm around me and warmly introduced me to my new teammates who were, to me at that stage of my career, superstars.

It was that unbelievable warmth which struck me immediately and stayed with me through the years right up until and beyond his memorable farewell in a packed Durham Cathedral 25 years later.

That first introduction also showed me the quirky side of the man for, on the night of the game, he looked across at me after about 70 minutes and shouted for Garth to get warmed up. It took a few moments to realise it was me he was talking to and it was my first experience of him and his now infamous problem remembering names.

I didn't get on that night but I made my debut later when I replaced Glenn Hoddle as a substitute against Scotland at Hampden Park, making my full debut the following season against the Irish.

Typically, he put an arm round me and told me he had a lot of faith in me, to do what I did every week and to enjoy myself. There were no long lectures about tactics or what I should do, just to go and enjoy myself. I scored and became a regular with most of my 80 caps played under Bobby.

I, and the rest of the England team, wanted to play for the man. He understood his players and the game and while many would say that his coaching was basic, his man management was superb. He knew when to pat you on the back and when to kick you up the backside and he always seemed to squeeze the best out of his players, as he showed around the world with all the trophies he won.

Apart from his unswerving loyalty, his infectious enthusiasm for the game captivated all of us. He was an honourable man who was loved by all of his players, even those who were on the periphery of the team.

Players are, by nature, selfish but every one of the squad in Italy was behind him to a man, especially when he was hounded by the media over the announcement that he was joining PSV after the World Cup. Some of the rubbish that was written was beyond belief, but it only helped in pulling the squad even closer together and becoming more determined than ever to do well.

He was so close to getting the rewards he deserved when we went out on penalties to Germany in the semi final. It was all a matter of inches and had Chris Waddle's shot that hit the post been half an inch the other way it would have left me with a tap in for what would have been the winner.

We would have been strong favourites in a final against Argentina who had shot their bolt with suspensions and injuries and it left us wondering what might have been. There were no regrets... but if only!

We were a much better side in 1990 than in 1986. We were not blessed with the best of luck in either tournament but we lost on penalties to a very good side. I watched a replay of the match recently in the company of Jurgen Klinsmann for a television programme and we agreed that both teams had played well and that it could have gone either way.

The levels of expectation in those days were ridiculous and we suffered with some unfair press but Bobby emerged from the tournament with his reputation hugely enhanced. He was seen throughout the world as a gentleman, revered by his own players and respected by the opposition.

It was, however, different in those days and it was sometimes easier to pick the journalists who would travel with us than it was to pick the team and only the odd foreign journalist or camera would intrude. It began to change in Italy and now it is different times with journalists and television cameras from all over the globe covering every England game.

In those days I would watch the journalists as they wrote their intros and put together their stories because I knew even then that I would like to go into the media when I finished playing rather than managing.

I was also interested in the way Bob Harris acted as a go between with Bobby and the players and it is something I have done myself with certain managers and players - without naming names!

What I learned was that we ALL wanted England to do well and as a television presenter I still want England to win every match just as much as when I played. I don't want to be a cheerleader but I am English through and through and some of the proudest moments of my life came representing my country.

The vast majority, perhaps all, of the players who represent the Three Lions feel that way and it was never simply a case of motivation. Bobby realised that it was just as important to manage the nerves, encouraging his players to be calm and confident, as it was motivating them.

He was brilliant at saying the right thing at the right time and we all trusted him because we all liked him so much. He exuded likeability; he was so infectious about everything. I recall being with him for a television programme at St. James' Park and he insisted on showing me round the ground and spent a good five minutes telling me about the big wooden double doors, where the wood came from and what they stood for. Ever the enthusiast.

Football is, by nature, tribal but Bobby eventually transcended that and was loved by everyone in the game. It was not how many trophies he had won but how he was as a human being and they didn't come much better.

His reputation and popularity grew when he finished his managerial career, as he battled with illness and channelled his efforts into his cancer charity in the North East.

In the end he had the adoration of the entire country, not just the football bloc, but everyone. A man no one had a bad word for.

Gary Lineker, June 2020

INTRODUCTION

I WAS ONLY TOO AWARE THAT THE EXTRA TIME THE brilliant surgeons had gifted to my friend Bobby Robson was almost over. The final whistle was due and no one knew better than this gentle, big hearted man when I visited him for the final time in his mini-castle in Durham, he shared with his wife Elsie.

It was June 2009. As a non driver I was fortunate that another close friend of many years, Paul Clark, a hotelier who had met Bobby on a trip to the Caribbean, volunteered to ferry me from one end of the country in the south east to Bobby's home in the north east.

We had cleared the way with Elsie and told her not to worry about food, that we would take a hamper to share lunch with them in their home and clear away the debris afterwards.

I admit I had to steel myself as we approached his home. Tears were close because I was more than aware that this would almost certainly be the last time I would share the company of a man who I had written five books with, covering his life, his times, his many high spots, the depths of sporting despair as well as his passionate love of his country and the worldwide game of football.

Memories crowded in of the many hours and days we had spent talking about the trips around the globe, the sights seen and the people met.

We were always an odd couple; a journalist and a football manager, not a happy mix, especially these days, but we came from a different, more forgiving and relaxed era in the game when the fans were on the terraces and not in your ear, the managers in their offices and the football writers in the press box. There was no social media to spit venom and uncertainty into a relationship – that was left to one or two of the red top newspapers – and we were able to have dinner in a restaurant or a drink in a bar without being abused and verbally assaulted. In fact, no one was more welcoming to the hesitant punter who wanted an autograph or just to shake hands so that he could tell his mates.

We even managed to get away on a few trips on our own to the West Indies and Spain, courtesy of another great mate Joe Sanchez and his private aircraft. We both became so used to the tape recorder, pen and notebook as we went headlong into another book, that we scarcely noticed.

Bobby, of course, made another difficult moment easier. Despite the creeping disease which was invading his body, he was his usual smiling cheerful self and Elsie also relaxed into the moment before leaving the men after our *al fresco* lunch to talk about… what else but football.

Paul just sat and listened – not his usual posture in a conversation whatever the subject – and then we were both enchanted as Bobby, in his wheelchair, gave us a personal tour of his gallery of signed photographs of the good and the great, not only of football but the world in general. Royalty, politicians, actors, film stars, all crowded in on the gentle world of the benign, smiling Bobby Robson.

Quite right, too. He was not only the man of the people but respected by all who came in contact with him, from the richest – and he knew a few of those – to the meekest. I came across precious few that expressed any dislike of the man other than the odd deskbound sports sub who had never met him.

As we drove away after our lunch I was enveloped in sadness, for I knew I had seen him for the final time but, as Paul reflected on the day, the photographs and the experience he had just enjoyed, I realised that tears would be misplaced and selfish. My memories of a truly great man of sport should, and would be, about the joy he had given me and the many people he came into contact with.

Now, more than a decade on, I remember him with a smile and more than just a fleeting memory. Never mind that he was a manager and I was a hack. We were mates.

+++

SIR BOBBY ROBSON WAS AS NICE A PERSON YOU could ever wish to meet. Polite, well mannered, humble and massively patriotic. In his working life, nothing could ever surpass his eight years as manager of England. So much so that when the vacancy rose again after Graham Taylor's failure to take England to the next level he offered to do it again – for nothing, until a full-time replacement could be found. What is more he meant it.

Not only was he a good person, he was also a huge success as a player, coach and manager, achieving what no manager had done since Sir Alf Ramsey won the World Cup in 1966, taking his beloved country to the semi-finals of the global competition. It would be another 28 years before another likable, respected figure, Gareth Southgate, also unexpectedly took England to within a game of the World Cup final in Moscow.

The massive difference between the two was that Southgate had managed to bring the press back to the side of the England manager. Without deviating from their job, they backed the quietly spoken, waistcoat wearing manager, criticising only when criticism was due. It worked at every level.

How different this was to Italia 90! This delightful Geordie who adored football above everything, other than his family, was totally bewildered as he found himself caught up in a tabloid war that was nothing to do with him, as the long established left wing red top, the *Daily Mirror*, fought for its status against the growing, burgeoning *Sun*, a paper prepared to thumb its nose at everyone and everything in their bid to steal a reader, or a thousand, from their great rival. It was not only the media Robson had to battle but also his bosses at the Football Association, some of whom failed to back him, and sometimes even the Wembley crowd, who occasionally believed what they read in the red tops.

Bobby's father, Phillip, was in the crowd at Wembley when England played Russia in 1984 and witnessed hate filled fans spitting at his son as he led the team out of the tunnel and onto the pitch. His mackintosh was covered in spittle but, as was so often the case, he refused to react and continued his walk with his usual dignity and head held high.

He sailed through all of the rubbish thrown at him, both physically and metaphorically, with great decorum, rarely taking his eye off the ball, culminating in the challenge for the World Cup in Italy in 1990, one of the great World Cups in a country steeped in football tradition and passion for the sometimes not so beautiful game.

I was privileged to witness his trials first hand, every one of his international matches, the tribulations and near success, from just about as close a vantage point as a journalist could get. His success was not in winning a trophy for his country but winning over his players, the media, the English public and, eventually, the football world.

We were writing one of our five books together at Italia 90 as I split my time covering England and the World Cup for the *Sunday Mirror*, while sitting with 'The Boss,' in his rare spare time, often on a daily basis to tape more information for the then current tome *Against the Odds* published by Stanley Paul.

Try and imagine my position in the middle of the brouhaha that surrounded England's growing bid to annexe the greatest sporting team trophy on the globe. A close friend, co-authoring an autobiography with him, while working as the newly appointed sports editor of the *Sunday Mirror*, one of those red tops embroiled in a tabloid sales war at the time. I had a foot in both camps and was in danger of being snapped in half as the chasm between the two warring parties grew exponentially in those early days.

But I had done it before, four years earlier when we compiled a World Cup Diary, often sitting on his hotel room balcony talking into a tape recorder in the balmy temperatures of Mexico, where you could almost feel the heat from the media gathered at the outdoor bar below his hotel room window.

Most people in sport – with just one or two exceptions – would have told me to keep my distance in the circumstances. Bobby didn't. He trusted me and I like to believe that through all his trouble and strife, I never once let him down and, at the same time, I did not cheat on my employers. That, he said, was why he wanted me by his side.

He proved it when he agreed to write another book based around the 1990 World Cup when the aggravation had been geared up several notches.

Yet, he would never have swapped his England experiences for anything else in this beautiful game of ours and, in fact, would have gone back to Lancaster Gate, the traditional home of the Football Association until they moved to the new Wembley in 2007 via a decade in Soho Square, at the drop of a hat.

It even superseded his beloved Newcastle United, the club he watched with his dad Philip as a football daft youngster, but who he overlooked when it became time to sign the professional forms as he went, instead, to Fulham where he developed as a player and a person alongside the likes of the first £100 a week professional footballer Johnny Haynes and future Chairman of the Professional Footballers' Association and television pundit in chief, Jimmy Hill.

Bobby was an outstanding footballer both with Fulham and with West Bromwich Albion, where he forged a lifelong partnership with his great mate and eventual England assistant Don Howe. The two were a perfect fit, often happy to disagree over football, and fight it out to a conclusion with a verbal discussion that would have made great radio or television.

Bobby used to cycle from his home in Handsworth Wood to the Hawthorns when he played for the Baggies and he remained a man of the people even when with the Football Association, regularly riding the Central Line to Lancaster Gate from Liverpool Street station, to the amazement of his fellow London Underground passengers.

Maybe it was the era in which he developed but Bobby was not just a man of the people but one of the people. He was down to earth, solid with no airs and graces whether it was riding his bike to training and games at West Brom or travelling on the underground.

There were no fancy cars; no sipping Cristal champagne in a roped off section of a fancy night club in the early hours of the morning;

no mingling with the pop stars and film stars, at least not until much later!

Even when his salary jumped as an international manager and then as the well paid servant of clubs like Barcelona and Porto he was still that same bloke from 'Up North'.

There were so many peaks and troughs during his reign and he was eventually forced into a position where he was levered by circumstance to announce his resignation from his beloved England job, even before stepping on the aircraft taking the team to Sardinia for the World Cup and even though he had a contract good for another year.

Italia 90 was more, much more, than Robson versus the press. It was an emotional roller coaster ride that saw England play through the tournament, gathering pace and winning friends with the likes of Paul Gascoigne, Gary Lineker, Terry Butcher and the rest, making their mark as England went unbeaten through the tournament until they were downed by the country's double bête noire – penalties and the Germans.

The only 'proper' defeat was in the soulless, pointless, third place play off against Italy. By then, who cared? Bobby did. He would have liked to have gone out on another win and survived the tournament without a single defeat. Terrible refereeing decisions, which dogged his eight years, dictated otherwise.

It was the end of an era for Bobby Robson and England, but far from the end of Bobby Robson, or Sir Bobby Robson, as he quickly became.

He was used to fighting battles all over the globe as his career took him to work in Holland, Portugal, Spain and the Republic of Ireland clashing swords with the cream of the coaches and the best players. But the final battle was one he could never win. Cancer. Even then, he battled the disease, which struck five times, and unselfishly used his illness for the good of others, setting up a charity which, to this day, raises a huge amount of money for a cancer charitable trust set up in his name in his native North East.

Shortly before his death I had the privilege of one last visit to his North East home for a picnic lunch in his kitchen as we talked over past times, surrounded by his mementoes and framed photographs of his lifetime in football.

He had one last task before that seemingly unquenchable spirit was finally exhausted. He attended a game in his honour and for his charity at St. James' Park and not only did he meet and greet all of the players who had given up their time and travelled from all points of the compass, he defied his doctors and insisted on being wheeled around the ground where he had stood as a kid, to acknowledge those who had come to say the fondest of farewells.

He passed on just five days later.

He was a friend like no other and this is his story from the eyes of an admirer, an occasional critic, and someone who will never forget a truly good man with a big heart who loved his country.

Bob Harris, June 2019

1

AS THE ENORMOUSLY SUCCESSFUL MANAGER OF Ipswich Town, Bobby Robson had little idea about the power of the press. In fact, Robson was actually mates with several of the country's top football writers, people like the late Steve Curry and Brian Scovell, and regularly welcomed them into 'his' club, at any time. The prospect of a press war between him and his friends was not a thought which would have crossed his mind. He got on well with them all, local and national. Ipswich were such a hospitable, friendly club, and the journalists, myself included, all enjoyed the short trip on the train from Liverpool Street station and the brief walk from Ipswich station to Portman Road.

It wasn't like it is now in the Premier League, where you encounter hundreds of staff, lots of closed doors and press officers at every turn. There was a plesant press room with finger food available before the game and a small bar which served a beer or a soft drink afterwards. Better still, for the regulars from Fleet Street, was the invite into the boardroom where the famous brothers, aristocratic brewery owners and directors John and Patrick Cobbold played host, often to the embarrassment of their manager if it had been a particularly bad or controversial day.

There was almost no pressure on their manager from the major shareholders, no matter the results and the famous quote, repeated many times and in many versions, was that the only trouble at the club was when they ran out of Sancerre in the board room – something I personally never saw happen.

I suspect that the social side and the interaction with football people from the boardroom through to the dressing room mattered more to these delightful brothers than what went on outside on the pitch. Indeed, one of Bobby's favourite stories from his time in the game came after his Ipswich side were thrashed by Leicester. Chairman John Cobbold was at Filbert Street for the match and collared his manager straight after the game, praising him for the innovative football his team had played. What Cobbold had not realised was that Ipswich, as the visitors, had played in their yellow away kit, while Leicester City were the ones wearing blue.

Bobby had a relationship with his board and the owners that I never saw matched at any other football club at any level in more than half a century of covering the great game. Liverpool was the only club to come close during the halcyon years of Bill Shankly, Bob Paisley and Joe Fagan. Even then, Shankly was a prickly character who would sometimes clash with the board, while his replacement Paisley was nearly sacked in 1981 after a poor run of results, only for things to change in spectacular fashion. At Portman Road, Bobby was never looking over his shoulder in the same way.

So it was something of a culture shock when he departed the homely atmosphere in Suffolk to become manager of England, following in the footsteps of another former Ipswich boss, Sir Alf Ramsey, forever enshrined in our football history as the only man to lead England to a World Cup victory. Through no fault of his own, Bobby was to quickly discover he wasn't as popular as he thought.

Far from being backed by Sir Alf, he found himself the unexpected target of the former England boss, a man he had cheered from the terraces of Wembley Stadium as a supporter. Sir Alf did an occasional column for the *Daily Mirror*, ghosted by Nigel Clarke, and it was always vitriolic when Robson was the subject. Nigel himself was set up by his sports editor to be the arch critic of the England manager, and he loved the attendant glory of headlines like 'FOR THE LOVE OF GOD, GO', and, after a 1-1 draw in Saudi Arabia, 'FOR THE LOVE OF ALLAH, GO'.

Sir Alf was not alone. Throughout Robson's England reign there was a long list of former England greats, led by ex-skipper Emlyn Hughes, and some not so greats willing to put the boot in as often as a cheque came their way. Give the circulation war waging at the time between the *Daily Mirror* and the *Sun*, those cheques were not short in supply. Many ex-players, who had not earned enough to be set for life, could not resist the tabloid temptations, and Robson and England subsequently found themselves in the middle of a storm.

While most of the experts in the game applauded the appointment of a manager who had taken Ipswich back to the heights, persistently chasing the First Division title and beating the odds-on favourites Arsenal to win the FA Cup in 1978 and then going on to win the UEFA Cup three years later on a limited budget, the tabloid newspapers were slightly less enamoured. They had put their considerable weight behind the controversial and very quotable Brian Clough –

a fellow overachiever with Derby County and Nottingham Forest – as Ron Greenwood's successor and were not best pleased when their choice was overlooked, despite their campaign for his appointment.

Clough frightened the staid FA to death, often relishing a scathing comment aimed in their general direction, regardless of who it was within his sights. He was a real character and much too much for the inner sanctum at Lancaster Gate. Robson, on the other hand, was seen as a safe and sensible choice, someone who would not attract such intensive coverage – at least so they thought.

They had not accounted for the Red Top War and the abuse Robson would receive, often from his peers in the game. Even though that hurt Robson, they were generally able to cope with such background noise. However, it was a sensational story that broke as England were preparing for the 1990 World Cup in Italy that they found harder to deal with, as it was completely out of their realm.

The bombshell came during the 1989/90 season. It was, at the time, a typical tabloid story, revealing a so-called affair with a red head many years before. Her name was Janet Rush and her sleazy revelations were just the fodder that the *Sun* editor Kelvin McKenzie loved for his front page. The 'splash' was justified by the 'fact' that she was soon to write her salacious memoirs.

Speaking as a former editor, sports editor and writer, the story was at most worthy of an inside splash, though the more you explored the more you wondered whether it was worth a story at all. I have looked through the records and can no find no trace of the book ever being published at all, which tells you all you need to know, yet this story of a long-finished relationship not only threatened Robson's much-cherished job but also his much-loved family.

The rest of Fleet Street were naturally on to it in a flash and hordes of the 'rotters', the self-titled name for the news pack who hunted down that type of story, along with the 'snappers' or 'smudgers' (the photographers) were on to Robson in tandem with the football writers looking for the follow-up story, crowding around Lancaster Gate and his smart corner house in the pleasant, quiet streets of Ipswich.

It was a nightmare and it literally drove Bobby and Elsie from their house and into a very, very private cottage they had purchased sometime earlier for the chance to escape the more normal run of journalists and the pressures of the job.

There was no telephone for the journalists to track down and no one knew of the address, and so one of the best-known faces in public life successfully disappeared off the face of the earth for a short while. It gave him and Elsie some precious privacy, but also gave even more incentive to the newshounds to be the first to find out where he had gone to ground. Money was no object.

Bobby had a private mobile phone, not so commonplace thirty or more years ago, which few knew about, and it was something he could simply turn off to regain his cloak of invisibility once more when he needed to.

But this was a game the papers, their news desk and their editors loved. It was a hunt for the big story, even if it wasn't really that big or that important. Bobby was backed into a corner and, for once, he hadn't a clue what to do. It wasn't football. With the lady in question promising a kiss and tell book to reveal 'even more', he knew that the pressure would be unrelenting. Sat in his company car, a Rover, in the lane which ran alongside his cottage, he reluctantly asked me over the phone: 'What the hell can I do?'

He wasn't impressed when I told him that the only way to get the mass media off his back was to front it up and answer their questions as honestly as he was able to and to do it immediately.

I was working on the basis that once everybody had the story it would eventually die a natural death. If one paper scooped the story it would be another massive splash and even more intrusion into his private life and his past, as the pack continued their search for a follow up. He wasn't at all sure that my idea was the right one but eventually he told me to go ahead and arrange it.

The venue, as it happens, was not a difficult choice. There was a lovely old pub and restaurant called The Bull at Bisham, owned by a mutual friend of ours named Joe Sanchez, a diminutive Spaniard, who would have laid down his life for the England manager he adored. Joe loved Bobby because he treated him as his equal and Bobby enjoyed his sometimes-lavish hospitality, including trips in his private plane. He was only too happy to oblige, especially when he considered the inevitable publicity it would bring for his hostelry and his car hire business, even if he was always wary of the media attention on himself because he was, in public anyway, such a shy, reserved man.

On the plus side it was a venue Bobby was comfortable in. The England squad stayed a little way down the road at the luxurious Burnham Beeches Hotel and trained over the road from the pub at Bisham Abbey. I rented the adjoining cottage to the pub from Joe whenever England were in town and it was so much 'home' that my office, with Joe's permission, installed a telephone for my use whenever I was in residence, usually with my mate Michael Hart from the *Evening Standard*. It also had a lawned area, just the right size to stage a press conference and, of course, an excellent restaurant where Robson and his assistant Don Howe often took the team to eat or joined Michael and I for a couple of hours away from the troops. It wouldn't have been large enough these days for such a press conference to accommodate all of the media that would have demanded attendance, but at the time it sufficed.

We talked it over beforehand and mutually agreed that it would not be in either of our interests for me to be present and I asked one of my colleagues to attend on behalf of the *Today* newspaper, for whom I was working at the time.

I waited anxiously by the television and radio at my home 70 miles away in Kent with my phone in easy reach, keeping my fingers crossed that I had not led my pal down a crooked path. Bobby called me immediately afterwards and, still shaken, told me how surprised he was at the number of media who turned up and even more amazed at how comparatively smoothly it had all gone. It was still, however, a very rough ride and he had to wait to see how the three-act play was going to develop.

His one remaining fear was that he would turn up at the office in Lancaster Gate the next day or at home in Ipswich and find the media pack still in hot pursuit. It didn't happen. Now that everyone had the same story it was the end of the chase and the pack prepared to move onto another victim.

It was undoubtedly a gamble, but it paid off. It was only one of many battles Bobby waged with the media in his eight years in charge of the English football team, but it was the dirtiest and nastiest of them all, as it threatened his family life as well as his treasured job. He survived and, as the years progressed, he became an increasingly iconic figure in the game.

Steve Bull, the delightfully grounded Wolverhampton Wanderers centre-forward, given an unexpected England opportunity by Robson, summed up how the team felt not long after in a magazine interview as they boarded their flight to Italy: 'The one thing I really remember is the uproar surrounding Bobby Robson over the affair with his mistress. All the players stuck together, got a load of bin liners on the flight and chucked all the papers away and said "That's it. We are sticking together. He's our gaffer, and we're behind him." And that was it. It was over as far as we were concerned. We were going there to do our jobs for our country and do it properly.'

If only it was going to be that easy.

2

*'Four hostile newspapers are more to
be feared than a thousand bayonets.'*
Napoleon Bonaparte.

THE LATE *NEWS OF THE WORLD*, SHUT DOWN IN 2011
by its owner Rupert Murdoch after scandals of its own, summed up
the daily damning of the gentlemanly Bobby Robson, when they
described him in print as 'the most vilified Englishman since Lord
Haw-Haw'.

Of course it was massively over the top, but that was the way of the
scandal sheet no one admitted they bought, but at one time was the
widest read news sheet on the planet. Often the tabloid was conve-
niently slipped inside the *Sunday Times* or the *Sunday Telegraph* at the
local newsagents so that the reader could hide it like some kid with a
pornographic magazine inside his maths book.

To put their comment into context, Lord Haw-Haw was the wartime nickname given to William Joyce, an Irish-American who broadcast Nazi propaganda to Britain from Germany during the Second World War, beginning his broadcasts with the words, 'Germany calling, Germany calling,' delivered in an affected cut glass English accent. Born in America and raised in Ireland, Joyce had first worked with the British forces, acting as an informant on IRA members during the Irish War of Independence. He took German citizenship in 1940 and following the conclusion of the Second World War was convicted of high treason and hanged on 3 January 1946 at HM Prison Wandsworth in London.

By contrast Bobby Robson was eventually a cherished icon of English football, loved even by those enemies who used his name, his position and his good nature to boost their own reputations and attract readers to the newspapers who were paying them. He was the ultimate patriot and definitely did not hang. Indeed, he couldn't have been more dissimilar to Joyce.

I can almost see the fingers pointed at me, having worked not only for the *Thomson Regional* newspaper group with their many newspapers spread across Britain, but also for the much-decried *News of the Screws*, the *Sun*, *Today* and the *Sunday Mirror*, to name just four.

The first time I got to know the man personally was when, while writing for Thomson Newspapers, I did a series with the Geordie managers of the time, long, in-depth pieces about them as people as well as their standing in the world of football.

I spoke at length to Bobby, the lovely Bob Paisley of Liverpool, Lawrie McMenemy and even Brian Clough. Bobby and I spent a long time in each other's company and soon discovered we had a number of things in common, including cricket, music and theatre. I had some connections in the latter world because of my elder sister Pam, who ran a famous pub in Stratford-upon-Avon called the Dirty Duck, a watering hole for the theatre brigade.

But the friendship really developed when he became manager of the England football team. Not only did a small group of us travel to all the England games, but also accompanied him when he went on spying missions to watch future opponents.

Quite often when the other press boys would go off on a long, boozy lunch, Bobby and I would do a bit of sightseeing and a little shopping and this led, eventually, to us writing several books together, and there is no better way to get to know someone. It wasn't always the most beneficial way, as I discovered with other subjects including his England successor Graham Taylor, but with Bobby it cemented our friendship.

Bobby and I worked together through some turbulent times and never fell out. Disagreed, yes, but never fell out. He accepted that we both had jobs to do and that I would criticise when I believed criticism was due and he would tell me when he thought my industry stank. I never once went behind his back.

That was how I worked. Honesty, I felt, was always the best policy, because you didn't have to remember what lies were made up. Throughout more than half a century in the game I only once attracted a lawyer, while sports editor of the *Sunday Mirror*. I knew my story on a certain Spurs footballer was true but, to my chagrin, the lawyers decided that it was cheaper to pay up the £5,000 libel demand than defend the story in court. Time proved me right – the footballer was a liar and my story was accurate. I won't give him the satisfaction of naming him, a journeyman who didn't even tickle the underbelly of international football.

I guess that is why Bobby and I formed a friendship over many years. We both shared the same working principles and beliefs. We were also both passionate about all sports and patriotic about anything English or, in the wider context, British. Football was the king for both of us, followed closely by cricket.

But Robson was bigger and better than anyone else I knew, for he always forgave his critics, no matter how vicious or how wrong they were, and maintained in print that the British sporting press were the best in the world.

He loved his newspapers, whether it was the *Journal* in Newcastle or the *Daily Telegraph* in London, and admitted that if he had more time he would read half a dozen a day, as he would on occasion when staying with his squad in hotels. He also wrote a column for the *Mail on Sunday* with journalist Joe Bernstein, not the sort that Sir Alf Ramsey or Emlyn Hughes put their name to, but a good read that was the result of long and in-depth conversations about the game written by a journalist he rightly felt he could trust.

During his eight-year reign in charge of the England football team he was the butt of some dreadful journalism, untrue stories based on nothing more than bar room gossip. People from all walks of life were more than happy to make a quick quid out of a man whose name was news, yet Bobby Robson put his England players and the team's results above all of the gibberish. He considered his job a privilege and was always confident his knowledge of the game and his desire for English success on the football fields of the world would carry him through against any verbal or written insult.

He quickly discovered that managing at international level was completely different from the life of a club manager. The tribe of lead journalists that followed the team around wanted a back-page story from every press conference, while their number two writers wanted something different for the inside pages. It didn't end there, as there were separate press conferences for the evening, morning and Sunday papers, and maybe another for the agencies, and that's all before you got to the radio and television stations. It was an endless cycle and if you didn't like the people you were dealing with it was never going to be very pleasant or uplifting.

With Bobby the problem wasn't so much being misquoted, more the downright untrue stories that seemed to come with the territory. There were a number of newspapers he could have taken to court and beaten, therefore enhancing his relatively modest earnings, but he didn't bother. He didn't even consider it until one paper, *Today*, headlined him as a 'Traitor'. Of all the words that were levelled at him, this was one he could not countenance. In his own words he was a massive patriot; the one to lead the players and the coaching staff in the singing of 'God Save the Queen' before games; attending St. George's Day celebrations and waving the flag, figuratively and literally, at every opportunity at home and abroad.

The 'Traitor' headline and accompanying story came on the eve of the squad's departure to Italy for the 1990 World Cup when it was revealed that Robson was to quit the England job after the competition to take charge of Dutch side PSV Eindhoven. The story had been circulating amongst the journalists for days and it was eventually confirmed via the Football Association – definitely not through me as many suggested – and what really annoyed Bobby was that he wanted to tell 'his' players and coaching staff the news before they heard it from anyone else.

There was still a year left on his contract after Italia '90, a regular feature of the England managerial contracts in those days, designed to allow a golden handshake of a year's salary when a manager left. FA Chairman Bert Millichip, who had always backed Bobby through some of his darkest moments, had told his manager earlier that the FA would not be renewing his contract whatever the team achieved in Italy and that he was free to find another job in the interim if he wished.

Earlier that year, in March, Millichip had been indiscreet again when approached by a couple of senior journalists in the executive lounge at Heathrow Airport and told them quite clearly that what happened in Italy would affect Robson's job. He must have got that wrong, forgotten or was simply too impatient, as he allowed a reluctant Robson to quit after he and his squad delivered England's best World Cup performance since Ramsey's triumph.

By April it had become widely known amongst the number one journalists of the national press, and one of the Sunday's even ran speculation as to who was to replace the incumbent boss after the inevitable failure in Italy.

That very story immediately prompted the PSV Eindhoven approach. The Dutch side, who had won the European Cup in 1988, were looking to replace Guus Hiddink after a couple of trophyless seasons, and their General Manager Kees Ploegsma contacted Robson to clarify the situation. They eventually met up secretly in Cambridge and verbally agreed a two-year contract, subject to Robson talking to the FA first.

Had Millichip or the FA Chief Executive Graham Kelly given their manager assurance that he could keep his job beyond the World Cup, even for that extra year on his contract, he would undoubtedly have stayed. He loved the job too much to walk away, either for money or glory. Millichip made his own position clear by giving his manager permission for further talks with the Dutch club, refusing to offer him any guarantees of retaining his England job regardless of success or failure in Italy.

Millichip was, of course, one of a group who made the decisions and I have no doubt that had he had his way Bobby would have stayed on, but he was put in a position where his loyalty and friendship to a man he had known for a lot longer than his tenure at Lancaster Gate was put to the test. Bobby found Millichip's position strange and hard to understand given that he had backed him through all the dark times, never once backing down to the power of the press.

In conclusion it was PSV Eindhoven who insisted on a decision so that they could plan for their new season and Robson promised them an answer by 17 May. He had a meeting with both Millichip and Kelly nine days before the deadline, and when the FA Chairman was not inclined to offer any further assurances on his future with the Football Association, it then became a matter of when and not if it would be announced.

Bobby did not want anything to disturb preparations for the World Cup and refused to travel to Holland to discuss terms himself, sending instead his financial advisor John Hazel to negotiate on his behalf, even if it meant losing the opportunity completely.

At the same time, it was known that a kiss-and-tell woman of the worst variety was going from paper to paper, looking for the highest bidder to tell all about a long-forgotten relationship with a now famous football manager, promising that her book would be published on the opening day of the World Cup.

It meant he was under intolerable pressure on two levels. Such was the intensity of the Janet Rush affair that he seriously felt as though he may have to resign and lose the opportunity of managing in a second successive World Cup after his controversial and narrow failure in Mexico via Diego Maradona's 'Hand of God'.

The FA, having effectively given Robson the green light to agree a deal with PSV, had to make contingency plans and they were actively looking for a replacement, with Howard Kendall of Manchester City, Joe Royle at Oldham and Graham Taylor of Aston Villa – the favourite and eventual replacement – all on their list. Even that path was fraught with difficulties as Peter Swales, both Manchester City's chairman and a prominent figure at the FA, made sure that the then City boss was never under consideration, while Royle felt such a job was too soon for him as a manager. Aston Villa, through chairman Doug Ellis, were indicating that they would want over a £1million compensation if they lost Taylor to England.

The sensible and unflappable Graham Kelly was unconcerned about the scurrilous sex story floating in the background and told Bobby so, but also stressed the importance of sorting out the announcement of accepting the proffered job in Holland. He could foresee the dangers that presented with the press.

Cracks began to appear when *Today* let it be known that they were going to carry a story saying that Robson had resigned and that he had personally given out handwritten letters to the FA officials in a London hotel.

Both Robson and Kelly made it clear to the journalist from *Today* and other reporters who were telephoning from their temporary base in Sardinia that there was no truth in the story and that it should be killed. Yet when Bobby went back home to Ipswich to pack for the trip he was doorstepped by a hungry pack of journalists from both the news and sport pages, and then the news came through that *Today* had not only ignored the advice of the England manager and his boss but had printed the story and also portrayed him as a 'liar, a cheat and a traitor'. Light the blue touch paper and stand clear. Robson, understandably, went berserk.

When it finally came out that Robson had accepted PSV's offer, the story quickly went viral and a small group of football writers decided that he had been underhand and was letting his country down, therefore making him a traitor. However, only one of them – Rob Shepherd, who had been my number two when I was at *Today* – decided to chance his arm and carry the entire thing a stage further.

Shepherd took a mixture of rumour and fact and launched himself into a story which, had it been thoroughly checked out, would not have stood the test. He was a young, enthusiastic journalist at the time and needed solid guidance from his superiors at his office, something he did not receive in the flush of the sports desk believing they had an international exclusive.

Robson was forced to confirm at a hastily arranged press conference at Lancaster Gate that he would be resigning after the tournament in Italy, but that he had not already resigned as newspapers were claiming. It was a common practice on the continent for managers to see out a two-year contract already knowing, and letting everyone else know, exactly where they were heading afterwards.

The furious England manager told the waiting journalists: 'I have never offered my resignation to the Football Association. It is appalling rubbish and there is no truth in it.

'It's garbage and I was stunned when I heard about this last night. The facts are that I received an offer from abroad and openly and honestly and directly went to see our chairman Bert Millichip.

'He said then that he did not think my contract would be extended as he did not know what would happen in the World Cup and I accepted that. I didn't think there was a job for me and he gave me full permission to speak to PSV.

'But resign! Why should I do that on the eve of going out with the players to try and win the World Cup? I have worked hard for four years to get us from one World Cup to another and on the eve of us leaving for the championships, this happens.'

The truth of the matter was that Robson had conducted his business in the most straightforward manner, conversing with both Millichip and Graham Kelly, and between them they decided that the announcement would be made immediately after England's first World Cup training session at their headquarters in Sardinia, although Kelly alone held reservations over whether the story would hold for that long.

Apart from his fury at my former newspaper, who had accused him of being a traitor, Bobby showed his sense of humour that evening when he laughed that the same journalists who were pillorying him for walking out on England had been trying for four years to get rid of him.

But on this occasion Robson was not going to let it go. He consulted his legal team, and, for the first time, they decided they would sue the newspaper, who did not have a leg to stand on. A settlement was hastily and sensibly made out of court, although Bobby would have been more than willing to stand up in the witness box and answer any question the paper's defence lawyer might have thrown at him. They were wise enough to realise and accept they had been caught with their trousers down.

The entire episode was especially embarrassing for me as I had recently quit *Today* to take up my new role as a writing sports editor with the *Sunday Mirror*, where the editor, Eve Pollard, was all too keen for me to pick up the story and run with it. No chance of that and I was quickly vindicated as the truth emerged.

Not that this meant she was going to give me a free passage where Bobby Robson was concerned. She had made her own mind up about him, and as soon as I arrived in Sardinia for the World Cup preparations I found she had forwarded a picture to me of Bobby sitting on some rock above the beach looking at the bevy of player's wives and girlfriends sunbathing in their bikinis.

I was instructed to write a suitable story to go with this latest 'proof' that the England manager liked pretty ladies. I told Bobby of the quandary I was in and he told me not to worry, laughed about it, asked for a copy of the photo and told me to get on and do my job. Needless to say, the headline was a lot stronger than the copy I had written. Sometimes you just had to swallow your embarrassment, get on with it and pray for the football to begin.

Bobby and I agreed that here was one talented but very dangerous editor. A year younger than me, she breathed fire. Lady Lloyd OBE, to give her full title, was not only a successful editor but also an author, television personality and a pretty good journalist herself, even co-authoring Jackie Kennedy's autobiography.

Bobby always said that his private life was private, and he worked diligently to keep Elsie and the three boys away from the rough edges of journalism, but he was game for anything as England manager who, as a public figure, was paid relatively decent money to do the job and was prepared to reveal his thoughts about the beautiful game to anyone who would listen.

I saw him angry and upset on many occasions, but he would quickly swallow it and get on with his job and his life. Incredibly, he bore few grudges.

The only other time he was moved to do more than shrug and ignore a journalist for a week or two was much later on in life, when he was at his beloved Newcastle. It was at the tail end of the 2003/04 season as Newcastle finished a more than respectable fifth and were ready to walk out and applaud their fans, only to discover that a mere 5,000 had remained in St. James' Park. On that same day Leeds were relegated and their entire crowd stayed on to cheer their team.

Bobby made a comment off camera and off mic and definitely not for publication. The journalists, happy to oblige for what was a non-story, agreed, all except for Alan Oliver of the *Evening Chronicle*, one of the provincials I wrote for in my days at Thomson Newspapers, who not only carried the story but gave it a bit of spin.

Bobby was incandescent and said that it was one of the most damaging stories about him in his career, describing it as a wicked piece of journalism with no semblance of truth. There were, of course, worse things written about him, but this was far too close to home. This was Newcastle and the place and people he loved, and what made it worse was the fact that it was penned by a football writer and not a news man.

You would think that by the time Bobby quit managing he would have had a Jack Charlton style little black book with all the names of those who had crossed him. Not a bit of it. There was a definite turn of attitude in Italy when the majority of the journalists finally came to the realisation that this Bobby Robson was not such a bad fellow after all, and we even organised a very pleasant *al fresco* lunch for him under the Italian sunshine.

In fact, when he returned from Italy he decided that, all-in-all, he had enjoyed a fair press and stated that while the media couldn't do without sport, professional sport could not do without the media, adding that he thought the sports journalists – not the 'Rotters'— did a job for the sport.

He went even further and, in an interview with Rob McGibbon of the *UK Press Gazette*, said: 'I think we have the best newspapers in the world for sport. There are some fantastic football correspondents and there is an incredible breadth of writing talent.

'And I firmly believe that the press would rather write a positive story rather than a negative story about England – unless, of course, you are Nigel Clarke on a special assignment [for the *Daily Mirror*].' It should be pointed out that while Clarke and I were neighbours and friends in Chislehurst, the *Daily Mirror* and the *Sunday Mirror* were two separate entities in those days and the only collusion would be over the sharing of the cost of a bought-up book for serialisation.

Clarke had infamously told a television journalist on camera on a flight to Greece for an England match in February 1989 that he was 'there to fry Robson' should England lose. They won 2-1.

Robson ignored Clarke from that day on until the writer approached the England boss before a big match, held out his hand and wished him and England luck. Needless to say Bobby forgave him, just as he forgave Brian Glanville, the grizzled, frumpy, veteran who had slaughtered him so many times in his *Sunday Times* pieces.

There is a funny prequel which shows up the character of both men. It happened in Sweden prior to an England game where Bobby and I launched our book, *World Cup Diary*, for the 1986 World Cup, a little ploy that worked well and gave us a great deal of publicity and the press boys a good story which required little effort on their part.

Glanville, however, had not flown out with the team and arrived on the day of the match on a charter flight. He had been in touch with me and begged for a rare one-on-one interview with Robson, with the promise he would review the book. Not a problem, even though neither of us had as much time for him as a person or as a writer.

Never shy of an audience, Glanville held forth to any fan who wanted to listen on the flight over to Stockholm, telling them what a poor manager Robson was and what a prat and poor writer Bob Harris was. What he didn't know was that the young lady sitting just behind him was the publicist for my publisher and she faithfully repeated every word to us when she arrived at the hotel.

Did we want her to cancel the interview? Not at all. Robson gave him a good half an hour on match day for an exclusive on our book. What did Glanville have to say? Haven't a clue and, quite frankly, I can't be bothered to look it up.

He was never a fan of mine and clearly my help in arranging an exclusive interview for him with the England manager did not put me in his good books (forgive the pun) and a few years later at Wembley, for a friendly against Brazil, he was holding forth in the press bar telling anyone who wanted to listen that Bob Harris, who had just left *Today* for a senior position on the *Sunday Mirror*, was, 'a moron and a buffoon'. This was reported in a book called *All Played Out* by an unknown young writer named Pete Davies.

Bobby had time for a number of writers, naming Paul Hayward, Ian Wooldridge, Jeff Powell, Brian Scovell, Henry Winter, Oliver Holt, Matt Dickinson, Michael Hart, David Lacey, Steve Curry, Hugh McIlvanney and Patrick Barclay amongst those he admired and respected. He also found himself both sides of the television cameras with Sky, BBC and ITV, and became particularly attached to Sky in his ten years abroad when he caught up with the home news and sport on his television.

Bobby told me that although he had been used as a pawn between the *Mirror* and the *Sun,* who saw him as fair game, he felt that he was old enough and experienced enough to take that and he made a point of never falling out with football writers, though he did hold the ex-footballers who so happily hung him out to dry in contempt, as he felt they should have known better.

He believed that these were the people who had briefly turned the public against him and he despised them for it. It meant he had to suffer the humiliation of being spat at by the fans at the two grounds he loved more than any others – at Wembley when England lost to Russia, and at St. James Park shortly after he had dropped Kevin Keegan from the England squad.

Robson reeled off the names of those who had pierced him to the heart, starting with the man who he had respected above all others: Sir Alf Ramsey.

Robson was anything but a vitriolic man, but he felt bitter about the way Ramsey had turned on him and when we published *Against the Odds* in 1990, he exercised his right of reply in a chapter entitled 'Thanks a lot, Sir Alf': 'Of all the abuse, both personal and profession- al that I suffered in my eight years at Lancaster Gate, the most hurtful from both points of view was the succession of attacks from Sir Alf Ramsey.'

Ramsey's abuse took Robson by surprise, and he had previous- ly been keen to bring the manager he had cheered for and admired back into the FA fold. Instead, Ramsey conspired with Nigel Clarke at the *Daily Mirror* to write a series of columns which crucified the man who wanted to do nothing more than try and emulate what he had achieved. He tried to talk to him, even offered him lifts back to Ipswich, but all were spurned.

For what reason? We could only assume it was for the money, for the big, fat cheques that were being waved in front of any name they could use as a byline to destroy the credibility of the England manager.

Robson didn't have to worry about naming them, for their names and the stories were already splashed across the tabloids. The former England manager would have been bad enough on his own, but he was only the start. Former England skippers Kevin Keegan and, in particular, Emlyn Hughes, joined the cash queue, as did Alan Ball, much to Bobby's regret as he held the World Cup-winning player on a pedestal. Newcastle hero Malcolm MacDonald also got in on the act, though Bobby somewhat excused him because he thought he was in need of the money after his own personal problems.

He was outraged at Spurs defender Steve Perryman, who based his thoughts of international management on the basis of one cap, awarded to him by guess who? Bobby Robson. Terry Fenwick was another introduced to international football by the manager he later traduced, and even a veteran rugby league player named Alex Murphy thought it fitting to climb aboard the bandwagon and expand his fame and notoriety beyond the confines of the North West of England.

These, he believed, along with the newshounds, were the people who caused him the most hurt, turning the fickle amongst the fans against him and causing not only him, but his father Philip, pain.

The news men were slicker, harder and nastier, and Bobby soon discovered they were after him by whatever method. He told me that they were there with their cheque books, sniffing at empty glasses to see whether the players had been drinking alcohol and offering cold, hard cash to anyone who wanted to spin a yarn.

Even the Queen acknowledged his problems with ex-players and a section of the media when she presented him with his CBE for his contributions to the national game in 1990 and showed how well she had been briefed, when she said, 'I understand you are in a very tough game.'

'Yes, I am, ma'am,' responded the ever-polite Robson, 'but it is most enjoyable.'

Her Majesty didn't leave it there, but added, 'I am sure it is, but you have done very well.'

It was a joyous occasion shared with Elsie and two of his sons, Mark and Paul. All the criticism, all the slander, all the grief, was forgotten as he shared his day with his goalkeeper Peter Shilton, former cricketer and official Raman Subba Row, Dame Mary Gow, television presenter Esther Rantzen and, with great irony, Brian Hitchen, then editor of one of those red tops, the *Daily Star.*

It was a special day but there was better to come.

3

'A right Bobby Dazzler.'
translation from Geordie – an exceptional person.

THERE IS A MYTH ABOUT FOOTBALL IN THE NORTH
East in the 'Good Old days', when a manager needed only to whistle
at the pit face for a couple of strikers to appear. But while it is true
that the thirst for the game in that part of the world is undoubtable,
it is also the case that one of the area's greatest footballing sons found
it hard to get an organised game of football when he grew up in the
village of Sacriston, County Durham in the heart of the North East
mining community.

The young Bobby loved his football, as did so many of his friends,
but they were restricted to kickabouts with coats and jumpers for
goalposts because there was no organised football for them to play at

their local school. This was the very beating heart of English football but playing in an organised game was out of reach for these football daft kids.

Born in 1933, Bobby was just seven years old when rationing was introduced four months after the outbreak of war, with limits imposed on the sale of bacon, butter and sugar. A couple of weeks later all meat was rationed and clothes coupons were introduced, promoting a flourishing black market.

It was not until Robson reached the age of fifteen that these restrictions were gradually lifted, starting with flour (bread had been rationed from July 1946), followed by clothes and then, in 1950, extravagances like canned and dried fruit, chocolate biscuits, treacle, syrup, jellies and mincemeat became available.

Rationing ended completely in 1954 and was celebrated with a special ceremony in Trafalgar Square but, as tough as it sounds, it did not leave an indelible mark on Robson and his friends. It was just something they had been used to and accepted.

Bobby remembered nothing of his birthplace as, within months of his arrival, the Robson family moved to a house in Langley Park, a two-bedroom terraced property that housed his parents Philip, a mad keen Newcastle United fan, his devout mother Lillian, along with his four brothers: Tom, Philip, Ronald and Keith.

The entire family was supported by Philip, a miner who spent 51 years on the coalface. He was the solitary wage earner in the family and missed only one shift in over half a century. It wasn't that he never got sick, it was simply that if he missed a shift he didn't get paid and there was no second income from Lillian as most women, particularly in the North East, did not go to work. Instead she stayed home to cook, wash and mend for the six men in the family. Had a job been available to her, she would not have had the time.

Needless to say there was not a great deal of money around for fripperies – clothes were passed down from boy to boy to boy until they wore out, and neither the Robsons nor the vast majority of their neighbours had a television. Entertainment for the adults centred around the many working men's clubs, a couple of local football pitches, a couple of cinemas and, of course, Newcastle United.

No one complained because there were no comparisons to be had – everyone lived in much the same fashion in a confined area with little contact outside their boundaries. Most of the men would socialise at one of the clubs, where they drank beer at a subsidised cost and smoked cigarettes and pipes like chimneys in the days when some of the tobacco companies claimed that sucking on the weed was good for your health. In Bobby's own words, they were poor but they were happy, not just him and his family but the entire village. Money was tight, but things never got desperate.

Entertainment was either kicking a football or playing cricket, depending on the season. For football, the ball was anything round, which at times meant a piece of coal, and for cricket a piece of wood for a bat and a tennis ball sufficed. At night the radio was the main source of indoor entertainment, while social life revolved around the Working Men's Club, an ice cream parlour and a dance hall.

Bobby's father Philip was teetotal, and because he never missed a shift he had enough spare income to treat the family to a radiogram, a piece of furniture that combined a radio and a record player. There was no greater joy for Bobby and his brothers than to put a 78 RPM record on after travelling home from football on a Saturday evening.

The music they played then carried Bobby through the rest of his life. Frank Sinatra, Nat King Cole, Lena Horne, Judy Garland, Ella Fitzgerald and Dean Martin all filled the Robson house with joy and as the boys grew and earned their own money they would buy the odd record or two to add to the collection. Bobby, to use the local vernacular, had a canny voice which was to stand him in good stead at family gatherings and then, in later years, when footballers had their own get-togethers and demanded a turn from each of the players.

Looking back now it was austere living, but at the time it did not seem that way. Nobody knew any different. There was no hot running water and the toilets were outside. It wasn't until much later that the coal board went around the neighbourhood replacing one of the bedrooms with a bathroom. The only thing that they weren't short of was coal.

Bobby often referred to the old, much used song refrain "We were poor, but we were happy," of his childhood, stressing the family values initiated by his non-drinking, non-smoking father Philip. Pleasures were garnered not so much from television and radio but family games and, most of all, from playing football and cricket whenever and wherever.

"When there was no ball to kick, we used a piece of coal, and when that broke into small pieces we simply found another, as coal was in plentiful supply. As we grew up there was not a lot more in the area: a couple of football pitches, the same number of cinemas, several pubs, the inevitable working men's club, which dad only used later in life to play cards or dominoes, an ice cream parlour and a dance hall.

"Because of Dad's example and our Methodist background, few of the family indulged in strong drink or tobacco. Tom was the only brother who smoked, and he stopped later in life.

"Socially I have enjoyed the occasional cigar and the odd glass of wine with meals, but I was never a compulsive drinker like so many British footballers who I watched damage their health and careers over the years. It was pubs and after hours drinking in the early years and night clubs later on. It was not for me. It wasn't how I was brought up."

Even then football dominated, which explained why Bobby flunked his eleven-plus exams and ended up at the local secondary modern school with most of his mates rather than the local grammar school. Every waking minute was spent with a ball of one sort or another.

He always maintained that the lack of organised sport helped him to develop his skills. Whereas youngsters are now forced almost immediately into the disciplined world of competitive football, Robson would hone his skills often by himself, either with a ball or a lump of coal. He did, however, later admit that he'd have played three competitive games a day if only he had the opportunity.

He frowned upon the drinking and gambling culture of his generation and was delighted when that culture was dramatically curbed in the 1990s, as foreign managers such as Arsene Wenger started to have an impact on the English game. Boozing was particularly rife at Highbury when the Frenchman arrived, with players often spending their afternoons after training in the local pub.

Living was comfortable by local standards and the boys rarely wanted for much as there was not that much to have. The youngest had to share bedrooms, but with an abundance of coal it was never cold. The priority was good, regular food and warm clothing and both were always available in the Robson household. One of the problems of the age was footwear, which was expensive to buy and expensive to repair. Kids often dragged their satchels to school in the rain with holes in their soles, letting in the wet and leaving their socks and feet damp all day. Luckily for the Robsons, Philip was an accomplished self-taught cobbler and was able to turn his hand to repairs when necessary. Given the amount of football played by the boys in the fields and in the backyard, it was a good job.

Before the coal board went around their housing estates replacing one of the bedrooms with a bathroom the indoor ablutions were chamber pots and a big zinc bath hauled into the lounge in front of the coal fire for bath time once a week. That bath was filled with hot water that was heated, of course, by coal. There was also an outside loo.

Because Philip spent little or nothing on his own social life, there were always coppers to spare for a family holiday, another rarity in the neighbourhood. A few pints after a shift down the mine soon bled the money away for most families. The Robson family would go away every summer, first of all to the local resort of Whitley Bay and then, later, when there was a little more cash coming in from the boys and from Philip's regular promotions, the glamour of Blackpool, the Las Vegas of the North of England. Regular coaches would be run from nearby Durham to the wonderful free street light display, the Illuminations, which you could catch from late August through to October. The spectacle was truly a magnificent one for a young child.

Even without the lights the resort was simply magic for the kids. The real joy was that glorious stretch of sandy beach, patrolled by the poor donkeys, who humped kids of all shapes and sizes on their backs while being lapped by the icy cold waters of the North Sea. The old joke asked the question: What did the donkeys have for lunch? Half an hour if they were lucky! The chill of the water was no problem to the Robsons after the equally cold waters of Whitley Bay, but the swathe of sand meant that Bobby could play football from dawn to dusk under the watchful eye of mam and dad in their deckchairs.

Although it was very much what he did at home this was a real, genuine holiday for Bobby and although he went on to experience some of the world's most famous resorts and luxurious five-star hotels, his days on Blackpool beach staying in family-run boarding houses remained amongst his happiest memories.

The memories came flooding back and stories were regaled when we met up on a holiday in January 1989 in the resort of Clearwater in the USA and sat and watched the San Francisco 49ers beat the Bengals 20-16 in the Super Bowl in a hotel lounge with dishes of popcorn and nachos. That is how much times had changed in less than a lifetime.

This was Robert William Robson (oddly enough the same Christian names given to me eleven years on), born 18 February 1933 and football daft from the moment he opened his eyes. He joined his dad at St. James' Park to watch Newcastle United just as soon as he could walk and remained a passionate Toon fan for the remainder of his life, even though the club was not always as kind to him and his loyalties.

Philip was no penny pincher, far from it, but he was a good accountant and from him Bobby learned the value of a pound, something he was to carry forward in his life and a skill that became particularly useful in his days as a manager. He hated waste of any sort. He treated every penny spent as if it were his own, particularly at Ipswich Town where the money was tight. At Portman Road each signing and every wage increase, including his own, was carefully weighed up. As a result, Ipswich finished in the black every year he was in charge apart from the summer they invested in building a new stand at Portman Road, money well spent and supervised by their diligent manager.

Bobby was happy to pass on his frugality to others and when Ipswich were playing Derby County at the old Baseball Ground he insisted on the Ipswich board joining him on a visit to the local mine at Swadlincote, where his brother Tom was working. It is funny just to think of the upper-class Cobbold brothers John and Patrick being dressed up in coveralls, wearing hard hats and carrying miners' lamps – it's likely they couldn't wait to get back to their bottle of Sancerre and let their manager get on with the accounting and the managing. Yet it left a mark on the brothers and gave considerable satisfaction to Tom, who was eventually to progress to chief engineer for the National Coal Board in Nottinghamshire and Kent.

It all harked back to Bobby's earliest days in the North East and the inspiration that football gave him. Imagine his sheer disappointment when he arrived at his junior school, Waterhouses Modern Intermediate, knowing that the miserable old goat of a headmaster was one of the few men in the region who didn't like football and therefore refused to enter a team in the local schools' league.

It meant that Robson and his school chums would play football all the way to school with anything worth kicking, more often than not a battered old tennis ball. Once home he would only break off from kicking a ball when he was called in for tea, supper and, worst of all, homework. Bed beckoned when darkness finally fell.

Sport dominated his life and, as was the case in those days, football stood proud in the winter and cricket the summer. He was proficient in both and it was thought he could have made his way professionally in either sport, so good was the hand-eye coordination. That coordination would serve him well in later life when he turned his hand to golf. Fortunately, his love and ability for sport was quickly spotted by his Physical Education teacher David Gilliland, who was acutely aware of the headmaster's strange predilections and sought to find his boys competitive games wherever he could. He would not only search out opposition but also grounds for them to play their matches on. As most schools had a regular programme, these were not easy to find and so the games were scarcely as regular as either the schoolmaster or his charges would have wished.

But Bobby, even then, was the eternal optimist and used his time playing with either a tennis ball or a cheap football to hone his skills. His salvation was the local Langley Park Juniors, but he had to wait impatiently for his eleventh birthday and the opportunity to play for them. When it eventually came he found himself playing with and against boys two or three years older than himself, meaning a big differential in physique and strength.

He played for Langley Park from the age of eleven until fifteen, with games taking place on a Saturday morning, allowing him enough time for the trip to Newcastle to watch his beloved Newcastle, making the seventeen-mile each way trip by bus and getting to the ground early enough to be at the front of the queue to watch the likes of Len Shackleton, *Wor* Jackie Milburn, Albert Stubbins, Charlie Wayman, Alf McMichael, Bob Cowell and the rest of the heroes make their way into the ground through the players' entrance.

These were the heroes he sought to emulate, impatiently hurrying the rattling bus along the country roads to get back home so that he could practice what he had seen that afternoon, becoming in his own mind the players he had just watched.

Bobby, even later in life, would talk reverentially about the players who influenced his early football and helped him to develop into the all-round footballer he was to become.

Had Durham County Cricket Club possessed first class status in those days things might have been different. Instead there was no first class county team to aspire to and his cricket was confined to Langley Park in the Durham County League. His brothers and father told me that Bob would have been good enough to join the group of talented athletes who made it as a professional in both sports in the days when there were two distinct seasons.

He was delighted to learn that his captain at Fulham Johnny Haynes, the first £100 a week footballer and an England international, shared his love of both sports and was offered a contract with Middlesex as a wicketkeeper-batsman. Indeed there is a distinguished list of dual internationals who won caps for their country at both sports, including the legendary C. B. Fry, who played football for Portsmouth and Southampton, and Willie Watson, who played in 23 Test Matches and four internationals, representing Yorkshire in cricket and mainly Sunderland in football.

But even had the chance arisen, football was still the all-consuming passion for the young Bobby, who left school at the age of fourteen and a half and who by the time he was fifteen was putting on the gear and heading down the mine himself, helped, of course, by the fact that his dad was the overman and his brother Tom the engineer. The overman was a deputy to the viewer and more involved with daily work of the pit and it meant that, rather going down to the coalface, Bobby became a 'sparks', a trainee electrician. He still had to go down into the depths with the rest, don his overall, his helmet and his lamp and repair the lights and other electrical fittings under the earth rather than hack away at the sedimentary rock, but he had it a little bit easier than most, and for good reason.

'In those days it was fairly common to play both cricket and football professionally as the seasons were so clearly defined, but I was steered to the colliery and a "proper" job by my father, despite him being such a huge Newcastle fan,' he told me years later.

'He and my brother Tom, who was an engineer, didn't expect or want me to work down the pit and I was given the "cushy" job of trainee electrician. I still had to go down the pit with the rest of the lads, something which taught me to respect the values of life, but, most of all, to appreciate and value my success in my years in professional football, being paid for doing something I loved.

'Had I not been good enough to make the grade as a professional, I guess I would have been like my father and Tom, with a lifetime working in mine-related business. But I was always determined that I should be different. I wasn't being a rebel, I just desperately wanted to become a professional footballer and earn my living doing something I really loved.

'Would I have survived a lifetime working in or around the pits? Probably not, as the pits began to close, but my training as an electrician would have kept me in work, albeit not nearly so happy and content as I was.'

He continued to play for Langley Park and continued to watch the Toon whilst working down the pit, until he eventually started to feature for the Under-18's, restricting his ability to follow his team. He was disappointed, but not so much that he would give up playing to watch the game.

Indeed, his performances as an underage player were attracting attention from the scouts who watched games at all levels in droves looking for the next Jackie Milburn. Wor Jackie came from down the road in nearby Ashington, the same village that produced Jack and Bobby Charlton. The slightly built Robson looked a good bet to follow in his footsteps.

When he was fifteen he was invited by both Middlesbrough and Southampton for trials and did enough to tempt both clubs into making offers. Saints followed it up, but in the end he chose the more local club in Boro and signed on schoolboy terms.

During this period Newcastle lost a lot of local, promising youngsters who saw a difficult path through to the first team, and history is littered with top players who quit the North East to find their fame elsewhere, places where there were more opportunities to make the grade in first team football. Robson, the Charlton brothers and the talented Howard Kendall are just a few of the names who left the area before they had made a professional appearance in the game.

He was far from satisfied with the attention he received from Middlesbrough, with invitations to travel to Ayresome Park for training and, more importantly, for games, all too rare and when they came back to him on his seventeenth birthday to sign professional terms, he stunned them by telling them he wasn't interested.

With Philip insisting that he served his apprenticeship as an electrician, he was a grown man by the time it needed a decision and the choices on offer were wide and varied. Although he admitted he would have crawled on his hands and knees the seventeen miles to Newcastle United, he made the decision that they were so full of the superstars of their time that opportunities would have been few and far between for him to make an impression.

He had made up his mind that playing professionally was his calling and the only decision left was where to go and who to play for. Southampton were back, Middlesbrough were desperate, as were the other local rivals Sunderland. Also in the frame were Lincoln, York, Blackpool, Huddersfield and Fulham. Blackpool, the land of his schoolboy holidays, were a top side, star-studded and finishing seventh in the top division that year, but behind third-placed Sunderland and Newcastle, who were fifth. Boro were ninth that campaign, Huddersfield were down in fifteenth, with newly promoted Fulham two places behind. Lincoln and Southampton were both promoted to Division Two from the southern and northern sections of Division Three respectively, while York City had successfully applied for re-election. All had something to offer this budding young man who was determined to become a successful professional.

Everyone, especially Philip, naturally assumed that St. James' Park would be his destination, but Bobby learned another footballing lesson that was to stand him in good stead when he went into management. He elected to travel south to London and Fulham because their manager Bill Dodgin had taken the trouble to drive north himself to talk to Bobby and Philip personally, not leaving it to a local scout.

Bobby met Bill for the first time when he finished his shift at the colliery and found the Gateshead born manager, who had first tracked him when he was at Southampton, sitting outside the house with his mam and dad. Neither were keen to see their youngest move away from home, but Bill had a persuasive tongue and he convinced Bobby that he would have a much better chance of making it at Craven Cottage where they encouraged young players and brought them into the first team, whereas at Newcastle he would always be subservient to the big stars brought in for big money.

Bobby was convinced but his dad wasn't, and it was only when Bill agreed that the youngster should carry on his electrical apprenticeship in the south that the deal was struck. Philip wanted his son to have something to fall back on if he failed to earn a living as a footballer and it meant that Bobby travelled to the banks of the Thames as a part-time professional, training in the evening with the other part-timers, instead of in the morning when the seniors went about their business.

It was a wise choice as several of the youngsters from his village team at the time joined professional clubs, with George Johnson and Dickie Brankstone signing for Lincoln, Leo Dale moving to Doncaster and one of the Kilkenny Brothers joining Newcastle – but not one of them made the grade. It did show, however, the enormous footballing potential of this tiny square of land in the North East corner of England.

4

'If my critics saw me walking over the Thames they would say it was because I couldn't swim.'
Margaret Thatcher.

IMAGINE HOW TOUGH IT WOULD BE, EVEN THESE days, to move away from your family, everything you knew and loved, and start a new life in one of the world's busiest capitals. That is just what Bobby Robson did in 1950 when he left County Durham aged seventeen and took the train to the great metropolis of London and joined Fulham.

He checked in at Craven Cottage, that lovely old ground on the banks of the Thames, and then into his digs in Inglethorpe Street just around the corner. Robson had never travelled further than Blackpool and was now on his own, timid, and a little shy in a city like London. Despite all those people it can be a very lonely place, as many who have made the journey south will assert, and a vast percentage of them were soon on their way home.

Bobby had an added problem in that he trained with part-timers in the evening, not mixing with the full-time players who were training while he was completing his apprenticeship as an electrician, and they had all gone home by the time he arrived for his training sessions.

His new club were nevertheless careful that he was set right. Firstly, his digs were next door to the ground, a quick walk and no bus fares to pay. Manager Bill Dodgin, a kindly, thoughtful man, took young Robson to Lloyds Bank on his first day and gave him a crisp pound note to open an account with. As far as I was aware, he stayed with the same bank until the day he died. More important was the man Robson ended up sharing digs with – a young Fulham apprentice named Tom Wilson.

It is not an exaggeration to say that Tom, two-and-a-half years senior to his new mate, was and would remain a major influence on his life. They made friends the day they met in 1950 and stayed close until Bobby passed away in 2009, with Tom making a moving speech at his memorial service at a packed Durham Cathedral, remembering their mutual fondness of spam fritters and recalling the problem of Bobby's snatched hours with his new wife Elsie, who was not officially permitted to stay at their shared accommodation.

Wilson was an outstanding full-back for Fulham and Brentford, having left his first club Southampton without having played a single game, following Dodgin to the Cottage. He was at Fulham for seven years, but in that time he suffered a series of dreadful injuries which meant he featured in just 45 league games for the club.

During their time together, the pair became such firm friends that he was best man to Bobby and Elsie at their wedding in June 1955, with Bobby repaying the favour when Tom married.

Wilson eventually left the Cottage in 1957 and joined Brentford, staying until the end of the 1961/62 campaign and suffering again from a series of injuries, though he managed to play 148 league games during his five years at Griffin Park. He was a bright man and he didn't waste his time when he was injured, training as a quantity surveyor and entering the property world on his retirement.

Even though fully qualified as a quantity surveyor, he loved his football so much that he extended his career with Folkestone Town in the Southern League and continued his friendship with Bobby.

Tom returned to Fulham in the late 1980s as a director and, linking up with another friend and Fulham teammate Jimmy Hill, used his business acumen to negotiate the purchase of the Cottage from the Bank of England, which saved the club from being merged with Queens Park Rangers and the famous old Craven Cottage being sold for redevelopment.

Wilson remained at the club until he was asked to remove himself in 1997 as his fellow director Bill Muddyman was negotiating the sale of the club to Mohamed Al-Fayed, the controversial owner of Harrods.

Bobby always maintained that there would be no Fulham Football Club but for Tom. He talked of him constantly and there was never any doubt over the strength of their bond, which survived until the very end.

The digs they shared together until they split to get married played an essential part in Robson settling into London and feeling at home in the big, wide world. Bobby told me he felt very special living in a house with hot and cold running water, an indoor toilet and, better still, a real bath in a real bathroom.

The landlady provided a fry up for breakfast and she also cooked them an evening meal, served when her husband returned home from his business in the City. But these were two growing young men who needed sustenance and every day they would repair to the White Horse in Putney or another of the local hostelries for a lunch with a soup to start, followed by meat and two veg and perhaps a spotted dick to round it off, along with a glass of lemonade. Never anything stronger.

The pair of them became quite adventurous as they settled in together, almost like an old married couple. With no television their evenings in revolved around the radio, while they would also save up to go into the West End to the cinema or the theatre to see a show and, for a special treat, they would splurge on tickets for the London Palladium to watch one of their American heroes, Frank Sinatra, Sammy Davies Junior or Nat King Cole, stopping on the way from the tube to gaze at the neon lights, watching the foreign tourists or pausing to have an ice cream cone from one of the hawkers.

It sounds like a wonderful life of leisure – but that was not the Bobby Robson I knew, and it was a wonder he found the time to cram everything in, as he also needed to complete his apprenticeship. To that end, he found an opening with an electrical company in Victoria which had a contract to work on the Festival of Britain.

This was just six years following the end of the Second World War, and after more than ten years of austerity, rationing and the grief of lost relatives and friends, it was designed to give Britain a lift and promote the feeling of recovery with an exposition of arts, science and technology.

The Festival came a century after the Great Exhibition of 1851 and and the centrepiece of it was a 27-acre site on the South Bank of the Thames and Bobby's first job was as an assistant to a senior electrician at the Royal Festival Hall to help install the lighting and heating.

The job quickly turned into a nightmare for the part-time footballer and trainee electrician as he watched in horror as one of his work mates stepped backwards into empty space over an unmade balcony onto the concrete floor below. He said his first thoughts were naturally of a selfish nature, that it could so easily have been him, especially given the lack of any real health and safety regulations, something which is too easily mocked these days.

Work took precedence over football and he had to rise early to catch a bus to Victoria Coach Station, where he would be picked up by a work mate in a van and ferried to his work at the Festival Hall. Starting his day at around six in the morning, he would arrive at home to his digs thirteen hours later. Three nights a week it was followed by training at Fulham.

It was an impossible schedule and Bobby remarked ruefully that when Saturday came around he felt shattered. He also felt it was seriously hindering his progress as a professional sportsman, a feeling that the club backed up. He told his mam and dad that if he kept up his current schedule he would become a very good electrician and a very ordinary footballer.

It reached the stage where Fulham invited his parents to the club to meet up with Dodgin, who promised Bobby he would do his utmost to persuade Philip that he should ditch his apprenticeship and have a serious go at football. Philip was still keen for Bobby to keep up both professions, which meant Bobby working this double life until he was 21, by which time he felt his football life would be in ashes.

Eventually his father reluctantly agreed to let Bobby give what he thought was a hobby a full effort and he was immediately put on £7 a week, which was roughly the average working wage at the time. Still, it bothered him that after paying for his lodgings and satisfying his healthy appetite there was nothing much left to send home to his parents. Whenever he had a few pence left at the end of the week he put it to one side and eventually saved up enough to present his proud parents with a seven-day chiming clock, which was religiously wound up every Saturday night and looked after so carefully that it lasted many years.

The switch from part-time to full-time paid off just in the way he and Dodgin had envisaged, and by the time he was eighteen, just a year on from quitting the apprenticeship, he was in the first team as a regular. Working as an apprentice electrician for a time had another beneficial effect: it meant that when he signed full professional forms on his seventeenth birthday he skipped straight to first team, missing out on the football apprenticeship most players had to go through in those days, which included cleaning the senior players' boots, scrubbing the toilets and painting the barriers on the terraces. He watched on as others like Johnny Haynes supplemented their playing wages by working in the offices at the club.

+++

IT SEEMS EVEN MORE RELEVANT NOW THAN BEFORE

when professional comedian and club chairman Tommy Trinder joked on stage, 'What's black and white and goes up and down? Fulham Football Club.'

The Streatham born son of a London tram driver was one of Britain's best loved comics and was particularly popular with the Queen but despite his many accolades, films and Royal Variety performances, he loved the football club at Fulham more than anything else and was chairman between 1959 and 1976.

The club reflected his happy go lucky attitude to life and the spectre of relegation was not as big a deal in those days as it is now, mainly because it would scarcely see a change in the club's finances. There was no television revenue, and the same 26,000 or so would arrive through the turnstiles for every home game, regardless of the opponents or the division.

Bobby experienced the up and down nature of life at the Cottage in his first campaign as a professional, the 1950/51 season. Fulham earned a spectacular 3-0 victory over closest neighbours Chelsea in the fifth round of the FA Cup after holding them to a draw at Stamford Bridge, only to crash out to Blackpool in the next round with their eyes firmly set on a visit to Wembley. Their conquerors went on to lose to Newcastle United in the final.

The next season, 1951/52, resulted in relegation from the top flight, but no one seemed to be that bothered and Bobby later reflected that the club never achieved what they should have done in the six years he was there. In fact, most seemed content with life back in the Second Division. Bobby found such an apparent lack of ambition hard to understand, especially as the squad resonated with quality players.

Bobby himself had, by this time, represented his country at both Under-23 and B team level. Johnny Haynes was considered to be one of the finest inside-forwards in the game and there were other quality performers in the squad, including Tom Wilson (when his fitness permitted), midfielder Jimmy Hill, goalkeeper Tony Macedo and England's classy defender Jim Langley. There were also huge characters at the club in Bobby Keetch, Tosh Chamberlain and former Manchester United player Charlie Mitten, players who kept everyone on their toes with their unpredictable antics.

The creative midfield partnership between Robson and Haynes was considered by some at the time to be not just one of the best in England but in the entirety of Europe. Why then, Bobby asked, did they spend most of their time outside the top division? It seemed to him that, sometimes, the football and the results were almost secondary to the good times.

Fulham were not alone. Down the road at Stamford Bridge Chelsea boasted a fine crop of players, and they were as noted as much for their performances on the King's Road as they were for the trophies they actually won. Arsenal's players were also renowned after hour pub attendees but others, like the Liverpool of the 80s, were able to balance the good times with a phenomenal success rate domestically and in Europe.

Craven Cottage was forever alive with reporters from the national newspapers because they were always guaranteed a story or two. Haynes became ever more famous as the first £100 a week football when the maximum wage was scrapped, while Hill was always the one with the loudest voice and the strongest opinions.

Everyone knows the stories of the gifted Haynes and the entrepreneurial Hill, who was an influential union man with the PFA, helping to break the maximum wage in 1961 and later in the same decade successfully managing Coventry City for six years before going on to become a major television celebrity. He was also heavily involved in coaching under the England manager Walter Winterbottom, though Robson himself preferred the style and thoughts of the cerebral Ron Greenwood.

Robson first came into contact with Greenwood while at Fulham. While Jimmy Hill was one of Walter Winterbottom's blue-eyed boys and had all his coaching badges, Bobby gravitated more towards the less flamboyant but deep-thinking centre-half Greenwood, who was finishing his playing career at the Cottage and was already well respected for his thoughts on how the game should be played.

Robson went with Hill and Greenwood to watch when Hungary trounced England 6-3 at Wembley in 1953 and was so deeply affected by the performance and the result that he joined them both at FA coaching courses at Paddington Street. Greenwood, of course, was England manager directly before Robson assumed control and their friendship was long-lasting and firm.

Bobby Keetch, a player Robson encountered in his second spell at the Cottage, was a horse of a different colour, and perhaps epitomised the Fulham dressing room at that time and the unpredictability of their performances. He was an extrovert in and out of football and although never a great player was extremely influential, a dominating central defender who would kick you up in the air as soon as he set eyes on you. You couldn't miss him wherever he was and whatever he was doing.

Built like a tank and with beautifully coiffured blond hair, he cut a dashing figure on the pitch, while off it he always had a beautiful girl on his arm in the best London night clubs and drove the fastest, most expensive cars.

He wasn't a man for the snooker halls or the cafe conversations on coaching after training, he preferred art galleries and antique shops, which laid the foundations for his success and fortune after he had left football behind. But he was appreciated on a Saturday afternoon on the side of the Thames where his abrasive style complimented the purity of Haynes, Robson, Alan Mullery and George Cohen, and if a strong arm was needed to protect Robson from a violent opponent, Keetch was always on hand, ready, willing and able.

He was less successful with Queens Park Rangers after leaving Fulham in May 1966. Rangers manager Vic Buckingham wanted a bit more culture in his side's play and told Keetch how tap dancing would help his balance. 'Fuck off!' said Keetch in a loud voice and he was to depart shortly afterwards. He eventually quit the English game altogether at the age of just 27 when he emigrated to South Africa to play for Durban City for a couple of years, while developing his art and antiques business.

Bobby claimed there was something a little odd about his sudden departure as if he was running away from something, but when he came back to London he was cock of the walk once more, great mates with Terry Venables and a prominent figure on the social scene where he was involved in the launch of the West End restaurant *Football, Football*. Tragically he died of a stroke aged 54 and left a big gap.

+++

KEETCH AND THE OTHERS WERE GREAT FUN, BUT

Bobby Robson had more on his mind and after watching England lose 6-3 to Hungary at Wembley in November 1953, deciding that the time had come to follow Jimmy Hill and Ron Greenwood into the coaching world – he would take his FA Coaching course to earn his preliminary badge in parallel to his burgeoning playing career. He was the youngest on the course, but his mind was already set on staying in the game after his playing days were over and contributing towards the English game.

Despite a relative lack of success Robson loved the gossip and the chat around the club, with so many bright minds having their own input, and the failure to regain top status in the league was offset by his own personal success as he continued to progress with England. He also began to see more of the world the higher he climbed, and in 1955, to his great delight, he discovered the Caribbean. As part of an FA tour, he played games against Trinidad, Jamaica, Bermuda and Curacao in an odyssey that sounds as though it was organised by the FA Board members rather than by the manager. The games were not accorded the status of official internationals and no caps were awarded.

The eighteen-man squad, including just three players who had been previously capped, flew to Bermuda on 9 May to undertake an eleven-match tour of the region which began with 11-1 and 14-1 victories over the local side, three of whom were English born players.

They also beat Jamaica 7-0 in the first game played under floodlights at Sabina Park, coinciding with 300 years of English rule, and finished the tour with successive draws against Curacao before returning to Jamaica to watch the Test match between the West Indies and Australia, much to the delight of cricket fan Robson.

He loved the atmosphere and the people of the islands so much that he returned later in his career, taking his Newcastle United side on an end of season tour to Trinidad and Tobago, while I accompanied him on a couple of trips when he did some coaching – free of charge – in Antigua and St. Lucia.

It was on his return from the summer tour that he married his sweetheart Elsie. They were wed in the local village church in the North East and honeymooned in Edinburgh at the splendid Waverley Hotel.

The two had met in their local Durham village in 1952 and they courted at the local dance hall and cinemas as Bobby enjoyed the close season before returning to London. Elsie was working at the Sunderland Infirmary and had to have permission from her parents and Bobby's landlady at his digs to visit and strictly in the spare room, with the older Tom Wilson acting as chaperone. There was no thought of sneaking off to each other's room for, as Bobby said, it was simply not done in those days.

Just a week after they were married they went boating on the Thames with friends Don and Helen Sinclair, travelling at a leisurely pace from Kingston in Surrey through the locks to Oxford and back. The weather was benign, and therefore a picnic stop was in order, but just after it had been spread out, Elsie realised that they were missing the butter and left the others chatting while she nipped back to fetch it. On her return the big, cumbersome boat shifted in its moorings and Elsie tumbled into the murky waters between boat and river bank. She was not a swimmer and struggled to keep afloat until Bobby glanced across and saw an arm and a hand holding a pack of butter. Bobby hauled her to safety just before the heavy boat from which she had fallen began to swing back towards her. Bobby remarked that he almost became a widower after a week of marriage.

Elsie, shaken but none the worse for her experience, moved to London where she worked as a state registered nurse at St. Stephens. Footballer's wages were still not enough in those days for a couple to live well in a city as expensive as London. Wages were only £20 a week in season and £18 a week in the summer for a player, no matter how good you thought you were or how many times you had played for your country. The average working wage by the mid-1950s was around £9 per week, so he was still comfortably off.

He now had everything he wished for – except for a clear direction in the game. He wanted to know just how good he could be, and he had reached the conclusion that he was not going to find out by playing for Fulham, no matter how happy he was there. He needed to move on and flex his muscles.

He never pushed nor asked for a transfer, but when West Bromwich Albion came in for him in 1956 with a £25,000 bid, just £9,000 short of the British record, he decided to take his chances and leave the club. Fulham had not only shaped his career but his long-term future through the discussions on the game, the advice and the coaching courses he encountered there.

Bobby was increasingly keen to further his career and felt that Fulham were holding him back because of an apparent lack of ambition on the pitch. No one seemed to be bothered that they had been in the second tier for so long, and for a man in his early twenties on the fringes of the England squad, that would simply not do. He wanted to test himself against the best and achieve more on the inter-national stage.

'Fulham was a nice club, and everyone involved was helpful in every respect,' he told me. 'There was no backbiting and no jealousy as a youngster quickly making his way into the first team. The senior players at Craven Cottage were, without exception, helpful and friend-ly, a good crowd of blokes and good footballers.

'Maybe that was eventually my problem. They were such a happy go lucky bunch of guys that I always felt that in my six years we never reached the heights we should have done, and with the addition of just one or two more top quality players, we could have achieved a great deal more than we did.

'It made me wonder years later what happened to the money that came through the turnstiles because we always had big crowds, a small staff and capped wages.

'Don't get me wrong. I was extremely happy in my years at Fulham, which helped form me not only as a player but as a person. In fact, it was a very sad day when I left Fulham for West Bromwich Albion because I had been very happy there and enjoyed my football, but I was fiercely ambitious and wanted more than playing for England at under-23 level and the B side. They hadn't held me back in any way, but I realised if I wanted to play at the very top level I needed to move on. Playing in the Second Division was not going to help me improve.'

Fulham were not going to stand in his way and he departed a club he truly loved after 152 league appearances and a haul of 69 goals from his midfield role.

5

'Nothing compares to the simple pleasure of riding a bike.'
John F Kennedy, United States President

WHEN BOBBY ROBSON MOVED FROM FULHAM IN
London to join West Bromwich Albion in the West Midlands he was
found digs – note *not* a hotel – in Handsworth Wood and he had three
options to travel to the Hawthorns from there: he could either take
the No.11 bus via the outer circle route, walk or cycle. Footballers
did not cruise around in Bentleys, Porsches and BMWs then. I know
the journey well – I was a schoolboy at the time at George Dixon
Grammar School in Edgbaston and my long journey from my home
in Erdington on the No.11 always paused at Handsworth Wood for
the driver to clock in on the green machine planted in the pavement.
On one of those green, smoggy days in Brum, that was often as far as

the driver would venture, leaving one very annoyed school boy half way between home and school with a very long walk either way.

Bobby's choice of transport was initially a bike, and he would cycle not only to training with his kit strapped to his back but also to the Hawthorns on matchday. It would be some sight now, the new signing – an England international – arriving on his bike as thousands of regular fans descend upon the ground. The club, or their insurers, must have seen it the same way for it was not long into the season when it was suggested to him that he might find some other way of getting to the ground, particularly on the day of a game.

The down to earth Black Country folk took no obvious notice but were just as clearly pleased to see their new star player had no airs and graces and was, indeed, one of them.

Neither was there a huge signing on bonus and consequently it meant that Elsie had to continue her working career and she moved to join her husband, taking a position at the Deritend Stamping Company, as an industrial nurse.

It is not so obvious these days why this area in the West Midlands to the north of Birmingham was called the Black Country. The reason was the area's proximity to the army of chimneys chasing each other across the countryside, reaching up to the sky and belching out clouds of black and sometimes multi-coloured smoke. It was just a little different to the park alongside the banks of the Thames as you left Craven Cottage and headed for the tube into London.

There was little respite – the training ground was surrounded on three sides by heavy industry spewing forth acrid smoke, while on the fourth side was the cut, local vernacular for the canal, a black ribbon of water skulking in the ground like a malignant moat round Dracula's castle. They used to say if the smoke didn't get you then the canal would, and they were nearly right when manager Jimmy Hagan drove his car straight into the murky water from the training ground exit and had to be fished out by the shocked players who, it is falsely rumoured, debated whether this sharp-tongued disciplinarian should look after himself and be left to swim to the bank.

Hagan was soon replaced by Vic Buckingham, who was completely the opposite in his approach, and, like Robson, a devotee of the push and run style, one-touch football, developed by Arthur Rowe at Spurs in the early-1950s, and refined in his time with Ajax in Holland.

Bobby coaxed in all he could from every coach he played under and worked with and was especially motivated by these two experienced old hands who had a vastly different approach. Hagan was abrasive and not liked by all of his players at The Hawthorns. He was far more fulsome about Buckingham who he described as an acute tactician and turned the Baggies form around before he was sacked after being named in a divorce action! They were both part of the Robson education but it was undoubtedly Walter Winterbottom who remained the biggest influence in coaxingthe future England manager into a coaching career.

Robson was not fazed by the move, the surroundings, his novel way of going to work or the almost incomprehensible local dialect straight out of an *Enoch and Eli* sketch on the radio. Although the language is supposed to be confined to the Metropolitan Boroughs of Dudley, Sandwell, Walsall and Wolverhampton, it was used all over that side of the Midlands, and to most of us Brummies it was as incomprehensible as the Dutch Bobby tried to learn years later.

Bobby always claimed he had no problem understanding the dialect as it was, he reckoned, close to his own native Geordie dialect. I beg to differ with the great man. I am a Brummie and I struggled to understand the lingo. For example, 'Bostin' fettle' means great food; 'Going round the Wrekin' means taking a long rambling route to a destination or taking a long time to get to the point of a story, with the Wrekin being a large hill in Shropshire. 'It's a bit black over Bill's mother's', means the sky is dark with coming rain and was a reference to Shakespeare (Bill) whose mother was Mary Arden of Stratford, with the showers invariably coming from that south-westerly direction. Goodness knows why but a 'Bobowler' is a large moth; 'Fizzog' is face; 'Half-soaked' is slow or stupid; 'Any road up,' is anyway or anyhow and, 'I'll go to the foot of our stairs,' is simply an expression of surprise or shock. I'm sure you get the idea.

The humour was just as dark, and Bobby found himself settling in well not only with his fellow professionals but also the neighbours and the Baggies supporters who welcomed him into their world. He felt quickly at home in his new circle of friends, especially with full-back Don Howe. He had Tom Watson at Fulham and now Don at the Baggies, not only colleagues but friends to last a lifetime. These friendships survived their various career moves, and his bond with Don was reignited when Bobby took over from Ron Greenwood as England manager in 1982.

He promptly made the shrewd Howe, who had guided Arsenal to their triumphant double as coach under former physiotherapist Bertie Mee, his right-hand man and there they stayed together for the full eight years, sharing the triumphs and disasters. Bobby desperately wanted Don by his side all the time, not just when England played their matches. Yet his request for him to be appointed as his full-time assistant fell on deaf ears and was rejected by the FA, because they claimed they didn't have the money available, a risible joke considering the cash that fluttered in and out of the headquarters at Lancaster Gate.

Howe was a great foil and allowing the pair to work full-time together would have potentially produced spectacular results for the national team. Though they didn't always agree they always debated rather than fell out with each other, one of the reasons they clicked so well.

Don was a quality left full-back immersed in the passing game encouraged by their manager Vic Buckingham, and a far cry from some of the Neanderthal, shaven-headed bruisers whose interpretation of a defensive tackle was to pick which row of the stand the winger would land. Aston Villa and Birmingham full-back Stan Lynn, lovely company but a bugger in the tackle, comes readily to mind from that era.

They were surrounded by like-minded players such as Ronnie Allen, a centre-forward but not in the traditional mould. Allen was small — only 5ft 8in — and relied on speed of thought and body rather than physical prowess, playing off the power and muscle of the giant Derek Kevan beside him. Allen, who won five caps for England, scored twice in the 1954 FA Cup Final, which Albion won 3-1 against Preston North End, and he was also part of an England team a few weeks later, featuring both Stanley Matthews and Tom Finney, who were crushed 7-1 by the brilliant Hungarian team, the Magnificent Magyars.

That was a result that cut English football deep, especially coming so soon after the 6-3 thrashing at Wembley in the November of 1953. Those two matches made a huge impression on Robson, who watched the first game from the terraces in utter amazement at the skill, guile and quality of England's opponents.

Allen also learned from his experience out on the field of play that day and was another manager that emerged from this flourishing group of thinking footballers successful abroad with Athletic Bilbao, whom he led to second in La Liga in the 1969/70 season, and Sporting Lisbon in Portugal. He had started his managerial career with Wolves and returned to the West Midlands on two occasions after that, first with Walsall and later with West Bromwich Albion, making it a complete tour of the Black Country.

There is no doubt that he and Kevan thrived on the service from young midfielder Robson and his teammates Jimmy Dugdale, Jimmy

Dudley and the abrasive Maurice Setters, who took his talents and his tackles to Manchester United. Robson said it was a team ahead of its time, a joy to watch and a joy to play for.

'When I moved to West Brom I found myself surrounded by quality footballers, people like my great friend Don Howe – my strong right arm when I was manager of England – Ronnie Allen, Jimmy Dugdale, Derek Kevan, Joe Kennedy, Frank Griffin, George Lee, Jimmy Dudley and Maurice Setters. We played lovely football, which gave me the ideal platform to launch my England career.'

Having already made his breakthrough at the lower level with Fulham, Bobby soon went on to win full international honours. It was a strange set up in those days. In Walter Winterbottom they had a bright, intelligent manager constrained by the archaic International Select Committee he worked under. This committee was an eight-man panel plus a chairman that selected the squad and the team, and naturally the various men involved tended to favour players from their own clubs, often leaving England's actual manager frustrated.

Even at this early stage in his international development Robson found this system a complete anathema, claiming it came from the Stone Age, leaving the manager with a hotchpotch of players that had to adapt to his favoured tactics. Fortunately for Winterbottom, English football was in a healthy state and there were enough players thrown at him with the skill and ability for him to blend into a team.

He also had a tactician's grasp of the game and liked Robson's style of play enough to give him his debut in November 1957 against France. He went on to win twenty caps and scored four goals, two of them in that debut against the French, a 4-0 victory, but such a fast start did not necessarily count for an awful lot in the England set-up.

'After my debut I was disappointed to be left out for the next game and learned to take nothing for granted at this level, because of the way the game was run and the team selected by committee men who had their own personal agendas when it came to giving Winterbottom the team he was expected to work with. Not surprisingly we did not achieve all we should have done with the constant chopping and changing.'

England's next game was a British Home Championship clash away to Scotland in April 1958, and Robson did not feature in that or either of the following friendlies against Portugal or Yugoslavia. His next appearance came in the 1-1 friendly draw with the USSR, a dress rehearsal for the clash against the same opponents under a month later in England's World Cup opener in Sweden.

Robson would start all three of England's group games in Sweden and was involved four years later in Chile as well. At both tournaments England failed to make the impact expected by their fans, not to mention those picking the squad, who took no responsibility for any failure.

One of the reasons they did not go further at either tournament was beyond anyone's control. The other two goals scored on Robson's debut, the 4-0 win over France, came from a trusted source: Manchester United's Tommy Taylor, a devastating goalscorer who was equally effective at club and international level. Robson revelled in the pleasure of playing with Taylor and the two other Busby Babes, the truly fabulous Duncan Edwards and Roger Byrne.

But Bobby's first international sadly turned out to be their last, as less than three months later they were killed in or as a result of the 1958 Munich air disaster when United were on their way home after a European Cup tie in Belgrade. Twenty-three perished on the snow and slush covered runway at Munich-Riem Airport, with Edwards dying fifteen days later from his injuries. United boss Matt Busby, given no more than a 50-50 chance, survived.

Bobby and I shared the same opinion of Duncan, just 21 years of age, as one of the very best players we had ever seen. As a schoolboy my view and opinion was of awe at a player who thrilled me whenever he walked onto the pitch, seemingly capable of anything. For Bobby, of course, he was an England teammate, and he described Edwards as a young man with the world at his feet.

I was at a school friend's house not many miles from his birthplace in Dudley when the terrible news arrived on 6 February, and it left two young boys sobbing. Our prayers for his survival fell on stony ground. We had lost a hero even though neither of us were supporters of his team.

Bobby, however, had lost a new friend and everyone at West Bromwich Albion and their fans felt it even more personally, because Duncan was a local lad born just down the road in Baggies territory. He was one of their own, even though he had played for the universally admired Busby Babes in Manchester his whole career. He had already won sixteen caps and the sky was the limit with his talent and personality.

I have no doubt, looking back, that he was going to be the forerunner of today's superstars. He had already gathered fans from around the world who had seen his explosive but controlled talents on their black and white television sets as United established themselves as favourites to win the European Cup.

'He seemed to be able to do anything on a football field and had an engaging personality to go with it. He was a perfect role model for any youngster,' said Bobby, who cried unashamedly along with his teammates when he heard the news.

+++

THERE WERE MANY PERIODS IN ROBSON'S FOOTBALL career that saw him despair of those who ran the game in this country. That was certainly the case for the 1958 World Cup Finals, when it was decided by the committee, to his absolute amazement, that the incomparable Stanley Matthews, Blackpool's Wizard of the Wing, and Nat Lofthouse, the Lion of Vienna, would not be in the squad of twenty travelling to Sweden for the tournament.

It was true that Matthews had not played for England in over a year, but there was particular controversy that the muscular 23-year-old Derek Kevan, Robson's teammate at the Hawthorns, had been selected over Lofthouse, who in May had scored both goals in Bolton's 2-0 FA Cup final win over Manchester United.

Years afterwards Bobby was still staggered at the decision which, he said, must have boosted their group opponents in Sweden – Brazil, the USSR and Austria – and disappointed many fans who had made arrangements to undertake the comparatively short trip to Scandinavia.

'My first taste of World Cup finals in 1958 showed the power and the stupidity of the autocratic FA when they decided to cut the squad from the regulation 22 by leaving two players at home [Alan Hodgkinson and Maurice Setters were included in the original list of 22 names sent to FIFA but did not travel with the squad to Sweden], presumably to save the cash. I can think of no other logical reason.'

Robson believed that both Lofthouse and Matthews were still in their pomp. The latter, admittedly, was 43 years of age at the time but there was no sign of wear and tear from the man who used to patrol the right touchline, embarrassing defenders and providing the sort of service loved by Lofthouse and his Blackpool colleague Stan Mortensen, who scored a hat-trick in the 4-3 victory against Lofthouse's Wanderers in in the 1953 FA Cup final.

Matthews was, according to Robson, still in full flow and had played in the World Cup qualifiers against both Denmark and Ireland.

Matthews was knighted while still playing football professionally, which he did at the very top level until he was 50 years old. He was the first winner of the European Footballer of the Year award and was suitably nicknamed 'The Wizard of the Dribble,' or, more succinctly, 'The Magician.' Yet his last match for his country was in 1957 at the age of 42 years and 104 days, with the wise old men at Lancaster Gate deciding he was not good enough for the Sweden trip and international football from that point on.

Two years earlier he was the star at Wembley when England beat Brazil 4-2, destroying the world class full-back and captain Nilton Santos in the process. To make his absence even more annoying to Bobby and his teammates, Tom Finney was injured in England's opening game against the Russians in the Ullevi Stadium. In those days there were no substitutes and the brave Finney dragged himself through the full 90 minutes in a 2-2 draw which left Robson fuming, as he scored what should have been the winner.

A shot from his Albion teammate Derek Kevan rebounded back off goalkeeper Lev Yashin and Bobby, following up, stuck it away, only for it to be ruled out by Hungarian referee Istvan Zsolt. He didn't know it at the time, but Bobby Robson had just discovered that he and referees were not going to be soulmates throughout the rest of his career, despite the unfailing respect he showed them.

The injured Finney bravely took and scored an 85th minute penalty which saw England snatch the draw having been two goals down early in the second half. Sticking it out came out at a price though, as the Preston winger did not play another game in the tournament.

Bobby's biggest regret in that competition was missing out on the opportunity to say that he had played on the same pitch as the man he believed was the greatest footballer who ever lived, Pele, who was just seventeen years of age but already recognised as a player with enormous potential. Bobby was also a big fan of the bow-legged Garrincha but he too was absent, with Brazil saving their two stars for greater exploits further down the line. They would soon go on to enchant planet football, winning the Jules Rimet trophy with a comfortable 5-2 victory over Sweden in the final and playing a new brand of exciting, attacking football.

Luck certainly seemed to be against Robson and the team, for not only did they draw 0-0 with the South Americans, they might have won the game when Kevan, a scorer in the first game against Russia, was brought down in the penalty area only for claims to be waved away, this time by German referee Albert Dusch. Nothing improved in the final group game, when England once more drew 2-2 with the USSR and again the frustrated Robson had a goal chalked off by Dutch referee Jan Bronkhorst which he later claimed was 'perfectly legitimate'.

Worse was to follow as Robson was axed from the team for the play-off with the USSR after the two teams finish level on points and goal difference in the group. Peter Broadbent was brought in and England, lacking the inspiration of a Finney, a Matthews, a Lofthouse or a Robson, tamely went out to a single goal from Ilyin.

Also missing that day was Bobby Charlton, a 20-year-old match winner who was supposedly left out because of the traumas of the Munich disaster. Robson was not convinced. If that were the case for his omission, why he was he selected for the squad in the first place?

Despite plenty of frustration, Robson still left Sweden enchanted by the competition and its excellence. He appreciated the huge difference between domestic and international football at its uppermost level where, he said, every player was of the highest quality with no apparent weaknesses and where mistakes were punished and the standard simply breathtaking. He wanted more.

He was picked for the next World Cup four years later in Chile when, with players like Bobby Charlton, Bryan Douglas, Jimmy Greaves, Johnny Haynes, Ron Flowers, Bobby Moore, Ron Springett, Ray Wilson, Gerry Hitchens and Maurice Norman, England were one of the more fancied contenders. By then he had retreated from his attacking midfield role to become a more defensive wing-half, with equal success.

When ill-fortune struck again he should have been forewarned that the World Cup was never going to be his competition, either as a player or a manager. He was injured in a warm-up game against Peru on the way to the finals, cracking an ankle bone. His replacement in the side was West Ham United's bright young thing, the blond haired, super cool Bobby Moore, who would end up keeping his place unchallenged for the next 100 games or so.

Robson recalled that if you were going to lose your place to anyone, then Moore was hardly the worst person to lose it to. The entire squad were aware of the potential of this bright young defender. Moore, according to Robson, 'had something about him. He came in and just grew and grew as a player.'

Robson was forced to watch from the sidelines as they lost to the eventual group winners Hungary, beat Argentina 3-1 and then drew with Bulgaria to progress through to the quarter-finals against Brazil, where two goals from Garrincha sent England home nursing a 3-1 defeat. The irony was that had England won, the older Bobby would have been available for selection having recovered his fitness, but he was wise enough to know that the youngster who had taken his place was destined for greater things.

Bobby knew that the defeat was almost certainly the end of his international career, along with his mentor Walter Winterbottom, whose departure after Chile was as widely known as Bobby's after managing England in Italia '90. The successor was to be Jimmy Adamson of Burnley, coincidentally Robson's roommate on that trip. But, to everyone's shock, the cerebral Adamson turned down the England job out of the blue and the FA turned instead to Alf Ramsey. The rest, as they say, is history.

When the next World Cup came around on home soil four years

later Robson was still impressing in a more withdrawn role back at Fulham, but he had not played an international game in four years.

'I would have loved to have played more for my country, but circumstances dictated otherwise,' he later told me. 'It was frustrating, especially as I felt that I was still good enough four years later when I was playing deep alongside the centre-half. I knew I was the best in London in the role and that I could have done a decent job at Wembley. The truth is, however, that Sir Alf Ramsey won the World Cup without me. So who was wrong?' He would have to wait until becoming a coach before rekindling his relationship with the national team.

As Robson took a step backwards, his replacement Moore was thrust firmly into the limelight and was to go on to become one of his country's most iconic figures, leading England to their one and only World Cup triumph in 1966 against West Germany at Wembley under Ramsey. He was widely regarded as one of the best defenders of all time and was described by Pele as the greatest defender he ever played against. He was certainly West Ham's best ever player, even ahead of the other World Cup winners, hat-trick hero Geoff Hurst and the brainy Martin Peters.

He was made captain of his country at the age of 23 and went on to win a then record of 108 caps, while his statue now stands outside the new Wembley stadium. Honours rained down on him and he was even selected in the World Team of the Twentieth Century along with Lev Yashin (Soviet Union); Carlos Alberto (Brazil), Franz Beckenbauer (Germany), Nilton Santos (Brazil); Johann Cruyff (Holland), Alfredo di Stefano (Argentina and Spain), Michel Platini (France); Garrincha (Brazil), Diego Maradona (Argentina) and Pele (Brazil). It would have been some team.

Moore was as laid back off the field as on it and found himself in trouble more than once, including being wrongly accused of stealing jewellery on his way to the 1970 World Cup in Mexico from a shop in Bogota, Colombia. He was released by police but then rearrested in Bogota and then placed under a four-day house arrest while the team headed out to Quito for a game in Ecuador. It took diplomatic pressure – not to mention a total lack of evidence – for him to be released, totally exonerated, and he rejoined his squad in Mexico to a guard of honour from the players.

There were, however, times when he was not so innocent, and he was often in hot water at Upton Park, particularly when he was once sent home from Blackpool in 1971 along with teammates Jimmy Greaves, Brian Dear and Clyde Best for drinking in boxer Brian London's nightclub the night before (or should that be the morning) of an FA Cup tie against the Seasiders. The reduced Hammers lost 4-0 to a team who were bottom of the league at the time and relegated at the end of the season. He liked a drink and convivial company, as did many of the footballers of that era.

Bobby Robson, along with the rest of us, could never understand why his friend and rival was never knighted and he watched with sadness as this great player's life deteriorated due to poor business dealings, ill health and a divorce before he passed away, ravaged with cancer, on 24 February 1993, aged just 51. His memorial service was at Westminster Abbey, only the second sportsman to be so honoured. He was one of the most modest, selfless, ordinary superstars I ever had the pleasure of meeting.

Robson's life was to alter considerably after the 1962 World Cup in Chile, but he acknowledged that playing for England and working under Winterbottom had shaped his future career.

It was in 1958 that Winterbottom approached roommates Howe and Robson and persuaded the pair to join him at Lilleshall, where they could take up coaching under his watchful eye, helping them prepare for a future in the game once their playing careers ended. Not even the cack-handed handling of the England management and team by the egoistical International Committee could dissuade Robson from joining his boss, although he confessed that he would have found it difficult to operate under the circumstances Winterbottom endured. Little did he know that he was to suffer far worse during his tenure, and not just from a different sort of International Committee.

The International Committee were a law unto themselves. As a panel they took over selection duties for England's first unofficial match in 1870, and this system continued right up until the last match before the start of the Second World War, against Romania in Bucharest. After the war Winterbottom was named as England's first official manager, but that did not mean he was in sole charge of selection, and the out of date system remained in place until Alf Ramsey took charge in 1963 and demanded control over selection, even though the committee still wielded enormous power.

+++

FOR ROBSON IT WAS BACK TO THE MIDLANDS AFTER the World Cup. He had recovered from injury and was looking forward to another season in the top flight with West Brom. He had left for South America after another excellent season and was now skipper of the Baggies. Although honours eluded him, his team were always up there challenging the Busby Babes; Stan Cullis and his great Wolves team; the fast-developing Spurs who were to go on and win the double; Burnley, an outstanding footballing side, neighbours Aston Villa and Arsenal.

Bobby and Elsie had settled well in the area and before that World Cup they had scraped together £425 in savings to put down on a house in Handsworth, borrowing £2,000 for the balance through the wise guidance of Bert Millichip, a solicitor and director (and later chairman) at West Brom, and eventually his boss at the FA. The two formed a firm and lasting relationship that was not, as many believed, spoiled when Robson was given permission to look for another job before Italia '90. They remained friends.

His advice and help meant that money was saved and the deal went through. Robson was happy to be in a pleasant neighbourhood within a twenty-minute walk of the Hawthorns, having now been banned by the club from riding his bike into work. The idea of purchasing a car was still out of the question due to finances. Instead he would make the half an hour walk or twenty-minute jog with his neighbour and teammate, Davie Burnside. The journey to the training ground was made quickly as the two grown men played headers and passing with a tennis ball on the way, with the climax coming as they reached the ground and hammered the ball against the long wall behind the goal.

There was no snooker hall or boozer after training as he, Don Howe and a handful of other genuine football enthusiasts would gather instead at the local cafe and talk football and tactics over coffee that would usually go cold due to lack of attention.

Yet his happiness at the Hawthorns soon came to a grinding, discordant halt when he was placed on the transfer list in August 1962. Robson had asked for a transfer and lost the captaincy to his friend Howe after a disagreement with the club over money. When the maximum wage was abolished in January 1961, Robson, at the time an England international, naturally thought he would enjoy a weekly wage increase, say from £20 to £25, but Albion's then chairman Jim Gaunt said an emphatic no.

Robson and his teammates responded by threatening to go on strike. At a time when his old Fulham teammate and England colleague Johnny Haynes was awarded £100 per week. Robson was offered £20 a week and a fiver a match in appearance money, with the extra £5 not guaranteed if injured or dropped from the team.

Although much of the talk of the abolition centred on Johnny Haynes's nice round figure, many of the clubs just ignored the brave new world. The players were used to low wages in a low wage society and there was no agent to argue their corner. Some managed to increase their appearance money and others didn't, while a great many accepted an increase of just a few quid and counted their blessings. Arsenal and Liverpool, after negotiations with their players, introduced an innovative crowd bonus, but even these amounted to little more than a few pounds.

It took a lot to upset Bobby at that time as he was so happy at the Hawthorns, settled in his home and looking forward to developing his career with his club. It wasn't the lack of extra income itself that Robson was upset by, although it would have been more than useful, it was the principle of the matter.

He wasn't on the transfer list long, and it was his old club Fulham who came in for him immediately with an offer of £20,000, and after six years he found himself on his way back to Craven Cottage. He would still be playing top flight football, as Fulham had finally won promotion back to the top flight.

Fulham hadn't made much of an impact on their return to the top flight, and only avoided relegation back down to the second tier by a point in the 1961/62 season, but the surroundings were all so familiar to the returning Robson, especially with his old inside-forward partner Bedford Jezzard now the manager. It was the still the same old Fulham, as illustrated by two games in the space of three days at the end of 1963, both against the same opposition. The Cottagers were on devastating form on Boxing Day, beating Ipswich by a staggering 10-1 margin by the Thames, only to lose 4-2 away to Portman Road just 48 hours later in the last game before the new year. It was not a formula that would bring trophies.

But there were other aspects which attracted him, particularly the quality of a young Londoner Alan Mullery, and they both fancied their chances of being the engine room of a new-look team with experience on one side and youthful, obvious talent on the other. The trouble is that while Bobby could see the potential so could everyone else, and the partnership was nipped in the bud when Spurs came in with a bid of £72,500 for Mullery, which helped pay a chunk off the new stand which was being built, wrecking the prospects of a side capable of challenging for honours.

It upset everyone as it was all done in secret in dark corridors and behind the manager's back. Jezzard left and the impetus vanished until the arrival of Robson's old Albion manager Vic Buckingham. Any chance he had of developing the team was halted once more when the club sold another bright young talent, Rodney Marsh, to Queens Park Rangers. History might have been different if Mullery and Marsh were allowed to develop their skills together at Craven Cottage. Football doesn't work that way, and at least the money was used to some good effect when a lean, young striker named Allan Clarke was brought in from Walsall before moving on to Leicester City just a few months later for £150,000.

Because of the comings and goings Fulham were never able to settle and were always one or two quality players short of a truly championship-challenging side, despite the presence of Haynes, Mullery, Cohen, a member of the 1966 World Cup-winning squad, Eddie Lowe, and the prolific Scot, Graham Leggat. Bobby was convinced that the addition of a couple of quality players would have been enough to push them over the line – though Fulham were regularly close to the relegation rather than the top of the table during his second spell at the Cottage – and the sales of the likes of Mullery and Marsh were clear evidence that the club were not prepared to take that final step to greater things. It was another lesson learned for the future.

6

'The only place that success comes before work is in the dictionary.'
Vince Lombardi. Legendary American football coach.

BOBBY ROBSON HAD NO DOUBTS WHERE HIS
career was heading as he approached his mid-thirties. He had fully
bought into Walter Winterbottom's modern approach, freely describing him as a mentor and describing himself as an FA disciple. He was
delving further into coaching all the time, and prior to Chile he had
earned his full badge.

As soon as he was back at Fulham former FA coach Alan Wade was
in his ear asking if he wanted some work. Wages were still not what
he might have hoped for in this newly enlightened era, especially with
three young sons and a mortgage on his house in Worcester Park, and
so the extra money would come in more than useful, while it also gave

him the opportunity to get some much-needed experience under his belt before retirement from his playing career.

He was offered the job coaching Oxford University and was thus following in the varsity footsteps of both Vic Buckingham and Ron Greenwood. Fulham were only too willing to give him leave to travel to Oxford twice a week – 240 miles all expenses paid, plus two guineas a session, a more than useful supplement.

Oxford were hoping for a lift having been on the receiving end of a loss in their traditional annual battle with Cambridge, and both he and they were delighted when he guided them to victories in their next two Battles of the Blues.

He readily admitted he probably learned more through the experience than the bright young things he coached had learned from him. He discovered how to stand up in front of a group and instruct them with confidence, and to his delight they took in every word and endeavoured with their limited skills but developing brains to put his ideas into action. He responded to their intelligence and eagerness and he soon discovered how to motivate and search out an individual player's qualities.

His expansion into this side of the game did not stop there: he was also a staff coach and paid up member of the Surrey Football Coaches Association. In this role he was in charge of coaches, taking the preliminary courses for school teachers and boys' club leaders and anyone else who wanted to increase their knowledge of the game.

Insatiable, he also worked out of the Crystal Palace National Recreation Centre, lecturing and assessing, trousering the standard fees. It meant he was coaching and teaching at least twice a week during his second spell with Fulham and added another string to his bow – not to mention a very acceptable fee of two pounds five shillings a session – when a friend persuaded him to prepare the players for the Pearl Assurance company for the forthcoming season, Monday and

Friday evenings after work.

The extra cash also allowed him to buy his first car in 1967 when, at the age of 34, he purchased a Morris Minor and was soon using it to drive down to the Essex coast to see Southend United, who had offered him his first coaching job as player-coach. He met up with another friend of mine, Trevor Bailey, then a director of the club. Trevor was a fine cricketer for England and Essex, not to mention our English Press Cricket Association, who he 'managed' on one of our two trips to the Caribbean.

He was a wonderful man, great company and a natural sportsman, although some would question that statement having watched the Barnacle bat for hours on end in Test matches, and Bobby could have signed just for the privilege of conversation with the legend of *Test Match Special*. But neither Trevor nor Southend were blessed with too much cash and offered him less than the £3,500 per year he was earning at Fulham and it also meant dropping down two divisions.

They shook hands and departed friends. Trevor, a brilliant radio summariser, sadly died in a fire at his retirement home in Westcliff, Essex in February 2011, aged 87. Undoubtedly one of my favourite people and a hoot after a drink or several.

Arsenal had shown an interest that never developed and Bobby thought that it was because Fulham wanted a fee, something the Gunners were not prepared to pay for a player reaching the end of his career. In those days there were still no agents and if a player dared to ask what was happening he was told to mind his own business. He was desperately close to joining a club he admired and respected later on in his development as a manager, and a club he agreed to join as George Graham's replacement in 1995, only to be let down by the dishonest Jorge Pinto Da Costa, who as president of Porto had given Bobby his word that he could leave the Portuguese outfit if a top English club came in for him. He was not true to his word. Had there been an agent involved in those early days, I am sure he would have ended up at Highbury.

By now he had decided that a player-coaching job was what he wanted so that he could enjoy another couple of years playing before being forced to hang up his boots. He quit Fulham at the end of the 1967 season and, after lengthy discussions with his family, accepted an offer from the Vancouver Whitecaps in Canada to put together a squad for the upcoming North American season. He was excited at the prospect, having previously enjoyed a stay in the Canadian west coast seaport town in British Columbia on an end of season tour with West Bromwich Albion.

Having seen so little of his wife Elsie and sons, Paul, Andrew and Mark towards the end of his playing career, he agreed the deal only if he could take his family out on the *SS Oriana* for the three-week trip across the Atlantic, first class, giving him his first holiday break for several years.

Doors were opening. The Whitecaps doubled his salary to £7,000 a year, and his duties did not finish with his own team. While he was in Vancouver he was tasked with holding coaching clinics, speaking at dinners and selling the game of football to the North Americans – all while playing and managing.

The Oriana was the last of the Orient Steam Navigation Company ocean liners, built by Vickers-Armstrong in Barrow-in-Furness, not a million miles from Bobby's boyhood home, and was launched in 1959 and sailed round the world until transferred to the ownership of P&O the year before the Robsons set sail. It was the fastest of the fleet and was an experience Bobby never forgot as they docked at exotic places such as Bermuda, Port Everglades, The Panama Canal, Los Angeles and San Francisco, meandering its way to a new life for the Robson clan.

In fact, he could hardly contain his excitement – until he started his job. With four months to go until the start of the season, Robson found upon arrival that not only did he have no players to coach and no money to pay the players he had recruited from around the world, he also had no wages for himself.

He felt desperate for the players to whom he had promised contracts, including two from Hong Kong he had spotted on a close season tour with Fulham, players who were meant to represent the growing Chinese community of Vancouver. He had also made promises to players from his old club, Fulham, and had contacted players from Blackpool and Huddersfield. He had even agreed to a deal with the Cyprus national team goalkeeper, who he was hoping would help attract the interest of the Cypriot community within the city.

Had he been a little wiser himself he might have considered the costs involved in his three-week holiday trip to the Canadian city before he had even started the job, but the owners of the club had sold him a crock of something nasty and had failed to reveal to their naive young player-manager that they were skint so close to their first fixture.

A search was underway to find a financial backer who could save the club and a solution of sorts seemed to have been found when George Flaherty, owner of rival club San Francisco Gales, stepped in and merged the two clubs. It did little to help Robson as the fabulous former Hungarian star Ferenc Puskas, one of the architects of the demolition of England at Wembley in the 1950s, had already been appointed manager of the Gales on a salary far in excess of Robson's.

Puskas, one of the great names of post-war football, was feted and Flaherty set him up with a training camp in Madrid, the city where the prolific goalscorer had finished his career with the world's greatest club side. Puskas was not only a legend but held on a pedestal by Robson, renowned for his performances with the 'Magnificent Magyars' and the scorer of 84 goals in 85 international matches for Hungary, plus seven goals in two European Championship Cup Finals.

Flaherty, unsurprisingly, wanted Robson and his salary out of the picture, but Robson played the aces up his sleeve, the fact that the team were still based in Vancouver and he still had a contract.

It is fair to say that at that stage of his managerial career Puskas was somewhat lacking, unable to translate his individual skills into a coaching platform, while he was unwilling to share the responsibilities with his English counterpart. There was also a language problem and a more fundamental disagreement over the coaching methods. The whole thing was a circus, with Puskas surrounded by friends and hangers-on from both Hungary and Spain. In fact, he allowed anyone who wanted a trial at the club the opportunity to simply turn up.

Despite the obvious lack of professionalism Flaherty would not hear a word against his illustrious manager, even when it became known that some of the players were having a slice of their wages deducted by Puskas's agents. Who did the aggrieved players turn to? Bobby Robson, who could do little to help them as he fought desperately for his own corner in a foreign land, trying to support his bemused family.

Robson had reached his nadir when he returned to Vancouver for Christmas with his family after a visit to England, where he often returned to scout players and catch up with business associates. He could see his first job in management was going nowhere, doomed to failure. It was not just Elsie and the boys he saw back in Canada but also his solicitor, as he sought to recover some of the thousands of Canadian dollars he was owed in wages. His contract as head coach looked watertight, and so he was told to forget the coaching for the time being so he could concentrate on fighting for compensation.

He ignored the advice and when Graham Hortop, secretary of his old club Fulham, called and asked him about his availability, he was up for it. Much against the advice of his legal team, he decided to up sticks and head back to the Cottage for a third stint after meeting up with Hortop, one of the original powerful club secretaries of the time, chairman Tommy Trinder and the money man Sir Eric Miller.

Robson's first job in management in Canada had lasted just nine months and the club did not last a lot longer after he left either, folding at the end of the season and going bust in spectacular fashion.

Fulham were, not unsurprisingly, in trouble when Bobby arrived back, with another relegation looming, but with the financial muscle of redoubtable Sir Eric Merton Miller, the long-term prospects appeared to be a lot brighter. He signed forms in January 1968, turning his back on the small fortune he was legitimately owed in Canada.

Robson confessed to me that he could have kissed Hortop when he offered him the chance to return to Craven Cottage, but he soon found that all he had done was to swap one nightmare for another. Within ten months his attention was drawn to an *Evening Standard* newspaper billboard as he drove across Putney Bridge from the ground announcing that he had been sacked, less than a year into his three-year contract. At first it did not register. He had only left Craven Cottage fifteen minutes earlier that afternoon and no one had hinted at what was to come.

'It was monumental,' he said later. 'I was extremely bitter and very angry.' No one had been brave enough to tell him to his face, but someone had been sneaky enough to let Bernard Joy at the newspaper know first.

Relegation was scarcely his fault – the club had won none of their last nine matches in all competitions when he took charge of his first game in the FA Cup against Macclesfield in January – and it was his understanding that he had been brought in to develop a plan for their immediate return the next season. He had already raised funds by selling striker Allan Clarke to Leicester for the then respectable sum of £150,000, bringing in the grizzled veteran Frank Large as part of the deal. He also invested £1,000 in an unknown Tonbridge full-back Malcolm MacDonald, who eventually became an England international striker and enjoyed a brilliant career with Luton, Newcastle United and Arsenal.

The club was in trouble and it would soon transpire that so too was Miller. Eight years later, he was dead by his own hand while under investigation for fraud, shooting himself in the head on the Jewish Day of Atonement. Miller received his knighthood from Harold Wilson in the controversial 'Lavender List' in 1976, shortly before the Fraud Squad and Department of Trade launched investigations, serving Miller with four writs and seeking restitution of funds he had allegedly taken for himself.

At the time of his sudden sacking Robson stopped the car to buy the paper and read the story written by former Arsenal centre-half Joy, who had become a football scribe at the *Standard*. Joy had telephoned Bobby that morning asking for team information without disclosing the real reason why he was calling or revealing his explosive information. Both Graham Hortop and director and personal friend Chappie D'Amato, a band leader in his real life, professed to know nothing about it and it soon became clear that it was the handiwork of Miller, who confirmed the dismissal himself with the curt acknowledgement that it was because results were not good enough.

Tossed on the scrapheap for the second time in a year, Bobby was distraught. He stood and cried on the centre circle at the Cottage and vowed to himself there and then that he would never return to Fulham in any capacity. Miller's suicide gave Robson no satisfaction, it just made the entire situation more ludicrous.

In all Robson had not managed a single game in Canada and had lasted just eight months in his first managerial job in England. His dismissal from the Fulham post also meant he was skint again, this time with a new house in the Surrey stockbroker belt and his three boys installed in fee-paying schools. He waited for a call, any call from anywhere, but nothing happened. This proud man was reduced to walking his dog on the local golf course and had to watch in anguish as his savings and pay off drained away. He didn't even receive a reply from the jobs he applied for and in the end he knew there was only one thing he could do and that was to sign on at the labour exchange. To his great surprise he found himself rubbing shoulders with bank managers, businessmen and even a retired army major as they all looked for work at a difficult time.

There was further humiliation to come, especially when he went to Radio Rentals to hire a television for the boys to watch while they were at home on school holidays, only to discover that because he was out of work and on the dole he had to pay up front.

Signs were ominous as Robson simply did not have the background in management he needed to secure a senior position and it was something of a relief, if not an answer, when the Chelsea manager Dave Sexton called and asked if he would do some scouting, which he readily accepted, an opportunity to show his face about the circuit and let people know he was in the market for full-time employment all while earning a few shillings.

The first game he was given was Ipswich Town against Nottingham Forest at Portman Road. As it happened, both clubs were looking for a new manager at the time, and so it clearly looked as if he was putting himself up for one of the jobs. Robson decided that he might just as well write to both clubs offering his services before he went to the game and although Forest ignored his letter completely, Ipswich responded as they looked to replace Bill McGarry.

They were a small club but had enjoyed amazing success under Alf Ramsey, winning the title in 1962. What he liked about them was that they enjoyed the reputation of looking after their managers. Since 1936 they had just five men permanently in charge and one of those, Scott Duncan, became secretary after eighteen years as manager, while Ramsey only departed after eight years to take over the England management.

It looked an outside bet, with the bookmakers cutting the odds-on Frank O'Farrell and Billy Bingham, only for Frank to decide to stay at Torquay while Billy remained at Plymouth. It must have been something about the south coast air, but there was no doubting that Ipswich could sniff out talent as Frank went on to manage Manchester United while Billy was a giant with Everton and also managed Northern Ireland.

As a result, just two days after his application in January 1969, Bobby Robson was to change his life when he accepted an invitation to meet the much-loved Ipswich chairman John Cobbold and directors Harold Smith and Ken Brightwell at the Great Western Hotel in London. They offered him a job but, remarkably, no contract. Mr John made light of it, telling him it meant at least two years but, after his recent experiences, Bobby was unsure. Still, he was in no position to turn the job down. After excusing himself for a couple of minutes away from the three delightful men, he returned to the room, shook hands and accepted the job. It ended a period of horrible uncertainty.

'I have to confess that I was concerned for my future,' he later admitted, 'but I had no thought of quitting, even though I had to go to the labour exchange and sign on the dole. I didn't know what else to do as I had no money.

'I was a young manager. I had no reputation. I had no credibility. I had no CV. I wondered who was going to employ me. It could have finished me in the game but, Ipswich came in and saved me by offering me their vacant job out of the blue. Six months after being sacked by Fulham I had a job at Ipswich on £6,000 a year.'

Welcome to the rest of your life, Mr. Robson.

7

'When we won, John Cobbold had a bottle of champagne and when we lost he had two bottles of champagne. That was his civilised way of looking at defeat.'

Bobby Robson, 2003

THE WORDS 'BOBBY ROBSON' AND 'IPSWICH TOWN'

are synonymous, aren't they? His success at the little club in Suffolk is legendary and led him directly to the job as England manager. His popularity was unquestioned, and he and his wife Elsie were considered part of the fabric of the town.

Yet that was not always the case. In fact, many of the Ipswich Town fans wanted the head of their new manager in his first two years as the club struggled to keep their heads above water.

It was a grim period and failure at Ipswich after his dodgy start in Canada and back at Fulham would have put his entire future in football under threat. He argued with some of his players and had the Tractor Boys supporters screaming such obscenities at him that it shook and upset Elsie as she sat in the stands. It reached a crescendo in the 1970/71 season when they were thrashed by Manchester United as George Best scored the perfect hat-trick. After the game he and his opposite number Frank O'Farrell agreed that if Ipswich had Best instead of United, they might well have won.

That admission was of little consolation to Bobby and he feared the worst, especially when John Cobbold called a board meeting the next day. However, he wasn't prepared for the chairman's opening statement to his fellow board members.

'Gentlemen,' he said, 'the first business of the day is to officially record in the minutes the apologies of this board to the manager for the behaviour of the fans last night. Agreed? If it ever occurs at this ground again, I will resign as chairman. Right. Onto the next business.'

Bobby loved both Mr John and Mr Patrick, as they liked to be addressed, and would delight in repeating their quirky expressions and transgressions just as much as they enjoyed hearing their manager's spoonerisms. One of Bobby's favourites came from Mr. John who, after Ipswich had qualified for Europe, commented, 'We're delighted to be competing in Europe. How else can we get our duty-free cigarettes?' Mr. Patrick, meanwhile, had his mind focused on similarly important matters: 'What constitutes a crisis at Ipswich? Well, if we ran out of white wine in the boardroom.'

His support was immense, as he showed in 1971 when Ipswich slumped to the bottom of the first division table and he promptly awarded Bobby a salary increase, saying, 'Our manager's name is not written on his door in chalk with a wet sponge nailed by the side.'

Bobby revelled in the tales of the two brothers, especially those of John, who loved a night out on the away leg visits to foreign towns and would write the name of his hotel on his shirt cuff so that he could find his way back to his lodgings, or so he could at least be helped to his bed for the night.

Sudden outbursts of bad language were accepted as the norm when it came to this genuine eccentric, although it often left his manager nonplussed. One such occasion was the time when Bobby was trying to sign a top player from Portsmouth and sought to impress him and his wife by taking them to Mr John's tranquil 2,000-acre home, where a pair of black swans floated gracefully on a lake. It was idyllic, and the manager was quietly rubbing his hands in glee, knowing that this sort of ambience would surely clinch the deal.

But that was without considering the impact of Mr. John's pair of donkeys, Alka and Seltzer, a mother and son, who produced a foal, aptly named Calamity. As they took tea on the lawn Mr John explained the illicit relationship to the couple and then, incredibly, turned to the player and asked, 'You don't fuck donkeys, do you?'

Bobby wished for the ground to open up and swallow him, while the young couple sprang to their feet and left in high dudgeon while Mr. John collapsed laughing. He did it again at the celebrations at the Copdock Hotel for one of their two FA Youth Cup wins under Bobby when he, to his great regret, persuaded his chairman to make a short speech to thank the parents, landladies and the players for their efforts over the course of the season.

Robson joined him on the stage as the chairman thanked everyone for coming, praised the young players and then turned to his manager and told the open-mouthed audience: 'The manager here wants to win the competition again in eighteen years' time, so I want you all to go home and have a jolly good fuck and produce another team.' The manager ought not to have worried, as after the audience got over their initial shock, they soon stood and gave the chairman a standing ovation.

My own favourite memory of the chairman came when Ipswich opened their new indoor training facility, heavily funded by their sponsors Pioneer, which was attended by local dignitaries, the players and some press from the local paper and from Fleet Street. No one had been allowed a preliminary look at the state-of-the-art centre, complete with the latest development in artificial grass, and so everyone stood gaping when they walked in to be greeted by an outcrop of mushrooms, seemingly growing in the Astroturf. The penny soon dropped as Mr John collapsed laughing. He had been out in the morning to one of the farm shops and returned to 'plant' the fungus ready for the arrival of his guests.

Soon after the chairman's apology for the poor behaviour of Ipswich's fans, he put his money where his mouth was, allowing his manager to invest £70,000 in Blackburn Rovers central-defender Allan Hunter, at the time Ipswich's record transfer fee paid.

Despite having little or no experience in the world of management, it quickly became obvious to Robson that he had to shoulder the major responsibilities – the boss did not have a large backroom team backing him up – and that there was little or no money to develop his first team. To that end he quickly decided that he needed not only to develop a youth policy but also Portman Road itself.

The support for a small-town club was quite impressive, with as many as 16,000 often in attendance for the bigger games. Only 2,500 were able to watch from the discomfort of a seat in the infamous 'Cow Shed' stand. In truth the whole ground was falling down, due in no small part to the previous angry young manager Bill McGarry, who went about kicking walls and doors after his many defeats, which had dragged the club into a relegation fight inherited by Robson.

The Cow Shed had to go and it was Robson himself who negotiated the sale of the old stand to the local speedway club and set about having the ground rebuilt, with a replacement stand the first priority. Many managers of the day had to contend with limited budgets, but not many were in charge of the redevelopment of the club's ground.

+++

FOR ALL OF BOBBY ROBSON'S SUCCESS WITH

England, Newcastle, PSV Eindhoven, Porto and Sporting Lisbon, his greatest legacy is probably with Ipswich Town. Yet had it been the cut-throat world of modern football of today, he probably would not have survived the two years of toil and struggle which allowed him time to develop his team and his ideas at Portman Road.

At first it was a struggle. After Bill McGarry left months into the 1968/69 season Robson steadied a rocky ship, leading them to safety and the relevant comfort of twelfth place, but in the following two campaigns the Tractor Boys slipped further back down the table, finishing in eighteenth and then nineteenth. 1971/72 saw Ipswich finish thirteenth, but it was the season after that when things really started to click into place.

Ipswich ended the season in fourth and demonstrated to the fans that there was real progress being made. In truth, they had been getting gradually better for a while. Robson's first three full campaigns in charge had seen his team accrue more points than in the last season on every occasion: 31 in his first year, 34 in the second and 38 in the third. In 1972/73, that points total jumped up ten to 48.

The icing on the season's cake came with a 4-2 victory over bitter rivals Norwich in the Texaco Cup in May, with Ipswich prevailing 2-1 in both legs, home and away. The cup was a competition that ran from 1970 to 1975 involving sides from England, Scotland and Ireland, and to get to the final Robson's men had to overcome St Johnstone, Wolverhampton Wanderers and Newcastle. It was the club's first success since the title win at under Alf Ramsey, and it also kickstarted Robson's success in cup competitions.

From that moment on Ipswich became an almost exclusively top half outfit under Robson, with the next four seasons yielding finishes of fourth, third, sixth and third, nearly emulating the title success of

1961/62 on a number of occasions. In the 1974/75 campaign, the season after Robson had rejected the advances of Leeds United as they searched for a replacement for Don Revie, Ipswich came particularly close to glory. They ended up in third place, though that only really tells half of the story. Clough's Derby were the eventual champions on 53 points, with both Liverpool and Robson's men finishing level on points with 51. Ipswich actually won more games than any other side over the course of the campaign, with 23 from their 42 games. Sadly, fourteen defeats meant they fell just short.

Ipswich had spent the season chasing an unlikely double and it looked to be on when they beat holders Liverpool and then Aston Villa in the FA Cup. Following those two impressive victories reigning First Division champions Leeds United were next up, the team he had so recently turned down. In those days in the FA Cup you'd keep playing and replaying your fixture until there was an outright winner of the tie, and so it took four energy sapping games plus three lots of extra time for Ipswich to finally beat Leeds 3-2 at the neutral Filbert Street.

In their semi-final against West Ham they were forced into another replay, and in that encounter Welsh referee Clive Thomas ruled out two Ipswich goals, both of which Robson claimed were proved to be good by the television cameras, even though it was long before the days of endless replays pored over by a host of pundits in the television studio.

Ipswich had looked tired and strained in the first match against West Ham at Villa Park, but they girded their loins for the replay at Stamford Bridge until, with the scores at 1-1, they were denied by the man in charge of the game. The most controversial of the two disallowed goals saw Bryan Hamilton adjudged to be offside and it so enraged Robson that he demanded an FA enquiry into the referee. This, in turn, inflamed Thomas, and thereafter the two loathed each other for the remainder of their careers.

Robson was always wary of the self-serving international referee and a reputation that went before him. Strict and over officious, he was perhaps the first celebrity referee who courted headlines and controversy throughout his distinguished international career, most famously of all in the 1978 World Cup in Argentina when refereeing a game between Brazil and Sweden. With the game entering injury time and the scores locked at 1-1, Brazil won a corner on the right but as Zico rose to head the ball home, Thomas blew his whistle for full time. Brazil's protests at the time and after the game fell on deaf ears as Thomas said he blew the whistle at exactly the right time whereas other referees, then and now, allow the passage of play to be completed before blowing up.

Thomas later exercised his right of reply in his autobiography *By the Book*, released in 1984. He believed that Robson should have been warned for his conduct and suggested that the reason he wasn't was because Bert Millichip, the chairman of the FA, would later appoint the Ipswich manager in the England post. Robson, meanwhile, remained furious at a man he described as a good referee but a big head who wanted to be the most important person on the pitch.

The disappointment of the defeat and all the replays that had led up to that moment took their toll on what was a small squad and their title challenge foundered, with Robson forced to introduce youngsters in place of his injured regulars. He always claimed to me that had he been able to afford to spend another £200,000, he would have won the league title not once but two or three times. He simply could not afford to buy players to sit on the bench in case of an injury crisis and he wouldn't put the club in hock to do so, and as a result he ended up falling just short.

After four consecutive finishes in the top six there was a drop off in the 1977/78 campaign, with Ipswich slipping down to eighteenth, but it is unlikely that the fans cared about their side's league travails – they had more important things to worry about in the FA Cup.

The Tractor Boys were on a roll in the world's most famous domestic cup competition, making their way past Cardiff, Hartlepool, Bristol City, Millwall and West Bromwich Albion, leading to a showdown at Wembley with Terry Neill's Arsenal, who were at the end of a strong league campaign.

No one outside gave Ipswich a chance of upsetting the mighty Gunners and all of that negativity was distilled in a terrible 6-1 defeat to Aston Villa just beforehand, with much of the trouble centring around the skilful midfield player Colin Viljoen, who Bobby admired as a player but not as a person.

Viljoen was not particularly highly regarded by his teammates either, reflected by his relationship with Derek Jefferson, the player who shared the same digs. The two would share a table for breakfast before Viljoen would set off for the ground in his car, leaving the full-back to catch the bus. This left the easy-going Jefferson shrugging his shoulders but the manager fuming and the other players seething on their defender's behalf.

Viljoen, like a lot of others, endured many injury problems during that campaign and found himself in and out of the side as the manager plotted and schemed to try and gather enough points to stave off relegation. What really annoyed Bobby at the time was that he felt some of his wounded warriors had an eye on the cup final and, sure enough, suddenly he had a full, fit squad from which to pick from ahead for the Villa game, the match before the final clash. Viljoen, when fit, was a key player and he was given his chance to prove himself in place of the popular grafter Roger Osborne, but it was such a disaster of a performance that only some outstanding goalkeeping from 18-year-old local novice Paul Overton kept the score under double figures.

As a result of a meeting with his staff after the crushing defeat,

Bobby made the bravest call of his Ipswich career, leaving out his schemer Viljoen for Osborne. In the process, he upset his own fans and received a panning in the newspapers, but it was a risk he was prepared to take. In truth, he was more concerned with his centre-half Allan Hunter, who faced a late fitness test. Hunter eventually declared himself fit and ready to play, but only after an unscheduled run out on the manicured lawns of Sopwell House hotel before breakfast on the morning of the game.

There was certainly no one complaining about their manager's choice after the game when Ipswich upset all the odds with a goal thirteen minutes from time by, of all people, Roger Osborne. There were scenes like never before or since as everyone threw themselves on their conservative young midfield player, who was suitably overwhelmed by the moment, so much so that Robson had to substitute him even before the game was restarted. A combination of emotional exhaustion and sunstroke meant he wasn't in the correct frame of mind to continue.

It was the highlight of Robson's time at Portman Road and more so because he held the FA Cup in such high esteem. In fact, he claimed that of all five cup competitions he won in his career, this was the best and certainly the most personally satisfying. Even before his team made it to the twin towers, he would make the pilgrimage every year he could, always using his players' ticket, never once tempted to bolster his wages by selling it on the black market as so many did in those days.

It would be nice to think that all players and all clubs were the same, but it is no secret that there would a designated man to sell on the team's allocation of tickets and such were the rewards that more often than not, the proceeds funded the family holiday in the close season or paid off debts to the bookmaker. Every time he watched the cup final he dreamt and hoped that he could one day be part of the celebrations himself, and how he enjoyed the walk from the dressing rooms into the May sunshine in front of the massed ranks of the blue and white clad Ipswich fans when he finally got his opportunity. Needless to say, every ticket of the allocation had been sold, and Robson always said they could have sold out the stadium on their own.

They overcame odds of 5/2 against but he and his team loved being the underdog and they were perfectly relaxed in the dressing room ahead of kick-off, and it showed on the pitch as Ipswich dominated for large parts of the final and hit the woodwork three times, twice through John Wark, before Clive Wood and David Geddis combined to tee up Osborne, who scored with his left foot.

The Arsenal team was stuffed with top internationals such as Pat Jennings, Pat Rice, Sammy Nelson, David O'Leary, Willie Young, Liam Brady, Alan Sunderland, Malcolm MacDonald and Frank Stapleton, but Brian Talbot, Allan Hunter and Kevin Beattie refused to be moved and goalkeeper Paul Cooper never looked like being beaten.

The final whistle sparked off a celebration in Suffolk which lasted for days, spilling over to Micky Lambert's nicely timed testimonial the next night, where 20,000 turned up to celebrate the substitute who came on to replace the hero Osborne at Wembley. A magnificent Suffolk Punch – a horse not a cocktail – joined the blue and white beribboned FA Cup on a lap of honour before the game. After the game the cup went home to the manager's house just up the road, and Robson kept it under his bed as he tried to sleep that night.

The FA turned a blind eye, allowing Ipswich to keep the trophy for eleven months. It was taken to schools, village fetes, shop windows and, of course, the Ipswich boardroom every other Saturday, while every night it was locked up in the local police station.

Before its return to Lancaster Gate it was taken to a local jeweller for a thorough cleaning and buffing and it was returned to the FA looking better than it did almost a year earlier. There were genuine tears shed when it was sent home before being presented to the next winners, Arsenal, the team they had beaten, who outlasted Manchester United 3-2 in a game with three goals in the final few minutes.

Robson and Ipswich returned to Wembley for the Charity Shield in the 1978/79 season curtain-raiser, but they looked to be carrying a hangover from the season before as, in Robson's own words, they were 'humiliated' by five-goal Nottingham Forest. There looked to be problems ahead for the club, and more concerning than defeat itself were the serious injuries to both key central defenders Allan Hunter and Kevin Beattie.

Ipswich needed inspiration and it came when the manager consulted his notebook and found the names of two Dutch internationals, Arnold Muhren and Frans Thijssen, who had performed well for FC Twente against his team in a pre-season friendly. He couldn't believe his luck when the Dutch side asked for just £150,000 for the skilful Muhren, a midfielder, and he almost bit their hands off five months later he went back and snapped up Thijssen for £220,000, which still left him with £80,000 from the sale of Talbot. Still, it did top his highest previous signing of £150,000 to sign Paul Mariner from Plymouth and was an indication that success at Portman Road had provided Robson with the opportunity to be a bit more ambitious in the transfer market.

Around the same time Trevor Francis became the first million-pound transfer when he joined Nottingham Forest from Birmingham City, while not long after that Manchester City spent almost £1.5 million to sign Steve Daley from Wolves, and Wolves later responded by paying a similar fee to take Andy Gray to Molineux from Aston Villa. Robson was still unearthing bargains.

Not only were they bargains, but Ipswich's deal with the Dutch pair and Spurs's capture of Argentine internationals Ossie Ardiles and Ricardo Villa at around the same time subsequently helped pave the way for many other foreign footballers looking to test themselves in English football, and from that moment on more and more started to arrive.

After the 1977/78 aberration in the league Ipswich returned to the higher echelons of the division in the next two campaigns, with finishes of sixth and third, and the Tractor Boys were really back to their best by the start of the 1980/81 season, finding themselves right in the hunt for silverware again. Their form was so good at times that they managed to beat eventual champions Aston Villa on three occasions, but once more a thin squad punished the frugal manager and his club. Even a change of rules in the FA Cup, decreeing for the first time that semi-finals could go to extra time, came to haunt them as they lost the hugely influential Kevin Beattie with a broken arm in their tie with Manchester City and were forced to play the additional thirty minutes with ten men with the game locked at 0-0. Injuries had the physio working harder than the manager and although they patched up the walking wounded, they eventually succumbed to a Paul Power goal.

Another win against Villa in the next league game re-established Ipswich as favourites for the title, only for them to stumble to defeats against Arsenal, Norwich, Middlesbrough and Southampton. Ironically, their only win in this dismal period came against the team who beat them in the semi-final – Manchester City. They ended up finishing four points short of Ron Saunders's Villa side.

There was so much promise and suddenly so little reward in domestic competition as injuries and a limited first team squad caught them out. But it was all so different in Europe, much to the delight of the Cobbold brothers, who were able to continue with their duty-free purchases as Ipswich progressed in the UEFA Cup.

Given the likes of Juventus, Manchester United, Barcelona, Porto, St. Etienne, Dynamo Moscow, Hamburg, Cologne, Stuttgart and Eintracht Frankfurt were all competing, everyone thought Ipswich's journey would be a rather short one. Because only the league winners went into the European Cup in those days, the UEFA Cup was a competition with brimming with quality and every game was a two-legged knockout tie.

Robson's side began with victories against Aris Salonika of Greece (6-4 on aggregate), Bohemians Prague (3-2) and then with Widzew Lodz of Poland, who had beaten Manchester United to get to this stage. After such an impressive result over fellow English opposition the Poles clearly fancied themselves, and Robson was left shocked when his Polish counterpart asked him, via an interpreter, if he fancied a bet on the result. Taken aback at the very idea of it Bobby said no, and the Polish coach must have been grateful as his side were on the end of a five-goal beating at Portman Road, thanks to a John Wark hat-trick. There were no similar offers forthcoming for the return leg in Poland, which was played in sub-zero temperatures.

Conditions were so bad that the referee offered Ipswich the choice of calling the game off, but it would have meant a return in March after the closure of the Polish season for their winter break. The timing simply would not work for either club.

They played and lost 1-0 against a team including the likes of top internationals Zbigniew Boniek, Wlodzimierz Smolarek and Wladyslaw Zmuda, but went through comfortably to earn a tie against the excellent St Etienne, full of sparkling international superstars like Patrick Battiston, Michel Platini, Jonny Rep, Gerard Janvion, Jean-Francoise Larios and Jean Castenada. As if that was not enough, they had not lost a home European cup tie for 26 years.

We on the press and the ambivalent Ipswich board had enjoyed top cuisine prepared by a world-famous chef at lunchtime, which turned out to be just the *hors d'Oeuvres* for a magnificent feast as Ipswich stunned the full house of 40,000, mainly Frenchmen, with a 4-1 victory.

The crazy celebrations in the away dressing room were only disturbed by the arrival of the St. Etienne president, who hugged Robson and told him he had never seen anyone tear his side apart like that. The Ipswich manager appreciated the compliment as much as the victory. From a personal point of view, it was the best I ever saw Ipswich play under the guidance of Bobby Robson and some of the best food and wine I have ever consumed.

The biggest problem was neither form nor goals, but the sheer volume of fixtures, and they soon ran into the usual backlog that faces any English side who do well in any of the cup competitions. Before they travelled to Germany for the second leg of the semi-final against Cologne, they had to play three crucial games in a matter of days: Arsenal at Portman Road on the Saturday, a match which they lost 2-0, then local rivals Norwich on the Monday, which slipped away 1-0, and then their German opponents at Portman Road in the first leg on Wednesday. They finally managed victory in that game courtesy of a John Wark goal, but Cologne must have had some confidence in the knowledge that their opponents still had to face Manchester City on the Saturday before travelling for the second leg.

Their team of internationals, which included England's Tony Woodcock, and Germany's Toni Schumacher, Harald Konopka, Herbert Zimmerman, Rainer Bonhof, Pierre Litbarski, Dieter Muller and Stefan Engels, clearly fancied their chances in the second leg in front of their 55,000-sell-out crowd against a team who had dramatically lost their form domestically and were on their knees physically. Ipswich Town were knackered, and Bobby Robson knew it.

He knew he had to think out of the box, and so he cancelled training and took the squad off to the local fairground for two hours, with riotous pictures emerging of the players laughing, joking, sliding down water shoots and riding the big dipper, causing much merriment and bemusement amongst the Germans. It worked. Ipswich defended like demons and not only kept a clean sheet against the free-scoring Cologne side but scored themselves through their young central defender Terry Butcher. They were into another final, this time against AZ Alkmaar.

Their joy was short-lived when they flew home from Cologne into Norwich airport – note the name – and were held up by customs officials who opened every skip and every case, taking an hour and half to do so. They found nothing but managed to take the joy out of the return trip for the Ipswich players and when Robson asked the simple question of why, he was given the old jobsworth answer: we are just doing our jobs.

As envious as Norwich and their supporters might have been, Ipswich were now in a European final against one of the other rank outsiders in the competition. The first leg at Portman Road soon became a party, and not only in the boardroom. The problems of the previous weeks, when the season had started falling apart, were simply shrugged off as Bobby sent his team out all guns blazing – this was the final hurdle. They responded with goals from John Wark once more, Frans Thijssen and Paul Mariner to take with them to Amsterdam two weeks down the line.

Bobby Robson was a big fan of Dutch football and their players and he was relieved to have a three goal cushion for the second leg of the final. He didn't need telling who their stars were, having watched Jan Peters score twice against England in an international while Johnny Metgod, Ronald Spelbos, Hugo Hovenkamp, Kristen Nygard, Jos Jonker and Kees Kist were all players he had watched on his scouting trips.

Thijssen scored first against his countrymen after just four minutes to give the English side what looked to be an unassailable four-goal lead, but Alkmaar lit up the Olympic Stadium in Amsterdam by throwing everything at their English opponents, defending with just two at the back despite Ipswich having Alan Brazil and Paul Mariner up front. It was shoot or bust and they pulled goals back through Welzl three minutes after Thijssen's goal and another when Metgod popped one in. Ipswich might have been in trouble but for a timely goal from Wark, setting a competition record of fourteen strikes, which made the aggregate score 5-2. Although Tol and Jonker added further goals, the two away goals meant that Alkmaar needed to score six. They couldn't manage it and Ipswich were champions.

Ipswich erected a huge marquee on the training ground next to the ground and the triumph was celebrated in true British fashion of the time – booze, booze and more booze, led by the indefatigable Cobbolds, who must have cornered the market in Suffolk for Sancerre that evening while the players drank beer and anything else that came to hand.

They were a lovely lot the Ipswich players, a good reflection of their manager, who was happy to stand back and take the congratulations of all of those around him with a glass of champagne which seemed to last him the night. Yet Robson was well aware of the importance of a triumph in Europe, not just for Ipswich Town but for England as well. There were only two European trophies played for by the top clubs in Europe and they won one of them. Some achievement.

The next season – 1981/82 – was even worse on the injury front and virtually every one of his squad suffered lengthy absences at one stage or another, including losing the outstanding Kevin Beattie for good, but it was an unusual injury to Terry Butcher which caused most concern. He missed fifteen games on the bounce through what everyone thought was a simple nose bleed. He was stretchered off in a cup game against Luton Town because the doctor couldn't stop the bleeding and instead of travelling back with the team he was kept in the Kenilworth Road physio room as the blood continued to gush.

In the end it was his father who insisted on taking him to the Luton and Dunstable Hospital because he was becoming weak from the loss of blood. He was eventually released but the next day, after lunch at the club's Centre Spot restaurant, the bleeding began again, so badly this time that the local Ipswich accident and emergency transferred him to a London hospital as no one was able to staunch or understand the frightening flow.

Eventually it was discovered that he had ruptured a nerve behind the nose but by that time it was reckoned that he had lost so much blood that he had to have nineteen pints of plasma pumped through his veins, almost three times the normal content of blood in the body. It was literally life threatening as Butcher lost a terrific amount of weight, and a simple cough could start the bleeding off again. Robson visited him on a regular basis and was genuinely concerned, not just for his football future but for his life.

But Butcher was made of sterner stuff than his manager or three hospitals reckoned, and not only did he return to the club, but played in the last nine games as they chased the title in vain yet again, finishing four points short of glory just like the year before, this time behind Bob Paisley's Liverpool.

The Ipswich injury curse struck again with Paul Cooper, Frans Thijssen, Russell Osman, Paul Mariner and Alan Brazil all missing for varying lengths of time. Mariner was off at the same time as Butcher with an Achilles tendon injury, while the influential Thijssen missed a total of thirty games.

The defence of the UEFA Cup disappeared in the first round, Ipswich losing to Alex Ferguson's Aberdeen, while the FA Cup proved to be the biggest disappointment, losing to giant killers Shrewsbury Town after putting out Birmingham City and Luton. The League Cup promised much with wins against Bradford, Everton and Watford, before Ipswich succumbed to Liverpool in the two-legged semi-final with a 2-2 draw at Anfield being spoiled by a 2-0 defeat at home.

They finished the season well in the league, losing just twice in the last sixteen matches, but in the same number of games Liverpool did not lose at all, demonstrating the kind of relentlessness and resolve that had seen them dominate English football for such a long period of time. Not even the coming of age of Alan Brazil and the prolific scoring of John Wark, who Robson likened to his future England captain Bryan Robson, could compensate for the absence of so many quality players for such a long time for Ipswich.

Though that league title remained elusive, Robson's success at Portman Road by this point was sustained, spread out across a number of years, with the manager consistently having to rebuild and replenish his first team, with players often arriving from the youth side he had helped to build. That self-sustaining youth policy reaped two successive FA Youth Cups in 1973/74 and 1974/75, without the help of any sort of grants. While the majority of the clubs spent any profits made on new players before tax kicked in, Robson and his willing board of directors paid their capital gains tax on the profits and then spent the residue on improving their ground, facilities and training pitches after careful budgeting and planning.

Robson's results were even more impressive given the problems he faced at the start of his reign. Not only was he fighting history and penury when he first arrived, but also some of his own players. Some of the senior figures in the dressing room were unimpressed with this young whippersnapper throwing his weight around and denying them their usual privileges, and so decided to take him on.

The tipping point arrived in the 1970/71 season when Irish international Tommy Carroll threw the rattle out of the pram after a verbal skirmish and went home to Dublin in an almighty huff, leaving Robson no option but to fine and suspend him for the upcoming game against Leeds United, which also saw another of the grizzled veterans, Bill Baxter, left out after pushing the envelope too far.

Ipswich crashed to a 4-2 defeat that weekend and the errant pair were rumoured to have celebrated with champagne and laughed at the result. Robson was a gentle gentleman but, like most sportsmen, when tested or backed into a corner he could turn into a whirling dervish.

He had had enough and when Carroll tore the team sheet off the notice board and thrust it into his face with a flurry of expletives it lit a short fuse, and when he then propelled his head towards the apoplectic manager all bets were off. Bobby, in self-defence, took a swing at the player, who was immediately joined by his cohort Baxter. Both threw punches at their boss until Bobby was reinforced by his faithful assistant Cyril Lea.

Robson quite rightly felt that he had his authority challenged one time too many. To him, the team sheet was revered, literally untouchable, and was not to be defaced, removed or, in this case, torn up and thrown on the floor.

He knew that had he backed down then it was the end of another managerial job, and he was furious when big full-back Geoff Hammond, backed by other shocked players, waded in to break up what was undoubtedly a brawl.

But it was Robson who emerged the victor as the rest of his squad backed him rather than Carroll and Baxter, who did not have quite the popularity and sway they thought they had in the dressing room. Their teammates wanted them completely ostracised but Robson, calming down, simply decided that they had kicked their last ball for the club.

Not only did the players back him but so did Mr John, who told him to get rid of the erring pair, even if this hand to mouth club had to give them away for nothing. In the end, he managed to raise a grand total of £31,000 by flogging Carroll to Birmingham and Baxter to Hull City. It was a key turning point: not only had Robson exerted his authority, he had done so and come out on top, receiving the backing of those above and below him.

'I couldn't have had a better job or better bosses,' he reflected. 'Brothers John and Patrick Cobbold let me get on with the job – every aspect of it.

'I had learned at Fulham, and when I stood in that centre circle I vowed that I would never be in that position – or put my family in that position – again. When I came up against a problem I would deal with it, and boy did I come up against some problems.

'Anywhere else I might not have lasted those two years the Cobbolds promised me when I first joined. They backed me every inch of the way. When we won, John had a bottle of champagne and when we lost he had two bottles of champagne. That was his civilized way of looking at defeat. He was a remarkable guy, an outstanding fellow.

'Everyone remembers it as years of unbridled success. It wasn't. I had fights – literally – with some players, the results were bad, but the board were always behind me, encouraging me, and gradually it began to turn around.'

Safe in the knowledge that he had the backing from the people that mattered, he continued to weather the storm. It took him three years to turn Ipswich round with the help of Cyril Lea and chief scout Ray Tyrell, who had mined the local talent and brought in the likes of Brian Talbot, Trevor Whymark, Mick Lambert, Clive Woods, Laurie Sivell, Roger Osborne, Colin Harper and Mick Mills, who Bobby made captain at the age of 21.

Not even the loss of the shrewd Tyrell could halt the progress as Bobby surrounded himself with Ron Gray, John Carruthers and George Finlay, who, from his base in Glasgow, brought in top quality players from north of the border such as John Wark, Alan Brazil, and George Burley, while Carruthers unearthed diamonds like Kevin Beattie, Eric Gates, David Geddes and Paul Gascoigne.

Gascoigne may have never played for Ipswich in the end, but he was mighty close. Aged fourteen at the time when he travelled south from Newcastle to Portman Road in 1981 – another player ready to leave the North East if the opportunity was good enough – he was clearly a youngster of immense talent and promise, but he was also as broad as he was tall, a roly-poly who looked more like a trainee Sumo wrestler than an apprentice footballer. With the club's tight budget, Robson thought it a gamble he could not afford to take, and Gascoigne soon made the grade at St James' Park.

Years later he did take the plunge with Gascoigne, introducing him to the England set-up shortly before Italia '90, and the country's most prodigious talent rewarded his manager by being elected the best young player in the World Cup. How Bobby loved him and how he loved Bobby. It was a football partnership made in heaven between two icons of the country born just over ten miles away from each other.

There was better luck when brother Bobby's brother Tom informed him that he had just seen a centre-half who could be another Kevin Beattie. He wasn't far wrong with his recommendation – Russell Osman would eventually become an England captain, and formed an excellent partnership with Terry Butcher, another man Bobby would come to rely on so heavily.

Osman was one of a number of Ipswich players, including John Wark, Kevin Beattie's legs and Kevin O'Callaghan, as well as international legends Pele, Bobby Moore, Ossie Ardiles, Kazimierez Deyna and Mike Summerbee and actors Michael Caine and Sylvester Stallone to feature in the legendary film *Escape to Victory*.

There were seven Ipswich players involved because, according to John Wark, Robson knew someone in the film industry. Kevin Beattie's legs were used as 'stand-ins' for Michael Caine's when the football scenes were being filmed. Beattie also managed to annoy Stallone when he beat him in an arm-wrestling contest.

Bobby's friends were wide and varied because he was such an affable, easy to get on with guy, but I have to confess that he never mentioned his contact in the film industry to me. That said, I can quite easily believe a couple of phone calls from Hollywood would have sorted it out.

Osman was just the type of player Bobby wanted to recruit, having set himself a budget between £40,000 and £70,000. He simply couldn't afford errors even at that price and scored some remarkable hits over the years with £20,000 goalkeeper Paul Cooper from Birmingham, tricky winger Kevin O'Callaghan from Millwall, as well as Frank Clark, David Johnson, Jimmy Robertson and Allan Hunter (who actually cost a whopping £75,000).

It wasn't just a question of buying but also selling at a profit, as he did with striker David Geddes, who later joined Aston Villa for £300,000, and wing-half Brian Talbot, sold to Arsenal for £450,000. Robson always looked to balance the books as if the money was his own, helping keep the club on even keel and helping him to fund the next crop of bargains.

Robson and Cyril Lea would often go to extreme lengths to scout players. On one such occasion they both made a dual trip up north using just Robson's car. They were going to separate matches, and so at the junction of the M1 and M62 Robson gave his colleague his keys so he could carry on to Leeds, while Robson himself hitched a lift to Manchester.

A big wagon was the first to stop and was delighted for the company, and luckily enough he was passing Old Trafford. Robson, wearing a 'disguise' of a flat cap and muffler, thought it wasn't the done thing to be seen rolling up at one of the world's most iconic grounds in a big eight-wheeler and got the driver to drop him off down the road where, he claimed, he was meeting his mates for coffee and a bacon butty.

It's a story that only demonstrates his commitment to the cause and he absolutely adored life at Portman Road, with England the only team that could have prised him away from a club and an area he had fallen in love with. It was, after all, the job that made him as a manager.

'I had difficult times. We won this and won that, but I also had it rough, and you don't get to the top unless it has been rough at some stage,' he would tell me. Some big-name footballers have tried their hand and given up at the first sign of problems or have packed it in because they have had the sack. To me that smacks of no character and no guts.

'I had a great quality of life. No one at the club had a better car than me, nobody at the club earned more money than me. I was the best paid person at Ipswich and the chairman would not allow players to earn more than I did.

'Some critics believed that had I invested more money in the players the club could have achieved even more, but it was a matter of personal pride to keep Ipswich in the black and to play good, attractive football. I always tried to spend the club's money as if it were my own.

'The right club came in for me at the right time. I finished up with a ten-year contract and finally finished working there after fourteen years.'

8

*'A successful man is one who can lay a firm foundation
with the bricks others have thrown at him.'*
David Brinkley, American broadcaster.

ONE AFTERNOON DURING ROBSON'S FIRST SEASON
as Barcelona manager, the 1996/97 campaign, he and I were sitting
quietly talking in his rented luxury apartment in Sitges, the seaside
resort a stone's throw from his workplace at the Camp Nou in
Barcelona, when an intense young man I didn't know came through
the unlocked back door unannounced. 'This,' said Robson, 'is my
assistant Jose Mourinho.'

I recalled the name from Bobby's time in Portugal with Sporting
Lisbon and Porto, but we had never met officially or unofficially and
clearly he was not best pleased to see someone taking up his boss's
time when he wanted to talk football with him. However, things soon
settled down and I was left with the impression that here was a young

man determined to make his name in football with the backing of the man he simply called 'Meester'.

One of the many things that the experienced, greying former England manager was able to teach the young Jose about was the side of the game outside the confines of the football pitch and the training ground, how he could defend himself against the brickbats that inevitably came his way as a number one of so many important clubs.

Football management remains one of the most unforgiving industries, but it was one that Bobby loved, another aspect he was all too happy to impress on those who looked up to him. With its gorgeous, tranquil beach, its verdant green hills, its restaurant and bars, Bobby also loved Sitges, and it was not hard to see why.

It was close to paradise and acted as a haven to Bobby, a place where he could reflect on the traumas and the joys of what had gone before, about those figurative bricks that were thrown at him and the not so figurative spittle that stained his mackintosh coat at Wembley as he went on a roller coaster ride as England manager for eight years.

Before taking the England job Robson had been on the receiving end of some cat calls and boos at Portman Road in his first three years at the club, but nothing he couldn't cope with and he soon won those critics over by turning Ipswich into one of the best and most consistent teams in the country.

Such success also made him one of the most coveted managers in the country, especially when the biggest clubs in the land realised that this boss, capable of building a winning team with virtually no resources, wasn't even properly contracted to Ipswich. That they could not prise him away from Portman Road was certainly not for a want of trying.

Everton, a giant in the English game who had enjoyed a golden period under Harry Catterick in the 1960s but had regressed in the 1970s, tried to secure his signature several times during his time in

East Anglia, while Derby County saw him as the man to replace the departing duo of Brian Clough and Peter Taylor in 1973. There were surprise approaches from Bilbao in Spain and another from Saudi Arabia, offering what was then considered to be fabulous wealth for his services.

In 1976 Barcelona also told him they were prepared to break the bank by offering him three times his salary to walk away from what was now a signed and sealed ten-year contract, while Don Revie offered him his job at Leeds United when he left to manage England. How ironic that Brian Clough should get the job at Elland Road instead, which lasted exactly 44 days. Sunderland, meanwhile, offered to make Robson the best paid manager in the land if he agreed to return home to the North East.

Perhaps the biggest temptation of all was when Manchester United threw their hat in the ring, albeit very quietly and discreetly, in the 1981/82 season after Ipswich had won the UEFA Cup and shortly before the larger than life Ron Atkinson took over from Dave Sexton at Old Trafford. Incredibly to some he turned them all down, leading to suggestions that this talented man lacked ambition. Few saw it fit to comment on his loyalty to his chosen cause.

It was not until FA secretary Ted Croker contacted Ipswich that his head was finally turned. It was Patrick Cobbold, who by 1982 had taken over the chairmanship of Ipswich from his brother John, who informed Robson of the approach. Patrick happily passed on the message, but also told his manager that there was a new ten-year contract on the table if he decided he wanted to stay, with a far better wage than the FA were prepared to offer him.

Robson's wage was already £72,000 per annum, and when Croker was informed of the sum he was taken aback, so much so that he even had the cheek to have the figure verified. Yet this was the one job that appealed to Robson above all others, and as much as he hated letting down the Cobbolds, the Ipswich supporters and, to some extent, his players, he soon displayed his patriotism and ambition by accepting the job and therefore a significant pay cut.

Bobby had discussed it with his wife Elsie, who could foresee the pressures he would be under from day one but also knew her husband would regret it for the rest it for the rest of his life if he did not accept the challenge. He was formally appointed to the role in June in 1982.

Yet he had not even set foot through the doors of the Football Association in its old home of Lancaster Gate when those bricks started coming his way. In May 1982 he had been asked by the FA to take an England side to Reykjavik to play Iceland in a friendly while manager Ron Greenwood was busy with the first team squad in Finland ahead of the upcoming 1982 World Cup. This second-string side drew 1-1 in a gentle game during which Bobby, at Ron's request, gave respected Spurs midfield player Steve Perryman a run out so that he could win his first – and only – England cap. Bobby was delighted for he held the hard-working player in the highest regard and felt the twelve minutes he gave him were well earned.

Not a lot of time for either, you'd have thought, to form any sort of impression on each other, but when Perryman brought out his autobiography in 1985 he slated Robson for the way the team was run and the lack of organisation since the heady days of Sir Alf Ramsey. It was all based on that twelve minutes and his involvement with a squad of strangers and a temporary manager, who only had two days to work with a bunch of footballers he had never coached before prior to the game.

Terry Fenwick, a defender who made all of his twenty England appearances under Robson between 1984 and 1988, was another to take a pop at the England boss later on. Fenwick was a neighbour of mine who often gave me a lift home if I was covering his game at Queens Park Rangers, and I know he liked Robson and was grateful for his international opportunity.

What led Fenwick to attack a coach he ultimately respected? The likely answer is money. Footballers, especially those in the latter stages of their career, knew they could generate extra income by creating tabloid headlines as the war between Britain's best-selling newspapers raged on, and many were quite happy to see their names in print as well.

Fortunately, Bobby could see the problems coming his way and was undeterred, especially as he knew that the red tops' preferred choice for the vacancy was Brian Clough. Around the time of his appointment he was more concerned about not leaving Ipswich in the lurch than any potential negative press. There was no question of them asking for compensation from the FA the way most clubs did, and they were delighted at the thought of their manager being the chosen one for the second time, as it reflected well on them and the club. However, they did float the idea of him taking on both jobs at the same time, encouraged by those who knew little of the England manager's workload thus saw it as a part-time job. Bobby always said that while club management was a seven day a week occupation, so was the England manager's job, albeit without the pleasure of the day to day contact with the players.

He tried to make the transition between Ipswich as smooth as possible by recommending his assistant Bobby Ferguson as the man to take the reins at Portman Road. Even that turned a little sour, as Ferguson laid claim to being the brains behind the Ipswich success, a difficult accomplishment considering he spent much of his time with the reserves. A singularly unimpressed Bobby Robson ignored the nonsense and moved on, leaving his successor with the greatest of gifts, a winning team, quality players, an excellent ground and not a penny owed to anyone. Ipswich were totally free of debt, which very few clubs in the top division chasing honours could boast at the time.

There were no millions coming in from television rights, no wealthy benefactor and just 18,000 Suffolk people putting their money into the club through the turnstiles every other week.

Bobby left Portman Road with one single regret, that he did not win the First Division title, but his legacy was there for all to see. He had spent ten seasons and had built the club into a considerable force, winning competitions at home and abroad. He professed to me that he was a little surprised when the FA came for him, but he shouldn't have been. He was an England man and an FA man, he had done all the coaching courses and was known as a steady ship by those whose responsibility it was to appoint the successor to Ron Greenwood, who had only good words to say about the man who was to replace him. He had certainly earned his crack.

9

'Cry, God for Bobby, England, and Saint George.'
(With apologies to William Shakespeare and Henry V.)

IT WOULD BE EASY TO RUN AWAY WITH THE IDEA
that Bobby Robson's eight-year tenure as England manager was a
constant battle with embittered ex-players and managers and that he
was continually under siege from fans, newspapers and the members
of the International Committee of the Football Association.

The truth is, though, he loved almost every minute of the job and
hated it when he was forced to walk away. Such was his commitment
to his country, there were also a couple of occasions when he offered
to return without payment while a more permanent commandant was
sorted out. The first offer came in 1993 when Graham Taylor was
on his way out after a disastrous spell, and the second when Glenn
Hoddle was sacked six years later

The battles with the media were so prevalent that he almost enjoyed the verbal swordplay, and the only journalists he was prepared to fall out with were the newsmen, the 'rotters', who, under instructions from those hidden away behind desks, did everything they could to unsettle him and the England team. That was something he loathed and despised, not because of the damage it could do to him but because it disrespected and disrupted his players.

He distrusted a couple of the regular football writers in the pack, but in general Bobby learned to embrace those he ended up spending so much time with on the job. Given the rough coverage he often received that might have seemed strange to someone outside of the industry, but the England manager knew that these were the messengers who got the word out to the supporters.

In return, even the reporters who had given him the hardest time over the years came not only to respect but also to love a man who was so forgiving and so forthcoming with his time, making their job easier than it might have been.

His view was that all of them wanted a successful England football team so that they could write positive things for their readers. Naive, maybe, but that was how he was. Intelligent without being a super intellectual, a great motivator of men without being the best coach in the world, Robson could inspire and more often than not he allowed his players to go out and express themselves. His trophies around the world are testimony to that and to the fact he was no mug in the tactical department, as some would have had us believe.

Even his England career was more successful than all his predecessors, with the exception of Sir Alf, and better than all his successors until Gareth Southgate quietly arrived at the Wembley offices and set about changing the atmosphere around the England team.

Bobby emerged at the FA surrounded by problems and obstacles, but none that were a surprise to him. Managers' talk to each other at every level and, in such a small world, news travels quickly.

It was perceived that Robson and the FA's resident director of coaching Charles Hughes were at daggers drawn, constantly at odds because of their differing views of the game and how it should be played, but in truth, Robson found Hughes good company, a stimulating conversationalist and someone he could bounce his own ideas off. They disagreed, often about the very basics, but Bobby claimed they never fell out.

Despite being close to Bobby during his eight-year England reign I never got to know Charles Hughes, a man who kept away from the media and the public as much as he could. Bobby had it right when he said that his colleague had no public persona because he didn't want one.

As well as the pair got on in private, Robson was always more comfortable around the likes of Don Howe, Terry Venables, Dave Sexton, David Pleat, Howard Wilkinson and Jack Charlton. There was nothing he would have liked better than to have brought his old West Brom teammate Howe on board as his full-time assistant, but the FA said they couldn't afford a second salary and the request was turned down. He did at least have Sexton available, as the former Chelsea, Queens Park Rangers and Manchester United coach was working at the FA's Residential School in Lilleshall.

Robson always said that he had good men around him: the smooth, articulate secretary Ted Croker, chairman Bert Millichip, who he knew from his days at West Brom and trusted implicitly, and Dick Wragg, the well-liked chairman of the largely unloved International Committee. They were all loyal to their man throughout his reign, no matter how tough things got either on both a personal professional level, and even rejected resignations from him on two occasions. The first time was after England had fallen foul to both Diego Maradona's gamesmanship and genius at Mexico in 1986. Robson had told Millichip that if they were thinking of replacing him, then after the World Cup would be the perfect opportunity, giving the new man time to bed in and prepare for the European Championships and the next World Cup in Italy in 1990.

When they told him to stay on he suggested that the FA should follow the lead of the Germans and appoint a young assistant who could be groomed over the years to take on the job when the time came. There were plenty of bright young things (and a few older ones) around at the time who could have slotted in alongside Robson; Venables, Wilkinson and Pleat were names that come to mind, with Graham Taylor, his eventual replacement, joining that list later.

Taylor, despite his club success and his popularity with the FA, later failed when in charge and Robson truly believed that had he enjoyed two years under him before his appointment it could have been so different for all concerned, and the bright young manager may have made the impact many anticipated and expected.

The FA could certainly have afforded an assistant at the time, but the belligerent and often unpleasant Manchester City chairman Peter Swales, a board member on the International Committee, dug his trainers (worn with a suit) in and reiterated his nonsensical stance that there was not enough work for one, never mind two.

Swales had never liked or approved of Robson and their dislike was mutual. The Manchester City man remarked before the European Championships in 1992 that Graham Taylor was a superior manager to Don Revie, Ron Greenwood and, especially, Bobby Robson, and went on to make such disparaging remarks that Robson complained privately to Chief Executive Graham Kelly who, in turn, suggested to Sir Bert Millichip that Swales should stand down for a while. Nothing happened, and Swales tried to smooth it over with a letter to Bobby, which was received with some level of scorn.

Swales earned more derision from the media when he addressed the press after Graham Taylor had steered England through qualification to the European Championships in Sweden in 1992 and told us that he was the most relieved man in England when they failed to win the World Cup in Italy as it would have kept Robson in the position. Any lingering credit he had with the football writers disappeared in a puff of smoke that day.

Far from it not being a job for one, as Swales and others thought, it would have still been a handful for two, but the FA, despite their consistent support for their manager, were too short-sighted to add Don Howe to the payroll. Robson was clear that Howe, an excellent coach, would have made his job easier and subsequently England would have become a better side.

The second time he offered to quit was after the three defeats out of three two years later in 1988 at the European finals in Germany. Robson told me that he expected to be fired after disappointing losses to the Republic of Ireland, Holland and Russia and couldn't complain if he had been, but Sir Bert Millichip once again turned him down when he offered to leave and, instead, asked him why he would do such a thing. Robson explained why he thought he would be sacked, but the chairman told him that there was no one they could appoint who would know more about the job and qualifying for Italy. He told him. 'If you can take the pressure we can,' he said, offering his manager unconditional support. 'We will back you and if you are happy to face the media and the public then so are we.' It was one of their shortest meetings.

I swear Bobby grew several inches, certainly around the chest, and he needed a boost after some awful performances in West Germany. They outplayed the Irish but couldn't put the ball in the net and lost 1-0, and they paid the ultimate price for such profligacy when they came up against the eventual tournament champions in Holland in their next encounter. At 1-1 England thought they were in with a good chance of getting something from the game and hit the woodwork twice, but a Marco van Basten screamer left them reeling, and the same man sent them packing a few moments later with a headed effort.

England were out of the tournament with a game still to play and Bobby addressed the players and the press, emphasising how important it was for his side to play with pride and to take something home. It fell on deaf ears as England lost 3-1 to the Soviets and delivered their worst performance under him throughout his whole tenure. To put it politely England were rubbish, and some of the players who were to go on and criticise the manager, including future England boss Glenn Hoddle, needed to take a look in the mirror at themselves. On paper it was a good squad, including the likes of Peter Shilton, Tony Adams, Bryan Robson, Gary Lineker, John Barnes and Chris Waddle who, along with Hoddle, was amongst the manager's biggest critics in future years. The pair were amongst the worst performers when it counted during that tournament.

As a journalist it is always easy to recall the shocking defeats and to point the finger at the manager and his players, but perhaps less easy to remember how you predicted glory and built the same figures up in the lead up to the tournament. Perhaps that is why it was always so vitriolic between the England management and the national press.

Gareth Southgate was, perhaps, fortunate that by the time he had arrived as England manager football commentators had been burned too often and rather than predicting unfettered success, began predicting defeat and destruction.

Bobby himself took great pleasure from a good victory but was never too self-satisfied, and I know he apologised to opposition managers on a number of occasions simply for winning. He was also honest in his press conferences after defeats, naturally shouldering the blame and deflecting the criticism aimed at his players.

Wembley was always a pleasure to him after his many visits there as a supporter, but it was those difficult away games which defined him, usually in crucial qualifying matches that just had to be won. Two other important victories to him were the single-goal win over the USSR in an intimidating Tblisi in March 1986 and the friendly victory over Brazil in Rio 1984, with a John Barnes special the highlight. In the latter Robson openly admitted his job was on the line after England had failed to qualify for the European Championships – even his old Fulham teammate Jimmy Hill suggested on television that it was all over for him.

Belgrade provided a threatening venue for the vital game against Yugoslavia in November 1987, when the minimum was a draw to qualify for the 1988 European Championship finals. England won 4-1 against an excellent technical side who were favoured to win. Of equal significance was the draw with Romania in Bucharest in May 1985, when England again needed a point to clinch a place in the 1986 World Cup Finals in Italy and did so with a hard-fought 0-0. At those finals in Mexico England required a victory in their final group game against Poland following two 0-0 draws. The critics had already virtually written Robson and his men off, but a memorable Gary Lineker hat-trick secured England's passage to the knockout stages.

Perhaps the most memorable for us was a trip to Istanbul in November 1984. I remember it well, for the Turks were convinced that not only would they score their first ever goal against England but were sure that their talented team could beat the team who invented football. As if to back up the point the stadium was already full to bursting point as I went for breakfast in our hotel, which was so close to the stadium we could hear the noise generated by one of the most passionate crowds I have ever encountered. When the two Robson's, Bobby and Bryan, went onto the pitch before the game they both claimed they could feel the ground trembling under their feet.

Had they come closer to the press box they would have felt me trembling as well, as we were the target not only for verbal abuse but also had all sorts of objects hurled at us, including a lethal looking potato with a razor blade embedded in it, which luckily flew over our heads and onto the side of the pitch.

God knows what would have happened if Turkey had won the match, but another Gary Lineker hat-trick, bless him, and a couple more from John Barnes didn't just silence the crowd but stunned them into silence as England won a remarkable game 8-0 and we all escaped safely.

There were some bad decisions, too, none more so than early in his reign as manager. Having replaced Ron Greenwood as manager just days after the end of England's 1982 World Cup campaign, his first task was to steer England to the European Championships in France. Just one team would qualify from a group of five consisting of Robson's side, Denmark, Greece, Luxembourg and Hungary. Denmark, who boasted Bayern Munich's Soren Lerby, Ajax's Jesper Olsen and the great Michael Laudrup in their ranks, were the clear threat. A 2-2 draw in Copenhagen in England's first group game therefore seemed a good result, though a late Olsen goal would later prove crucial.

Comfortable wins against Greece and Luxembourg followed, but when England hosted the former at Wembley in March 1983, they were unable to register what should have been a routine three points. It meant everything was riding on a clash with the Danes at Wembley in September of the same year. Robson's men had beaten Hungary 2-0 in the intervening period, but this was the game that would determine the outcome of the group, and England's new manager knew it. Robson was keen to stress to his team how good the opposition were – too keen. His players subsequently did not rise to the occasion, and a first half penalty from Allan Simonsen – who had spent the 1982/83 campaign at Charlton Athletic – condemned them to a 1-0 defeat.

'All managers make bad decisions at some point or another,' he told me, 'and I certainly had my share with England, but the biggest was undoubtedly the 1-0 defeat to the Danes at Wembley, when I was guilty of overestimating them. I overemphasised the Danes many qualities before the game, not only to the England fans but also to my own players.

'They did prove to be an outstanding side as it happens, but I admit that I pushed it too hard at the time and it eventually became a negative.' Denmark would go on to reach the semi-finals of the European Championships in France, beating Yugoslavia 5-0 in the group stages and only going out to Spain on penalties, and two years later at the World Cup in Mexico they won all three of their group games, including a 6-1 thrashing of Uruguay and a 2-0 victory over eventual finalists West Germany.

Yet England had been still been overwhelming favourites at the time of the game: they had reached the second group stage of the 1982 World Cup and been knocked out by the narrowest of margins; their opponents had not been there at all. Laudrup, undoubtedly Denmark's star man, was still at Lazio and yet to reach the heights he would achieve at Juventus and Barcelona. Preben Elkjaer, the striker who would later star for the national team and fire Hellas Verona to an unlikely title win amidst the glitz of Serie A, was still playing his club football in Belgium for Lokeren. It was a chastening evening for Robson at the beginning of his England career.

'International football is unforgiving, and I feared the worst when we failed to qualify for the finals in France,' he would recall. 'That defeat to the Danes at Wembley was one of my worst nights in football, with the result only part of it. The way we played; the walk back to the dressing rooms after the final whistle; the abuse of the crowd; the feeling of total confusion all contributed to the desolate feeling.

'I wasn't just feeling sorry for myself, but it was a blow to our football pride in the country, our status in world football, not to mention the subsequent effect on my personal life. All I wanted to do was go home to Ipswich and bury my head, but instead I had to face the gloomy dressing room, the after-match press conference at the stadium, with another scheduled with the media big-hitters for the next morning at the Wembley hotel.

'There was little or no sleep and I was seeing the headlines in my head long before they were delivered to my hotel bedroom. The team I selected did not play and I had to shoulder the responsibility for a result which affected every person who was interested in football in England.

'My mistake was exaggerating their ability in my own mind and then transmitting those thoughts to the players. I put our opponents on a pedestal and, in so doing, knocked our own confidence and belief in our performance.

'It earned me a reputation of being indecisive and that rankled. For fourteen years I had pitted my wits and my little club against the best in England and Europe, making important decision day after day. But this time I wanted, for the first time, to know the names of my opponents before naming my own line-up and it was not until lunchtime on the day of the game that I named my side.'

'The great irony is that after my bitter press conference at Wembley I bumped into Soren Lerby, who told me that his team were afraid of playing England at Wembley, but by half-time were convinced they could win because of our timidity.

'I learned a great many lessons that night but wondered if I would ever be able to use them when we were knocked out of the competition we had been tipped to win. There was no way I was going to quit but the pressure would be on my employers at Lancaster Gate.

'I had to attend a meeting at Lancaster Gate the next day to discuss the development of Centres of Excellence. I vowed after that

I would never put myself in that position again and would be better off walking my dog, taking the phone off the hook and cancelling the newspapers. The following Saturday I was at Villa Park for a game against Southampton when the big scoreboard flashed up my name, welcoming me as one of the guests, it was greeted with a storm of boos.

'To have any chance of qualifying for France we needed to beat Hungary away from home and hope that Greece would beat the Danes when we were playing Luxembourg in their tiny stadium. When we arrived, some smartarse told us that the Greeks, who had already kicked off, were a goal up, but we rushed into our dressing room to discover he had a cruel sense of humour, as the Danes won by a couple of goals.

'We were out and, to make it worse, our hooligan element had trashed the Duchy [20 England fans had been arrested in Luxembourg after clashes with police in and out of the stadium] after the game for a second time, and we were shunned by our neighbours when we went to the World Cup draw in Zurich soon afterwards. There was a growing lobby of countries in Europe who simply did not want a visit from English football fans.

'It was so bad that both I and Bert Millichip felt that we could be thrown out on our ears before a ball was kicked. But at least Bert was backing me and had dismissed any thoughts projected by the English press of me being sacked before I could seek to rebuild my battered reputation.'

Not qualifying for the European Championships was a serious blip early in Robson's tenure, and so it was a surprise when he selected an inexperienced outfit in England's first game following the qualifiers, a friendly against the hosts of that tournament, in February 1984. He fielded the raw Brian Stein and Paul Walsh up front against a team led by the brilliant Michel Platini. He scored both the goals in a 2-0 victory, a scoreline that didn't reflect the dominance of England's opposition that evening.

Robson accepted full responsibility for that defeat as well, accepting he was wrong to plunge a team full of youngsters into the deep end against a team who would go on to claim European glory just months later. Luckily for Robson, he did not get too much more wrong in the ensuing years.

It would take until the 1988 European Championships for him to receive the same level of criticism and pressure again, and those who doubted his technical nous felt they were vindicated following the 3-1 loss to the Netherlands in the group stages of that tournament, when he got two of his players to tightly mark Ruud Gullit and Marco van Basten. The latter scored a hat-trick that day.

It was a defeat that led to the realisation he needed to field a sweeper against strong sides possessing a dangerous front two, evident two years later at Italia '90. Robson thought about tactics far more than he was ever given credit for, and learnt from his mistakes quickly, such as when he unsuccessfully tried to shoehorn Bryan Robson, Glenn Hoddle and Ray Wilkins into the same midfield. They were England's three best players, but it was soon evident they couldn't all fit in the same side.

It was to Robson's credit that he learned from these errors of judgement. After all, who doesn't make mistakes in their place of work? The question to be asked is who admits to their errors? I have to hold my hand up as well – my colleagues and I in the press were always too quick to praise before a game and too quick to criticise afterwards. Perhaps we were not the experts we thought we were.

Bobby was often so distracted, usually by football, that he also gave great enjoyment to us with his occasional mangling of his home language, although that was nothing compared to his attempts to speak Dutch when he later left England to manage in Holland.

My favourite was when he passed his skipper Bryan Robson in a hotel corridor and as he hurried by, said, 'Morning Bobby!'

'No, I'm Bryan, you're Bobby,' was his skipper's response. For every daft thing he was quoted as saying there were a dozen pearls of wisdom and, in the end, it was considered one of his many endearing qualities, although not something he readily owned up to.

I witnessed plenty of these moments, such as the day he was autographing one of our books and the man politely requested if he would sign the book to his son Peter and then, making conversation, asked him if they had had a lot of people buying the book. 'Oh yes, hundreds,' Bobby answered as he continued to write his message. When the man got the book home and gave it to his son Bobby had written, 'To Peter, all the best, Bobby Hundreds.' How much is that copy worth?

Italia '90 provided a feast of quirky comments. In the tunnel before the quarter-final against Cameroon, the England manager clapped his hands and shouted to his players, 'Come on lads, this lot don't look up for it,' to which one of the Cameroon players politely responded in amused fashion: 'We speak English Mr. Robson.' After a very tight game which England won with two late Gary Lineker penalties, Robson said of his tough and, it has to be said, unlucky opponents, 'We didn't underestimate them. They were a lot better than we thought.'

He wasn't on his own with Big Jack Charlton getting away with murder when the Irish manager, asked which Egyptian players had caught his eye in England's group, responded: 'I couldn't tell you – I don't know any of their names.'

Most of the time Robson talked a lot of down to earth sense, and I can certainly vouch for his vast, encyclopaedic knowledge of football. He truly adored the game, and one of his most famous quotes would have touched even the hardest of hearts:

'What is a club, in any case? Not the buildings or the directors or the people who are paid to represent it. It's not the television contracts, get-out clauses, marketing departments or executive boxes.

'It's the noise, the passion, the feeling of belonging, the pride in your city.

'It's a small boy clambering up stadium steps for the very first time, gripping his father's hand, gawping at that hallowed stretch of turf beneath him and, without being able to do a thing about it, falling in love.'

I don't know who he said it to, nor do I know where it first appeared, but whoever it was on the receiving end of that magnificent Kipling-esque quote, I offer my thanks because it is exactly who the man was. I just wish he had said it to me.

Every so often he dropped out little gems that were as worth collecting as rare stamps. 'I think I have the best job in the country,' was his genuine response during one particularly tough period as England manager, while he was also defiant in the face of the media abuse he received: 'I will not let these people get to me or rattle me. They have no qualifications. They have never been anywhere or done anything in football. Why should I listen to them?'

After he stepped down in 1990, he was equally honest in his assessment: 'I was just a victim of the tabloid newspaper war. I had watched this cancer spread over the eight years. It was ugly and damaging.'

'I'm here to say goodbye – maybe not goodbye but farewell,' he later added. Clumsy, but everyone knew what he meant. He was leaving but he was going nowhere – he would be around the beating heart and soul of football for plenty of time to come.

Naturally, he was a staunch defender of his own profession, under-appreciated until too late: 'If you are a painter, you don't get rich until you are dead. The same happens with managers. You're never appreciated until you're gone and then people say, "Oh, he was okay." Just like Picasso.'

It certainly took a long time for Sir Bobby Robson to be fully appreciated, not just being an outstanding manager but also a true patriot with a big, big heart. Allied to that, he had some smart observations not only on the game, but on life as well.

10

FORGET ALL THE SKIRMISHES WITH THE MEDIA AND
the issues with his fellow managers and former England internationals determined to earn a bob or two with their vitriol, there was one problem Bobby Robson could not come to terms with during his England reign – hooliganism.

This ugly side of the beautiful game reared its head frequently and tainted the name of every Englishman and woman in its wake, destroying a reputation built on centuries of sportsmanship and gentlemanly behaviour. It was a problem that Robson was all too aware of before he had taken the England managers' job.

'I first came across it [hooliganism] in a serious way when I was manager of Ipswich and we played at the Old Den against Millwall,' he told me. 'I admit I was frightened at the time as the so-called "fans" were throwing lumps of concrete down towards the pitch.

'I should have been more circumspect, but I made my strong feelings known in the Millwall boardroom and my comments were passed on to the media by someone present. I commented that the police should have turned the flamethrowers on the hooligans who threatened serious injury by throwing concrete. That went down well.'

The match in question was Ipswich's 6-1 victory over their opponents in the quarter-finals of the 1978 FA Cup, the Tractor Boys' biggest victory en route to their first and only FA Cup triumph. The violence that day was serious enough for the referee John Gow to take the players off the pitch for around 20 minutes, though Robson's men were seemingly unfazed, returning to wrap up a resounding victory after the delay. Still, the trouble clearly left a lasting impression on Robson, and sadly it was not confined to domestic football – English fans took it across the globe.

Along with many others I found myself trapped in the heart of it at football grounds around the world as violence erupted with the help of the men and boys who preferred to fight rather than support, whilst wrongly believing they were doing both. For a long while I seemed to be writing front page stories rather than back page sports stories. There were a number of incidents involving English clubs in European competition down the years, from trouble between Leeds United and Bayern Munich fans at the 1975 European Cup final in Paris, to the Heysel disaster ten years later, which led to the deaths of 39 Juventus supporters after Liverpool fans caused a wall inside the stadium to collapse.

Liverpool had to bear the brunt of the blame for the tragedy, and deservedly so, but it has been easy to forget the behaviour of the Italians at the other end of the stadium, many wearing face masks and carrying weapons, while one was pictured actually wielding a gun. It was an intimidating atmosphere at the end of a glorious, sunny day which should have provided the backdrop to one of the matches of the season.

While I sat in the press box and later walked amongst the dead – just as I later did at Hillsborough when police errors before the FA Cup semi-final between Liverpool and Sheffield Wednesday caused a crush which resulted in 96 deaths – Bobby and his England team sat in their luxury hotel, the Camino Real, in Mexico City to watch the game on television.

He was in one of those periods when bad results on a tour including games against World Cup holders Italy, the World Cup hosts Mexico and one of the favourites for the upcoming World Cup in Mexico, West Germany, could have meant the sack. By the end of that black day he was wondering whether he would have a team to manage at all.

The European final was on England's first full day in Mexico, having been given the usual sparse time for preparation at the end of the domestic season. Watching their Liverpool rivals and some of their England teammates perform was a form of relaxation, or so Bobby thought. They all took their seats in front of the giant television screen in the hotel lounge which remained obstinately blank. I can picture Bobby fussing about the problem which went on and on and on for a full 90 minutes at a time when the game should have been concluding.

Gradually news began to filter through of fighting fans and even a death or two, but this was all dismissed in the English camp as exaggeration, a feeling which seemed to be confirmed when the television showed the game kicking off, and it was only when players began ringing home at the half-time break that their families revealed to them the dreadful, shameful news that stunned not just Britain but the entire world.

The full horror of that fateful day on 29 May gradually began to filter through to management, staff and players in Mexico. There were, at the time, 38 confirmed deaths and ignominy came down on the English game and everyone connected with it like black shroud. Even in faraway Mexico the England squad couldn't escape.

Robson was naturally mortified, but as a manager he realised there were obvious ramifications and decisions to be made. England were due to face, of all teams, Italy at the Azteca Stadium on 6 June, and players from both Liverpool and Juventus were to join up with their national sides in Mexico City straight after the game in Brussels. It was quickly decided between the two associations that the scheduled game should go ahead, otherwise an unbridgeable gap could have formed between two football loving nations. Both Robson and his opposite number, the vastly experienced Enzo Bearzot, were in agreement and it was also decided that both teams should attend a memorial service for the dead in their temporary home of Mexico City.

Both associations felt that there was enough time between their game and the horror show for the match to go ahead without accusations of having a cruel disregard for those events in Belgium. The two involved nations might have agreed, but many of those in Mexico City for the football took the opposite view and felt that the entire English party should pack their bags and disappear back home. The atmosphere was febrile amid talk that England's top teams were to be banned from all European club competition and the country from all international football.

In the meantime, myself and other journalists due to fly out to Mexico after the final instead found ourselves at the wrong end of another news story as we gathered details of how a slender chain-link fence was all that separated the two groups of Liverpool and Juventus fans and that it collapsed the instant the Liverpool fans surged towards the Italians, leading to a retaining wall collapsing at the end of the terraces.

At the time we were led to believe that it was this which caused many of the deaths, but it transpired that the crumbling wall in the dilapidated stadium in fact saved lives as it allowed an escape route to many who were otherwise left trapped. After the 'game' had been played, I was invited and attended the pre-planned Liverpool 'celebrations' at a castle like building later in the night, travelling with the shocked wives and backroom staff in their coach to join the players at the venue. It was the most surreal and unforgettable 'party' I have ever attended.

Some players just found the entire episode too hard to take in, while others were jubilant that family members and friends were all safe and had not been injured or worse. Drink pumped into dehydrated bodies from the stifling weather, the adrenalin and the effort didn't help. I was relieved when it all ended.

I was grateful that there were no television cameras or press photographers at the dinner because it would not have looked good and would certainly not have reflected the players' exemplarily behaviour on their return. Indeed, no team could have reacted better than Kenny Dalglish's Liverpool, who also worked so diligently to soothe the grief and heartache after Hillsborough four years later.

By the time I arrived in Mexico City, the English were persona non grata with everyone whether you were a footballer, a fan or a journalist. Only around 8,000 fans turned up in the vast stadium for the game against Italy, with every Mexican firmly and understandably on the side of the Italians. The English, quite rightly in the circumstances, were painted as the villains, even though, in my opinion, it could have ignited at the other end just as easily.

Bobby had told the English players that they were to behave immaculately whatever the provocation, and that anyone who didn't heed the instructions would be given an instant plane ticket home and would end their international careers in disgrace. Fortunately, under Robson, England were noted for their fair play, a non-violent team who tried to play football the proper way.

The two teams stood side by side for two minutes of silence before the game which was, indeed, played in the spirit hoped for. Salvatore Bagni had put the Italians ahead after 73 minutes before Mark Hateley equalised a minute later for the English. With the clock ticking down and the game heading for a draw, Pietro Vierchowod hurled himself across the outstretched leg of Gary Stevens as he attempted a back pass to Peter Shilton and the Mexican referee Antonio Ramirez Marquez could scarcely conceal his delight at awarding the dodgiest of penalties.

Alessandro Altobelli scored from the spot and even then, with seconds remaining, England may have rescued the draw they deserved when Gary Lineker was upended in the penalty area, only to stare in disbelief as the referee waved play on. There were no protests at either penalty decision and neither could there be. England and Robson just had to swallow it, grit their teeth and smile their congratulations.

It was much the same story in the next game against the Mexicans with top notch German official Volker Roth giving England nothing, including ruling out a valid equaliser. But this was no time to moan, and the players were constantly reminded of this by their manager – a stiff British upper lip demeanour was required and was maintained. Mexico satisfied their own 15,000 fans with a 1-0 win, the goal scored by Luis Flores after nineteen minutes.

Strangely, or perhaps not, attitudes began to change ever so slightly. England and their gentlemanly manager were earning grudging respect and even admiration for the way they had handled the hatred aimed at them, and there was certainly some sympathy as they approached the third and final game against the Germans, facing the prospect of three successive defeats for the first time since 1959.

Again the stadium was hauntingly empty, with an exaggerated 10,000 given as the attendance in an Azteca Stadium which could hold ten times as many fans, and again England had a penalty awarded against them by a Mexican referee. This time it was a correct decision by Jorge Leanza Sansone, and Peter Shilton saved Andreas Brehme's spot kick.

England then went on to win 3-0 against a German side who had inexplicably and against all best practice flown in at the last moment in a bid to overcome the altitude problem. Coach Franz Beckenbauer was made to look somewhat silly as skipper Bryan Robson and Kerry Dixon's first goals for his country set up a surprise and welcome victory against a German side visibly struggling with the thin air.

England and Robson had survived the trip and they enjoyed a beer back at their hotel before setting off for Los Angeles and the final game of their tour against the USA before the players scattered for a well-earned holiday, wondering what their future held in the circumstances. They were none too happy at having to play an extra game at the end of a stressful few weeks, but the rest of us looked forward to a pleasant few days sampling the LA hospitality and the plethora of restaurants and bars.

It was an even better chance for Bobby to relax along with our mutual American-based friend, Dr. Mike Shapow, who showed us around the town and Hollywood like a couple of good tourists. Bobby was to wave goodbye to his team after the game as he planned to stay on and seek out suitable training facilities for the pre-tournament preparations the following year – if England were allowed to compete.

There was an end of term feeling amongst the players as well and they had to be reminded of the American disaster in the 1950 World Cup at Belo Horizonte in Brazil, when an English team stuffed with big names like Bert Williams, Alf Ramsey, Billy Wright, Tom Finney and Stan Mortensen were turned over by a group of players scraped together from around the globe to represent the USA.

Needless to say, there was still a little frivolity amongst the players that the manager turned a blind eye to and they didn't let him down later, gently running five goals past their opponents, enough to satisfy everyone without humiliating the hosts as they so easily could have done.

That was it. It was all over. It was a happier group who headed back to their hotel for a final beer or two, which was followed by a deserved night out. Unfortunately, there was one last bit of bad news, and one by one the players went to their rooms to discover they had been robbed. They came back with tales of missing money, credit cards, personal stereos and anything else that could be shifted quickly and quietly.

Lists had to be made for the hotel security and the local police of exactly what had been thieved with the embarrassed US Soccer Federation, who had been such good hosts, mortified at what had happened to their illustrious guests.

The consequences of Heysel were far-reaching, and the Prime Minister Margaret Thatcher, definitely no fan of football, became heavily involved. English clubs were kicked out of Europe and only a backs-to-the-wall defence by the Football Association stopped FIFA kicking England out of the World Cup. English club teams were banned for six years from European competition, eventually reduced to five, while Liverpool suffered an extra three-year ban, eventually reduced to one, while fourteen of their 'fans' were found guilty of manslaughter and sentenced to three years in prison.

The consequence for Robson was that his best players from the best teams were deprived of the experience of playing in Europe against the best opposition, while the memories of Heysel were still vivid when he took his team back to Mexico for the World Cup the following year, a side written off and unloved.

Robson was a great believer in planning ahead and he was immediately struck that England would begin their group matches at sea level in Monterrey but then, if they qualified, they would be transferring to 6,000 feet above sea level for the knockout stage. England could do with getting used to such conditions before potentially playing in them, but Robson was also aware that if he based them at a high-altitude camp for the whole tournament then it would only accentuate the distance they had to travel in the short-term. Added to the antipathy felt towards the English team, the oppressive heat and the health hazards from simple eating and drinking, it was going to be a very difficult World Cup.

A compromise was found, with England staying in the small town of Saltillo, a little over 4,000 feet up in the mountains, which meant a hairy 90-minute coach ride downhill through bandit country for training and the games at the stadium in Monterrey.

The press also stayed in Saltillo and, of course, made great fun of the coach ride down to the stadium and the threat of highwaymen – that was until we were included with the England contingent, and raced down the mountain at hair raising speeds escorted not only by police cars and motorcyclists but also by a helicopter and armed guards. You can be sure we kept a wary eye on the countryside for the first few trips before the novelty wore off with not a single 'Stand and Deliver.'

It was such a contrast from our pre-World Cup camp at the fabulous Broadmoor Hotel in Colorado Springs, a magnificent hostelry on the edge of a lake with every facility, including even an ice-skating rink where one of the winter Olympic skaters was going through her routines. It was also handily placed for an American Airforce training base situated at 7,350 feet, almost the same as Mexico City. It was clear, fresh air, and there was plenty of opportunity for the players to sunbathe, swim and relax between hard training sessions of a couple of hours. Ice skating, however, was banned.

It was definitely the lull before the storm as far as the England manager was concerned and his quiet excitement at the prospect of having his whole squad available for longer periods in the year ahead of the tournament in the wake of the European ban on top English clubs was quickly dashed by the officious Football League President Jack Dunnett and then by the absolutely ridiculous inception of the Screen Sports Super Cup, a competition for the teams who would have qualified for Europe, and the Full Members' Cup for those that hadn't.

Robson could scarcely contain his anger at this wasted chance for the national team to become more familiar with each other. Instead of added training sessions and extra friendlies, he saw his players corralled into performing in a competition which lasted precisely one season and another one which lasted for seven years and changed its name twice during that time.

Liverpool won the Screen Sports Super Cup, beating Everton in a home and away final with two cups awarded. Ian Rush gave his away to a ball boy, showing how seriously the competition was taken. At least the Full Members' Cup final was played at Wembley, won twice by both Nottingham Forest and Chelsea before it faded into obscurity and then thankfully into total oblivion.

Robson couldn't even fit in a date for a game at Wembley before the team left for the USA as the Rugby League Cup Final was scheduled for the Saturday immediately prior and Wembley's owners were too afraid to gamble on two events in as many days.

The England manager's argument was that if his team could prepare properly and subsequently perform well in Mexico, they would be able to restore some of English football's lost pride and credibility and increase attendances across the board. Instead, Robson was left to worry about the effect that 42 league games, the FA Cup, the Full Members' Cup and the Screen Sports Super Cup would have on his players. How were they supposed to prepare for a World Cup halfway around the globe after all of that?

After a number of man-made catastrophes at the hands of hooligans, ahead of the World Cup there was another problem, but this time of no-one's making. On Thursday 19 September 1985 there was a catastrophic earthquake in Mexico City and the World Cup, already shifted from Colombia because they couldn't afford the cost of the upgraded competition and new stadiums, was in serious doubt, with the USA promptly considered a viable alternative.

The earthquake was a really bad one. How many died on that morning no one is really sure, with estimates ranging from a ridiculously small 5,000 to an exaggerated 45,000, with a seemingly random number of 10,000 eventually agreed upon. The earthquake had a magnitude of 8.0 on the Richter scale and a Mercalli Intensity of IX, in other words violent in the extreme. There were still aftershocks seven months later, but it was decided the show must go on.

There were discussions of a twelve-month delay or even cancelation. Chile had suffered an even more devastating quake in 1960 – registered 9.5 on the Richter scale, still the largest ever recorded figure – but that was two years before the World Cup was scheduled to be held in the South American country. This earthquake arrived ten months before the tournament.

When Bobby and FA Secretary Ted Croker arrived in Mexico City the apparent damage was seemingly slight, although there were remarkable scenes in pockets of the city, with hotels literally being held up as they leaned in towards each other. Some were still in that state when we returned for the tournament.

The Mexicans did a remarkable job to ensure they kept the competition in their country, a hotbed of the game, and were delighted that the English were backing them and had taken the trouble to visit and select their hotels in advance, showing solidarity.

It was all a far cry from when Sir Alf Ramsey led his world champions to Mexico in 1970 to defend their title and upset the nation with his comments about the food, the water, the sanitation and pretty much anything else he could possibly criticise.

The Mexicans were ready for Robson and England, but he had been there before, overcoming an intensely difficult set of circumstances after the Heysel disaster, and was widely admired for his deportment along with his team.

The football journey to Mexico had been far from trouble-free – there were unwelcomed innuendos from the Romanians at the end of qualifying suggesting that England were conniving with the Northern Irish to play for a draw in the final round of group stage fixtures, which would ensure that their neighbours qualified ahead of the Eastern European country, whose game against Turkey kicked off half an hour earlier.

England were already confirmed as group winners but the manager was apoplectic at the suggestion that he would do anything underhand or collude with his opposite number Billy Bingham to fix the result.

The big problem was that England did draw and Northern Ireland did qualify for Mexico ahead of Romania, and no great imagination is needed to understand the indignation and anger that ensued from Izmir where Romania beat Turkey 3-1. How do you work that one through in a game England were expected to win on their home ground in front of more than 70,000 fans? As the game petered out to a goalless draw there were even chants of 'fix' coming from the Wembley terraces, albeit tongue in cheek.

England were soon cleared by the FIFA observer, and those who watched the game either on television or live could have had no doubts as the Irish clung onto the result, with their hero 40-year-old goalkeeper Pat Jennings, the man with hands like meat dishes, who produced world class saves from Glenn Hoddle and Kerry Dixon, while the Swedish referee Frederik Eriksson missed a clear handball by QPR defender Alan McDonald, which could have seen the Irish go out.

Bobby was spitting feathers over the accusations and made the telling remark that if the Romanians wanted someone to blame it should be themselves as they were beaten twice by the Irish, with Bingham's team conceding just the one goal in their final five qualifiers. It left a bad taste in everyone's mouth and Bobby, for all his admiration of the great Pat Jennings, wished that Gary Lineker and company had stuck five past their neighbours.

Qualifying as usual was not enough for some, with former England captain Emlyn Hughes launching yet another personal attack on Robson, annihilating his team in print, which was then followed up by the most spurious of articles by the former Spurs captain Steve Perryman, all gracing the pages of the *Daily Mirror*.

It was only after qualifying that Robson began to realise the weight on an England manager's shoulders. Those such as *Sunday Times* columnist Brian Glanville, who should have known better, and others that suggested that managing England was a part-time job, should have had a random glance at the manager's diary, which showed just three nights in his own bed out of 25 and visits to half a dozen countries for matches, along with the usual distractions of speeches at dinners and guest appearances on television shows. The return home to Ipswich was only ever really an opportunity to swap suitcases and wash clothing.

The 1986 World Cup Finals were fast becoming a reality and the process soon sped up dramatically when Robson flew out to Mexico for the third time in a year for the draw and to confirm England's hotels, training pitches and bases for when it really did begin.

England were seeded in the second pot behind top seeds Italy, Mexico, West Germany, France, Brazil and Poland, alongside Argentina, Paraguay, the Soviet Union, Spain and Uruguay, with South American papers claiming that the draw was fixed and had already been made in advance. It was not the only time accusations like this were made and each and every one of them could be traced back to the television rehearsal, where a practice draw was made out of necessity.

Had it been prearranged it would have certainly helped England, for it had been organised that the moment their name came out of the hat Bobby Robson would leave the prolonged ceremony to head straight to the venue to confirm bookings of hotels and training centres, which had been earmarked on previous visits.

Best laid plans of mice and men … the carefully constructed arrangement inevitably disintegrated as England's was the last name out of their seeding section, and they soon found out they were heading for Monterrey and its altitude problems. It was more Johnny English than James Bond, as the English contingent hastily rearranged their meticulously-laid plans to prepare for the games against Poland, Portugal and Morocco. Naturally, they were followed by a retinue of television crews, photographers and journalists.

Chaos reigned but England eventually prevailed, with the designated plane turning back to the gateway to pick up Robson and the rest of his contingent. They were so delighted at their last-minute stroke of luck that Bobby made instant friends with the flight captain Hector Alcocer, posing for pictures with him and inviting him to World Cup games as his personal guest.

The efforts proved to be worthwhile as the representatives of both Portugal and Morocco arrived at the Camino Real hotel while Robson was already in talks with the hotel director to confirm the bookings, which had been tentatively made in advance. All that was left to do was to placate the local media, who had headlined their front page, 'The animals are coming,' when England were drawn to play at their local stadium. All three games were to be played at four in the afternoon to avoid the cruel midday sun, but still too early for the northern Europeans.

In the meantime the hooligan element of the English fans continued to cause problems – even when there was no game. Robson desperately wanted to test his team against a top nation in a fallow period between playing Northern Ireland in November 1985 and Israel at the end of February 1986, preferably in a warm climate with no chance of disruption. The opportunity arose for a fixture against Spain, the 1984 European Championship runners-up, in Seville, but the FA put the block on it because they felt they couldn't have any disruptions abroad ahead of draw for the European Championships in Frankfurt on Valentine's Day. It was the same story with other willing countries until they settled with a game against Egypt in Cairo, the first time the two countries had ever met.

The details of the games against Egypt and Israel prompted another flurry of criticism from Hughes and the rest, but the biggest disappointment for Bobby was that Brian Clough, who had backed him since being rejected in his favour, called the trip laughable and then went on to claim there were ten places up for grabs in front of goalkeeper Peter Shilton. None of these experts mentioned the problems the hooligans had created, nor the fact that England would have been without a fixture for three and a half months if Robson had listened to them.

It gave the England manager an opportunity to play a couple of fringe players and hopefuls, and a 4-0 victory satisfied most and helped the team spirit. There was further good news for the manager when, while on holiday in the Alps with his wife, he heard that England had again drawn Turkey and Northern Ireland, as well as Yugoslavia, in qualifying for the 1988 European Championships. He knew that the Romanians thought they had an axe to grind over the Irish result, but he felt blessed that they had a four-team group instead of five and that each away venue had their own way of coping with the rough element of visiting fans.

Only Israel – and a few injury problems – were left in front of them before the World Cup began. Israel was an easy choice. Only a nutcase would try to start a riot in Tel Aviv where the weather was balmy, and therefore also an aid to Mexican preparations. It could have backfired when Eli Ohana, a talented player who went on to become chairman of Beitar Jerusalem, put Israel in front. I watched some of the English reporters sharpen their pencils and lick their lips in anticipation of defeat, but they were disappointed when skipper Bryan Robson scored one glorious goal and then added the winner from the penalty spot.

This was a warm-up match but it still did not satisfy some. Television commentator Barry Davies took Robson to task, as did BBC radio man Kevin Cosgrove, who asked him what he was going to do to put things right. Bobby scratched his head for, within an hour, the team were on their way back to the airport and he wouldn't see them or even know who was going to be in the squad until a month later when they met before a game against the USSR. Robson himself had another trip to Mexico scheduled, as well as a visit to Cairo for the African Nations Cup and a first look at opponents Morocco.

The game against the Russians also threw up some typical East against West problems. The hosts had insisted that England should fly via Moscow, stay the night and then repeat the two-day journey on the way home from the game in Tbilisi, over 2,000 kilometres away from the capital. You can imagine what the First Division clubs thought of that arrangement and, risking an international incident, Ted Croker and Robson himself approached a dozen or more countries, trying to find an alternative fixture in the middle of a designated international week.

The FA were ready to pull the plug and have a training camp instead when, three days before the game, England were finally granted permission to fly their charter aircraft directly into Tbilisi, the first country to be allowed to do so. The media thought Robson's stance was a bluff. It wasn't. England were prepared to do without a game rather than be messed about and their decision was to be proved correct when Italian-based players Mark Hateley, Ray Wilkins and Gordon Cowans arrived in Georgia by way of the route the FA had refused to take. One look at them was enough to convince the England coaching staff that they wouldn't be ready to train before the game, while Hateley was clearly injured and unfit to take part in the match itself.

The media mob were satisfied on their way out when it was announced at the airport that Don Howe had quit his job as manager of Arsenal, providing them everything needed for the next day's back page. To hell with fitness tests and a game against a team with one of the best home records in world football. They had their story.

Had local hero Aleksandre Chivadze, who played his entire career with Dynamo Tbilisi, scored from the penalty spot it might have been a different night, but he missed and England went on to record a 1-0 victory, with a world class goal from Chris Waddle in front of a 62,500 crowd who seemed to want England to win rather than their home team. This unexpected support was confirmed later in the players' hotel when Russian spectators from all over their huge country arrived with all sorts of English paraphernalia for them to sign.

England were on a run as they headed to Mexico, beating Scotland 2-1 in the Rous Cup, the World Cup hosts in Los Angeles and then Canada in Burnaby, east of Vancouver. It did little to discourage the detractors, with Sir Alf Ramsey still finding time to criticise a dozen of the selected players, while Clough dismissed Glenn Hoddle, Mark Hateley, Kerry Dixon and Chris Waddle as not good enough on the morning England played Scotland.

It was generally thought in the world of football that Robson and Ramsey did not get on at all, but the truth was that Robson had huge respect for his predecessor and what he had achieved in the game. When Ramsey was sacked by England in 1974 – leaving the former Ipswich manager a 'broken man' – it was the current Ipswich manager that offered him support.

'When he was sacked from the England job I wrote a personal letter to him and sent two directors' box tickets for himself and his wife with the invitation to come to Portman Road whenever he wished,' Robson said. 'He attended a couple of games but never took the trouble to look me up and say hello, never mind thanks.

'I could understand his anger at the FA for the way he was treated but could never understand what I had done to be attacked in such a scurrilous way. I even asked for his advice and help but he never responded, and when I offered him a lift back from a game at Stamford Bridge, he told me sharply that he had come by train and would return by train.

'Most of all I wanted to talk to him about his experiences of the World Cup in Mexico before we went there but he never allowed it to happen.' In fact, Robson was stunned to read Ramsey saying in print that the England manager had said three times he would like to meet up for a chat and three times he couldn't make it. The truth was that Robson had phoned once to ask for a meet and was told Ramsey was too busy to see him. It was at that point that Robson wrote to him thanking him for his interest and left it at that.

'I vowed when I left my job with England that I would never criticise another England manager while he was trying to do his best for himself and his country. I never did because I knew just how much it could hurt.'

11

*'The general who wins the battle makes many calculations
in his temple before the battle is fought. The general who
loses makes but few calculations beforehand.'*

Sun Tzu, Chinese military general and writer

WHEN BOBBY ROBSON MADE HIS ENGLAND PLAYING
debut against France in November 1957 he was privileged to sit beside
Tom Finney on the coach from the hotel on the way to Wembley.
To many who saw them both Tom was considered better than the
man on the other wing, Sir Stanley Matthews, but with so little to
choose between two world stars, the difference whichever way would
be infinitesimal. Bobby admired Sir Stanley, but his respect for Finney
bordered on awe.

Bobby marked his debut that day with two goals in a 4-0 victory,
with Tommy Taylor scoring the other two. Perhaps that is why he
remembered, word for word, what Finney said to him on the way to
Wembley.

'You will find it the hardest game you have ever played in,' said the Preston North End winger. 'It is not only physically but also mentally demanding. The pace is difficult to cope with because your opponents think so much more quickly. Remember, however, that though they are the best in their country in that position you too are now considered the best in your country in your position and you will find you are being backed up by better, faster-thinking players than you are used to. The more you play the easier it becomes.'

Bobby was no great writer, no great orator, but he loved carefully crafted words. He liked the theatre, loved Shakespeare on the stage in Stratford-upon-Avon, recalled the lyrics to favourite songs and could always direct me to a favourite piece of literature. He also had a great passion for life and this is what came across to his players.

Of course, he sometimes found himself tangled up in tongue twisters or mixed up names and faces, usually because his mind was elsewhere, often to the next little speech he was to deliver, whether to a single player, to a team or to the press.

He took on board the problems players had at the top level, the mental strains that came with being on show to the world, having to prove themselves to their peers, performing in front of family and friends, coping with being away from loved ones, cooped up with other men you did not necessarily choose as friends but who you were expected to bond with.

Those were the thoughts of the international manager when he whittled his Mexico World Cup squad down to 22. He despised the onerous task of telling those who had failed to make it, particularly the million-pound striker Trevor Francis and defender Dave Watson. After 42 games and having used 61 players, Bobby Robson presented his final squad to the FA, with a further six on the standby list in case of injury or other problems.

The squad was as follows: Peter Shilton (Southampton), Chris

Woods (Norwich City), Gary Bailey (Manchester United), Gary Stevens (Everton), Viv Anderson (Arsenal), Kenny Sansom (Arsenal), Terry Butcher (Ipswich Town), Terry Fenwick (QPR), Alvin Martin (West Ham United), Gary Stevens (Tottenham Hotspur), Bryan Robson (Manchester United), Ray Wilkins (AC Milan), Glenn Hoddle (Tottenham Hotspur), Peter Reid (Everton), Trevor Steven (Everton), Steve Hodge (Aston Villa), Chris Waddle (Tottenham Hotspur), John Barnes (Watford), Mark Hateley (AC Milan), Gary Lineker (Everton), Peter Beardsley (Newcastle United), Kerry Dixon (Chelsea).

The six told to keep fit and be on call were Martin Hodge (Sheffield Wednesday), Dave Watson (Norwich City), Paul Bracewell (Everton), Stewart Robson (Arsenal), Trevor Francis (Sampdoria) and Mick Harford (Luton Town).

The journey started from Ipswich under a cloud. Bobby's companion in the car to the meeting place at the Post House Hotel at Heathrow Airport was his old friend Terry Butcher. Terry was down and depressed as only Terry could be, especially as his team, Ipswich Town, had just been relegated and he had the prospect of being in Division Two when he returned from the World Cup unless there was a move for him in the summer. Having spent so long turning Ipswich into top flight contenders, Bobby was also saddened by their demise.

It was all soon forgotten, however, with the excitement of the departure to a major tournament and Bobby, in particular, busy checking on the injuries from those weekend games. Two of his standby players were already ruled out, with Mick Harford hospitalised for a knee operation and Francis recovering from an operation on a fractured cheekbone. Bobby observed that had it been an international the next day instead of a flight he would have been without the spine of his side – Peter Shilton, Ray Wilkins, Bryan Robson, Steve Hodge and Alvin Martin – who were all suffering from a variety of knocks, bumps and lumps.

Also missing were the Everton players who were to fly out after the cup final against Liverpool, leaving on Sunday. West Ham manager John Lyall requested that Alvin Martin should stay behind to recover from his physical and mental exertions after the Hammers had gone so close to winning the league title. It was a testing time, especially with the hangover from Brussels and ensuing European ban, ill-discipline on and off the pitch and near riots at Luton and Birmingham.

I stayed behind to cover the 105th FA Cup final, a Merseyside derby between Liverpool and Everton. I had friends on both sides and remained unbiased in my role as a working journalist, but still enjoyed the Reds' 3-1 victory, with Ian Rush scoring twice and Craig Johnson once after Gary Lineker had opened the scoring for Everton. Wembley had the usual raucous atmosphere but there was an undercurrent because both clubs were not able to compete in Europe despite their success. Having completed the double Liverpool would have ended up in the European Cup, while Everton would, under normal circumstances, have automatically gone into the Cup Winners' Cup after finishing behind The Reds in both league and Cup.

Oddly there was not a single Englishman in the Liverpool team – John Barnes and Peter Beardsley would both join the club in 1987 – but I joined Gary Stevens, Trevor Steven, Peter Reid and Gary Lineker on the flight out to America on the day after the final. I was able to inform the players that all of Bobby Robson's promises of hot sunshine at the Broadmoor Hotel in the Rockies and warnings of sunburn and sunstroke could be ignored. It had been snowing heavily and was now raining. It came as a body blow to that professional sunbather Gary Lineker.

I had called Bobby at his hotel on their first full day and he told me that they had woken up to a blizzard so heavy they couldn't see the nearby Rocky Mountains, with temperatures ducking below 50 degrees Fahrenheit. It snowed for seven hours and the acclimatisation programme was hastily switched to the steam rooms in the American Airforce Academy. After the steam, the heated indoor pool was just the ticket to unwind, as the players watched the young air force recruits jump off a ten-metre board, simulating leaping off an aircraft carrier – all except one youngster who couldn't do it and retreated in distress as his courage continued to fail him in front of an international audience.

When Bobby returned to the pool it was to find his very expensive, very fragile players leaping off the same high board under the admiring gaze of the instructors. It was, he said, something he would never have allowed had he been present, but at the same time he admired their courage and was privately pleased that there was plenty of bottle in his squad.

The weather slowly began to change and by the time our little group arrived from London the temperatures had soared. The players were relaxed, demonstrated by an 11-0 win over an Airforce Academy team, a decent outfit who had only lost by a single goal to Canada's national team. England's next opponents were the improving South Korea team at a local school ground with Peter Shilton, Bryan Robson and Ray Wilkins all volunteering to play. It was a carnival atmosphere with barbeques, flags, banners, a couple of thousand people and not a hooligan to be seen anywhere. The Koreans took the game seriously and even more so when Fenwick elbowed one of their players in the face. It was a 4-1 win, with Kerry Dixon making it five goals in two friendly games.

Next up it was the Mexicans in their Los Angeles base. The World Cup hosts had enjoyed a seventeen-match unbeaten run, including a win against the South American champions Uruguay, but England put them away comfortably with three unanswered goals. However, unknown to us in the press box or the 63,000 fans in attendance, Robson's fears were realised when his namesake and skipper Bryan dislocated his shoulder for the third time. Physio Fred Street was able to pop it back in without anyone noticing, but the recurring problem was a real worry. All the players who performed had lost around five or six pounds in weight, but Robson was more concerned about his captain and how to protect that now suspect shoulder, which, he was told, could go again at any time. Any other player he would have sent home, but Robson was key to his plans and England's immediate future.

The week in luxurious surroundings went well for all of us. The players had their wives over – paid for by the FA – and the manager and his wife even found time to do a little sightseeing. The only minor setbacks were news from back home that Sir Alf had published the private letter Bobby had sent him and the dressing room had been closed down by men in white suits following a dangerous spillage of mercury. Both poisonous.

It was time to bid farewell to the wives and girlfriends before travelling to Burnaby for the final friendly against Canada. The hotel staff impressed on me and other journalists how much they had enjoyed having the English team, describing them as first class sportsmen and first class people. Needless to say, the flight out was dramatically overbooked, with twelve passengers giving up their seats for considerable reward from the airline, while John Barnes nearly missed it altogether as he had dawdled on his way to the gate, plugged into his earphones.

The team arrived into Vancouver on the Friday evening, with the game kicking off at eleven the next morning. It was one the manager must have wished he had crossed off the list, for England put in a tepid performance in a 1-0 victory and, much worse, star striker Gary Lineker broke his wrist.

It looked like he had ruled himself out of the World Cup, at least according to the dispatches we sent home, but to everyone's relief it turned out to be nothing more than a bad sprain. Very sore, but with the right strapping he would be able to perform. A nice little sidebar was that Lineker's obvious replacement, Peter Beardsley, asked Robson if he could skip the official reception later that day to visit the injured player in hospital. It seems hard to equate this thoughtful young man in 1986 with the problems of his own making which led to him leaving Newcastle under a cloud in 2018/19.

Robson was beginning to wonder whether someone had the evil eye on him and his team, for rarely did they move without some drama enfolding them. It was the same again when we all left Vancouver to fly to Los Angeles. Despite confirming and reconfirming the 11.40am flight to Monterrey, it was full, and the England group were not registered. It took a lot of shuffling and a lot of time to sort it out.

Just when it seemed all was well in the world again there was an angry shout from an American sitting just in front of me: he had spotted his luggage still on the ground, with plenty of other bags surrounding it as well. We could manage without ours for a day or so, but in his bag were his samples he needed for his job and without them his trip was a total waste of time and money. He disembarked in high dudgeon and we were delayed yet again.

Before arriving in Monterrey we still had time for one more further delay, with the plane unexpectedly making an unscheduled stop at a tiny airport in the Mexican city of Chihuahua, where a great many small packages were uplifted onto the aircraft. I don't think they were dogs!

Eventually the team arrived at the Camino Real, but with everyone ready to drop the manager was again disturbed, this time in his luxury suite, by an urgent call from FIFA official Ivan Toplak, telling him he had made a dreadful mistake and named Gary Stevens twice in his squad. The same message had also come from another FIFA representative, Walter Sieber in Monterrey. Surely there was only one Gary Stevens. Incorrect. England, just to be difficult, had named two

– Gary Stevens from Everton and Gary Stevens from Tottenham. To make things more complicated, Trevor Steven, also of Everton, was in the squad as well.

The problems didn't end there as popular team physician Vernon Edwards, on his last England trip before retiring, suffered a massive heart attack and was temporarily replaced by the ITV medic Lesley Young, while arrangements were made to bring replacement Dr John Crane out from England. The press contingent were as upset as the players over the loss of Doc Edwards, who was a beautiful man and always available, unofficially, to help a media man in distress, as we often were.

He was also a huge loss too for Bobby: a quiet right-hand man who was always there when needed and totally efficient in everything he did. Robson said it was like losing one of his best players.

+++

DESPITE THE FACT THE WORLD CUP WAS TAKING place on another continent, and despite all of the recent trouble engulfing England's club teams, it soon became clear that the National Front, who by now had hooked themselves onto the national team, would be in Mexico.

Bobby was never more embarrassed than when he willingly posed in front of a group of 'England supporters', only for them to unfurl their sick banner proclaiming their evil politics behind his back, and he was a very wary man from that point on.

These were, according to Robson, the scum of the earth. He had come across them two years earlier when England travelled to South America and beat Brazil 2-0 with goals from John Barnes and Mark Hateley. This mob had refused to acknowledge Barnes's brilliant solo goal, and on the flight from Rio to Argentina they had racially abused both him and Mark Chamberlain until a delegation from the press fronted them and told them to shut up.

These same faces were in Mexico and Bobby, quite rightly, pondered how they could afford these expensive trips halfway round the world. He debated whether they were being subsidised by some politically motivated group back home in England, recalling how they had devastated the streets of Luxembourg ahead of an earlier England match, turning over cars and attacking the locals.

When Bobby was free, he and I would sit on his balcony outside his room in the balmy Mexican evenings to bring our *Diary of the World Cup* up to date. Often my colleagues would be sitting outside the bar after dinner on the ground floor by the swimming pool, glaring my way – they were concerned that I was going to scoop them from what they saw as a privileged position. There was, of course, no way that could happen and if something did come up, I felt obliged to share the information with everyone once I had cleared it with Bobby, and eventually they became used to me and my evening duties to publishers Collins Willow.

There were no problems with sunstroke as the rain poured down in torrents, forcing England to hastily switch training grounds, and it became so bad that there were even thoughts that the opening game against Portugal might have to be called off. Reflecting later, Bobby Robson wished it had. It was another of those days he was becoming used to. It started with Bobby rambling on for 50 minutes to the players with his pre-match lecture, and then Lineker reporting stomach pains and sickness.

Fortunately, everyone reported fit for the kick-off and it was largely one-way traffic until Portugal scored the first time they entered into the England eighteen-yard box. Bobby blamed the entire back four of Kenny Sansom, Terry Butcher, Gary Stevens and Terry Fenwick as Carlos Manuel converted Diamantino's cross. It was the only goal of the game, and England's lengthy unbeaten run was over at the very first hurdle and at just the wrong time. As part of both of our duties for the diary, Bobby would sit down with me in the aftermath of each game back at the hotel to reflect on what had happened out on the pitch.

PORTUGAL 1-0 ENGLAND, 3 JUNE 1986:

It was not a promising start to our opening match, especially when we arrived at the ground to discover it locked, barred and bolted, and when we did finally gain entry there were no lines marked out and no nets in the goals. How could you possibly plan free-kicks and such the like with no penalty area marked out? I had a good moan and managed to squeeze an extra 30 minutes of practice on the pitch where we were to open our challenge. Worse was to follow when a car arranged by FIFA to take me back to the hotel after an official meeting failed to turn up.

Both my skipper Robson and my main man Lineker were declared fit, and apart from the weather we were in good shape, and as I sat in my hotel on the eve of the game I felt good.

Rain and more rain. It was more like a February day in Birmingham. It was so severe that at one stage I feared that our long-awaited opening game would be called off. In retrospect that might not have been a bad thing.

I thought we were going to win and win comfortably. Score one and more would follow, but we missed three good chances in the first nine minutes of the second half and Portugal were not in the game at all. But the first time they entered our box they scored after a host of errors. Starting with the reliable Kenny Sansom stumbling as he attempted to tackle Diamantino. All of our back four were at fault one way or another.

Goals change games and that one certainly did, and we were lucky not to concede more, especially when Terry Fenwick fouled substitute Paolo Futre and German referee Volker Roth waved play on. It was annoying to lose a game we should have won but I remained optimistic as we had not suddenly become a poor team in one game, and I had not seen anything to frighten me in the other games I had watched, either live or on television. I still felt we had considerably more chance of winning the World Cup than the team who had just beaten us.

There was very little time to put things right before they met the challenge of Morocco, one of the more unfancied teams in the tournament. It looked as though England might soon be packing their bags when the injury prone Bryan Robson put his shoulder out again and was helped off the pitch, while his midfield partner Ray Wilkins was sent off not long after. An unimpressed Wilkins had been given offside in the corner of the pitch, and upon walking back to his own goal tossed the ball back in the direction of the referee and was promptly given his marching orders. He had let his frustration get the better of him, but it was a travesty of a decision.

Morocco, as it happened, were only too pleased to take advantage – they subsequently played for and got a draw against ten men. It left England needing to win against the group seeds Poland in order to progress. Temperatures soared and so did Bobby's when he was left having to answer a number of untrue media claims before the match – claims that he was rowing with his captain Bryan Robson; claims that his wife Elsie was receiving obscene phone calls back home; claims that Ron Greenwood had to step in between Bobby Robson and Bobby Charlton as they argued over Bryan Robson's fitness. A little digging traced the Charlton story to Italy and the dodgy phone calls to Oslo, with Elsie not even being at home at the time of the so-called heavy breathing at the other end of the line.

ENGLAND 0-0 MOROCCO, 6 JUNE 1986:

In the space of five minutes I thought my world had collapsed and our World Cup hopes had gone out of the window. It was bloody hot, but it was cooling down and I fancied we would win it in the second half.

My injured captain Bryan Robson was helped off and my vice-captain Ray Wilkins was sent off. Something you would not expect to happen in an entire World Cup campaign, let alone in five minutes of one half. I feared the worst when Robson was heavily tackled in the penalty area and landed with a sickening thump on his elbow, just as he had done against Mexico in Los Angeles. He had put his shoulder out again.

I was still trying to reorganise the team when I noticed out of the corner of my eye Ray Wilkins being fouled in the far corner of the field. I was surprised when the Paraguayan referee gave him offside and saw Ray toss the ball in a lazy arc towards the official. I was totally shocked when he brought out the red card.

Our ten out-passed and outplayed the timid Moroccans in the second half despite the heat and ten men against eleven. It was a priceless point and my shattered and worn out team now had to beat our groups' seeded team to qualify.

There was more criticism in the lead up to that crucial Poland clash when Robson picked Trevor Steven ahead of Chris Waddle and selected a team devoid of both the injured Bryan Robson and the suspended Ray Wilkins, with Steve Hodge and Peter Beardsley introduced to the side in their place. The pressure on the manager and players was enormous and it showed as they began horribly, giving the ball away with their defence all over the place. Yet by half-time England somehow led 3-0, with the remarkable Gary Lineker scoring all three. It still needed a couple of world class saves by Shilton from the flame-haired Zbigniew Boniek to keep that clean sheet and every England player improved as the game progressed, especially central defenders Terry Fenwick and Terry Butcher, who saw out the 90 minutes despite debilitating injuries. England were through.

ENGLAND 3-0 POLAND, 11 JUNE 1986:

Ron Greenwood was very supportive when he visited us and told me of the criticism I was facing back home, not helped by some of the off the wall quotes from Bryan Robson, which he later denied. Rise above it, said Ron, and that's what I tried to do.

My most difficult moment was telling Robson I couldn't risk him and his four times dislocated shoulder in such a crucial game. It was not easy for either of us as he was my best player. It was a gamble I couldn't take and it left both of us depressed.

The mood amongst the squad was good and there was a little link to the crucial game when Gary Lineker came back from 2-1 to beat Terry Fenwick 3-2 in the pool final organised by the players on the eve of the big game.

Everything looked normal on the 55-mile trip to the game, with the usual cards and dreadful music provided by Gary Bailey, but the nerves were evident as we gave the ball away several times, and it took a marvellous save from Peter Shilton and a last-minute lunge from Terry Butcher to foil the dangerous Boniek.

But by the time we walked into the dressing room at half-time we were three goals to the good — all of them scored by Gary Lineker, and each was a beauty. The first, after only seven minutes, was critical to settle the nerves after our awful start, and the second a classic set-up by Peter Beardsley, and the third by Steve Hodge.

I was not at all nervous and I knew we would win given a decent bounce of the ball and a fair referee. We had both, and the atmosphere on the coach back to our headquarters in Saltillo was terrific, and even better when we arrived at the hotel to be greeted by all the staff, most of the guests and a mariachi band.

With England's luck it was a bold decision to fly out from

Monterrey on Friday the thirteenth to Mexico City. However, this time it wasn't the airline that was the problem, it was the smoggy Mexico City and the rather bleak Valle de Mexico Hotel, based on an industrial estate, which was a stark contrast to the plush surroundings of the Broadmoor and Camino Real. It was not what the journalists wanted but, as Bobby remarked, the players would have settled for tents on the motorway for the chance to play against Paraguay in the last sixteen a couple of days earlier, when they looked more likely to be flying home instead. They were also more than happy to be back at the plush Reforma Club for training and relaxation during the day.

However, that only served to emphasise the disparity with their hotel in Mexico City and gradually it became clear it was not the ideal place to prepare for such an important game, with traffic noises from the street and nightly orchestral concerts from the wonky plumbing.

The final insult came when coach Mike Kelly, along with Bryan Robson and Ray Wilkins, had no water in their rooms for showers, a shave or to flush the toilet, somewhat essential in Mexico City where hygiene, particularly after the earthquake, was not at the highest level.

The one advantage was the hotel's close proximity to the training ground, but everyone was eventually delighted to give that up to be in the much quieter Holiday Inn, with its first class rooms and swimming pool, especially important now the sun was out and the temperatures closer to what had been expected. The new practice pitch at the Club Atlantic was also well received.

So was Sir Stanley Matthews, who Bobby invited into the England dressing room along with the television cameras for the benefit of those back home before the kick off against Paraguay and to give his players a lift. It didn't work. England once more began lethargically and once again had Peter Shilton to thank for his early save against Adolfino Canete. Yet Linker soon showed his composure and poacher's instinct in front of goal once again, tapping the ball home from no more than a couple of yards after Steve Hodge's pass on the half-hour mark.

From that point on England were palpably on top and the South Americans didn't like it, and they began to exert some verbal pressure on the inexperienced Syrian referee, Jamal Al Sharif, as well as fouling and provoking the English players. It exploded in the second half when their skipper Rogelio Delgado elbowed Gary Lineker in the throat. Gary was a popular boy, not only with his appreciative teammates, but with the press contingent as well, and I have rarely seen such anger as Lineker was stretchered off struggling to breathe.

It also infuriated the English players, especially as the Syrian referee saw it and gave a foul but did nothing else. He should have seen red. Revenge was extracted with another goal as Peter Beardsley did a Lineker in his partner's temporary absence, tapping the ball home after the goalkeeper couldn't hold a Terry Butcher effort. This only provoked more antics from the South Americans, who hurled themselves to the ground at every opportunity and harassed the referee constantly.

Lineker returned after lengthy treatment and finally put the appallingly behaved opponents to bed with a typical goal, rounding off an incisive move that flowed through Hoddle and club mate Stevens to set up the tournament's leading goalscorer. England had progressed and were now scheduled to meet Argentina, the country the United Kingdom had been at war with just four years earlier in the Falklands.

ENGLAND 3-0 PARAGUAY, 18 JUNE 1986:

Throughout the tournament I had been inundated with calls and messages of goodwill from all sorts of people back home, and I was particularly tickled on the morning of the game with one which read simply 'Wishing you the best of luck against Paraguay,' signed: Bert Humphreys, Chimney Sweep, Birmingham. Another came from Mrs Porter, the old age cockney pensioner who lived in Newcastle and who had called me before every game. She told me she worried she couldn't afford it [the call] but felt that if things did not go well it would be her fault for not wishing my luck.

The players were delighted with the atmosphere at the Azteca Stadium when we arrived and fears over the heat had been allayed by a decent cloud cover. The pitch was in poor condition, but no one made an issue of it and everyone was thrilled when Sir Stanley Matthews overcame his shyness to pop in and wish us luck. The vibes were so good I even invited the cameras into the dressing room to share the moment.

Things went downhill a little when, within the first five minutes, Peter Reid took a knock on an already sore ankle and the quick South American forwards gave us a few problems. Once more, we needed a Peter Shilton save to keep things on par and, just as in the previous game, we responded with a goal, again scored by the inevitable, lethal Lineker, a goal that gave everyone on the pitch and on the bench confidence that we could go and win again.

Paraguay had suddenly turned from a happy-go-lucky group of youngsters to a snarling bunch, attempting to intimidate the Syrian referee and to provoke our players. Some of their challenges made me wince and fear for our players' health and safety.

Cold towels to bring down the temperature and oxygen to compensate for the altitude were administered at half-time. I don't know what the opposition were given but they came out more desperate than ever and Lineker was carried off after being elbowed in the throat. Beardsley nipped in to score a crucial second and the Paraguayans ratcheted it up even further as they became increasingly hysterical, chased the poor referee and behaved in a disgraceful manner.

We kept our cool and ruffled our opponents with the speed of our counter-attacks, and with Lineker back on after his scare, he scored his fifth goal of the tournament.

The joy in our dressing room was unconfined, and I even allowed FIFA to bring in their cameras to film the delight English players had in winning, but I was quickly brought down to earth at the press conference with the *world's media already concentrating on our next game at Argentina. It seemed that the world were rubbing their hands in glee at the prospect of the two countries, who had so recently been at war over the Falklands Islands, clashing in such an important World Cup match.*

No matter how hard I tried to avoid politics in the build-up to the game it was impossible, with the conflict only four years in the past, and I went out of my way to warn the players to avoid becoming involved and to stick with football. We were there to play football and I am a manager, not a politician.

Ahead of the game, the FA announced that they would keep to their promise and they had managed to charter an aircraft to fly out the wives and girlfriends for the last week of the competition providing, of course, they managed to beat Argentina.

Yet there were more warning signs, particularly when the team turned up on Saturday for their scheduled training session at the Azteca Stadium in the morning rather than the afternoon so that they could return to their hotel in time to watch France play the favourites Brazil. When they arrived, they found the dressing rooms locked and no one around with the keys to open them up. They made their way to the pitch where the groundsmen were still cutting the grass, and even had the strings out ready to mark up the pitch for the game. There was no way they were going to allow England to disturb their work and said graciously that Robson's men could walk carefully on the pitch providing they wore trainers and not boots.

World Cup regulations permitted teams to train for 45 minutes on the match pitch and England had even had it confirmed it with FIFA beforehand. Hasty calls were made to their headquarters but there was no one there with any authority, and they were then informed they could train after Argentina at 11am.

As an alternative they contacted the Atlantic Stadium to ask if they could use their facilities and were told that it would not be a problem, but again when they arrived the doors were locked and the police escort refused to break open the bolts, instead sending for a locksmith who let England into the ground – but not the dressing room. It was fast developing into a farce.

Perhaps FIFA had done them a favour, though, as the Azteca pitch was like a cabbage patch, worse than ever, with clods of turf lifting as the players walked on it, while in other areas their feet sank into the soft earth below the grass. FIFA themselves eventually started to show their concerns on the day of the game with no heavy roller available to flatten out the bumps, and farcically they used a little mower-roller to flatten the huge divots that littered the surface just half an hour before kick-off.

When the game itself got going, there were early signs that the Tunisian referee Ali Bennaceur was not as good as he had been billed. Best referee in Africa, we were told. Fenwick's very first tackle on Diego Maradona after just nine minutes brought a booking, leaving the tough-tackling defender walking a tightrope for the rest of the game. Bobby had warned the entire team that this man Maradona could change the course of the match in an instant, but no one could believe how the referee and Maradona combined to puncture an English dream.

After 51 minutes Maradona blatantly punched the looping ball past the oncoming Shilton just outside the six-yard box, an action seen by everyone in the stadium except for the referee and his assistant Berny Ulloa Morera from Costa Rica. Maradona himself couldn't believe the goal stood and suddenly went racing off in celebration. He should have been cautioned for deliberate handball, but instead he was up with the gods and four minutes later he showed the other side of his game when he slalomed through the English defence to beat Shilton and put Argentina two goals ahead. No one was at fault this time – it was just sheer, outrageous brilliance and the goal of the tournament. The best and the worst of Maradona was there for all to see in the space of just four minutes. For Bobby and his side, it never rained but it poured.

It would have been understandable if England had laid down and given it up, but they had come too far for that and soon Robson had his two wingers, Chris Waddle and John Barnes, off the bench and on the pitch for Peter Reid and Trevor Steven and they began to turn the screw. With ten minutes remaining the dazzling winger Barnes waltzed past two defenders and crossed for Lineker to head home for his sixth goal of the tournament. Another cross from the Watford man in the dying seconds saw Lineker head goalwards again from close range, only for the striker to end up in the net without the ball, which had somehow been scrambled to safety.

Conspiracy theories abounded when the Tunisian referee blew his whistle 45 seconds after the 45 minutes were up, despite the Argentina time-wasting, the celebrations and complaints for the goal and the substitutions. This was a World Cup quarter-final played on a disgrace of a pitch with inferior officials, but Bobby Robson remained a true gentleman, keeping his darker thoughts to himself as he went through the interview routine before he made it back to a dressing room filled with tears, anger and bitterness. There were no public protests or complaints and Robson told his players over dinner that night that they could hold their heads high and they were a credit to their country. They didn't want to hear, they just wanted to leave Mexico City and go home to lick their wounds.

ENGLAND 1-2 ARGENTINA, 22 JUNE 1986:

I took all my usual calls and messages, spoke to my senior citizen from Newcastle and busied myself with interviews with BBC and ITV before 9am, before heading out for the Azteca Stadium with our usual escort of police cars and outriders, always something of an event.

There were problems with the ragged pitch, especially the goalmouths, which concerned Peter Shilton. Senior FIFA officials were also concerned but there was no sign of a heavy roller to flatten the bumpy ground and it was no more than a gesture when, half an hour or so before the kick off, they brought on a little mower-roller, which made no appreciable difference.

They had the edge in the first half but I was more concerned with the Tunisian referee, who reached for his book for our first foul on Diego Maradona ten minutes in to caution Terry Fenwick, but worse was to follow when the referee ignored a blatant Maradona handball to score the opening goal. Our players were going crazy because they knew full well that the only way the brilliant Argentine could have beaten Shilton was by using his hand. But all our complaints were to no avail, and I was left with a hollow feeling in the pit of my stomach.

The goal lifted Argentina and especially Maradona, and four minutes later he showed the other side of his football brain when he ran through our defence to score a second. It was staggeringly brilliant. A solo goal which saw him go through half our team.

Lineker's sixth goal of the tournament gave us a chance, and we had Argentina on full retreat as shots hit bodies, flew wide and did everything but go in. I still felt we could pull it back but, despite all the time wasting that been going on, the referee added on just 45 seconds at the end of the 90 minutes.

I was devastated and in the dressing room there were tears, anger and annoyance. They were sick and bitter, and nothing I could say could help them, as they felt they had been cheated out of the World Cup by the tournament's best player and the worst referee.

There was no blame attached to anyone in our team, and in the end they had their Maradona, and we did not have our injured Bryan Robson. The thin line between winners and losers at this level.

I told them they could all go home with their heads held high. Every one of them had been a credit to their country and two months had passed without a single sour incident.

Time capsule as a youthful Bobby poses for a pre season Fulham photograph on August 1 1951. (PA)

A whole life in front of them. Bobby and Elsie look carefree as they pose on 2 September 1955. (PA)

Bobby Robson and the legendary Bill Dodgin at Fulham in October 1950. (PA)

Never mind Fog on the Tyne, this was a wraithlike Robson emerging from the Mist on the Thames to score against Brentford at Craven Cottage on 2 January, 1954. (PA)

Bit of class side by side as Bobby and Ron Greenwood sit shoulder to shoulder on August 2 1954. (Colorsport)

Just imagine heading one of those old leather balls on a cold wet day! Fortunately it was early June 1960 when Bobby was at West Bromwich Albion. (PA)

Playing for West Brom at home to Chelsea in April 1961. (Colorsport)

Memorable victory as England beat Italy 3-2 at the Olympic Stadium in Rome on May 24 1961. (Colorsport)

One of my favourite pictures of two of my favourite men. The incomparable Gentle Giant John Charles and Bobby Robson get together in November 1960 after the Italian League had beaten the English League 4-2 in Milan. This very picture, signed by both, hangs on my wall. (PA)

Walking on the beach at Worthing in Sussex in January 1968 having just been appointed manager of Fulham. Don't know why but it's a good picture! (PA)

Wall of Fame or Wall of Shame? We will never know as Bobby pins up another head and shoulders of an unknown player at the Portman Road Rogues Gallery in October 1969. (PA)

Little did either of them know what lay ahead as the newly appointed Bobby Robson shakes the hand of his new chairman John Cobbold on 13 January 1969. Nothing unlucky about that date for Robson, Ipswich or football. (PA)

This is my home! The manager takes his guests on a tour of Portman Road at the start of the 1972 season. Home was literally over the road. (PA)

One of the greatest days of his life! Bobby begins the year long celebrations of winning the FA Cup when they beat Arsenal 1-0 at Wembley on May 6 1978. (Colorsport)

This what the FA Cup meant to the town of Ipswich as everyone turned out for the celebrations - and continued to do so for the next twelve months! Here skipper Mick Mills and unassuming goalscoring hero Roger Osborne show the crowd what it was all about. (PA)

The day that couldn't come soon enough for a football nut like Bobby as he prepares his Ipswich troops for the 1973/74 season. (Colorsport)

Bobby Robson with his first team coach Bobby Ferguson watch with some satisfaction as their Ipswich team brush aside Cologne with a 2-0 second leg UEFA Cup semi final success on April 22 1981. (Colorsport)

A day of huge regrets and anger after losing to two Diego Maradona goals, one a worldy and the other a hand ball, in the World Cup quarter final in Mexico City. Bobby tries to keep a lid on it as he talks to the nation via ITV's Jim Rosenthal. (PA top & Colorsport)

Another book; another launch; another treasured dedication. (Authors' collection)

"Hello Bobby".... "No I'm Bryan. You are Bobby." It actually happened but not here as the two Robson's share a chuckle during training at Bisham Abbey on 25 March, 1985. (PA)

Queen Elizabeth II looks on (disapprovingly?) as Bobby Robson announces his departure from his England job at Lancaster Gate on May 25 1990 amid a media frenzy. (Colorsport)

"Gazza!! Move your hand, immediately!" (PA)

The manager tells it how it is while the media, with Harris sitting on the radiator at Bisham Abbey, listen and take note. (Author's collection)

Whatever he said it didn't work! Bobby talks to his senior penalty shooter Stuart Pearce before the shoot out in Turin against the Germans in Turin. (Colorsport)

The England players and their wives join Bob Harris for dinner at his hotel – with permission, of course – perhaps proving that the mass fall out between the media and the players wasn't quite all that it was cracked up to be. The photo when attached to an expense form gave the editor palpitations. (Author's collection)

No one better to celebrate another triumphant season with than his close friend Frank Arnesen, who he promoted to assistant and unearthed an excellent coach and a lifelong buddy. (PA)

This was always a big one. Bobby at PSV versus Ajax on 28 October 1990. (Colorsport)

Two of the Royals of football Peter Shilton and Bobby Robson celebrate their Royal honours together at Buckingham Palace. (PA)

Guess who that is sitting on Bobby Robson's left? Give the man a coconut if he guessed Jose Mourinho. Pictured soon after Bobby took over at Porto with Jose moving swiftly from his left side to the right side! (PA)

Another trophy for the Robson cabinet, this time it's the Cup Winners' Cup where Barcelona beat PSG 1-0 at the Feyenoord Stadium. Flanked by his assistant Jose Mourinho and the character that is Ronaldo. 14 May, 1997. (Colorsport)

Robson enjoys the glorious flora of the Caribbean island of St. Lucia and a training session on the beautiful island of Mauritius. (Author's collection)

Sir Bobby Robson and Sir Viv Richards enjoy each others company in Antigua. While Robson played international football for England Richards went one better and played cricket for the Windies and international football for Antigua. (Author's collection)

Arise Sir Bobby! Invested as a knight in 2002, as a proud Elsie and sons Paul and Andrew look on. (PA)

You have to be special to have a statue in your image, which makes Sir Bobby extra special as he has two! This one at St. James' Park and another celebrating his years at Portman Road with Ipswich Town. (PA)

Bobby finally returns home to his native north east after nearly half a century in the game. (PA)

Sir Bobby's first game in charge of a struggling Newcastle United on 11 September, 1999 at Stamford Bridge and an unfortunate 1-0 defeat. (PA)

Two Bobs together for the last time. This was taken on my final visit to Sir Bobby in June 2009. (Author's collection)

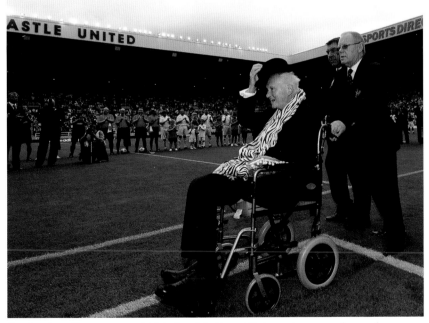

One last lap of honour around his beloved St. James' Park as a huge crowd turned out to pay tribute to their hero days before his passing. (PA)

Football fans from the world over paid tribute to one of the gentlemen of the game after his death. (PA)

Sir Alex Ferguson, Paul Gascoigne and Alan Shearer mourn at Sir Bobby Robson's Memorial Service in Newcastle on September 21 2009. (Colorsport)

Bobby stayed on. As much as he would have liked to fly home to his family he also, as a football man through and through, wanted to watch the semi-finals and final of the competition he had contributed so much towards. Outwardly he remained totally calm and together. Privately he was distraught and felt he had been cheated out of the competition.

Never having been a cheat himself, never having resorted to gamesmanship, he felt it was unfair on him and his players to have been dealt such a bad hand and, quietly, there were senior FIFA members who agreed with his complaints. He watched the semi-finals unfold, putting his personal hex on France by supporting them against the Germans. They lost 2-0. Returning to the Azteca Stadium for the second semi-final between Argentina and Belgium, he was convinced that his side were good enough to have beaten outsiders Belgium had they been given the chance.

He hadn't forgiven Maradona for his Hand of God goal, but he loved watching him perform against the Belgians, turning it on in the second half just as he did against England, scoring another spectacular solo goal after the cheekiest of openers early in the second half. It was a performance that had him purring.

With a couple of days off Bobby, myself and some of the ITV crew took off for the beautiful Pacific Ocean resort of Ixtapa. I should have known better than to chance my arm with this unlucky man. What could possibly go wrong? A nice swim in the big rolling waves underneath the lovely sunshine was just the ticket after weeks away, until a woman started running along the beach shouting, 'Big Fish, Big Fish.' We swam back for the shore as quickly as we could, certainly I was faster than I have ever moved in water before, scrambling onto the sand and turning to see the slick black fin of a shark gliding through the water no more than 30 yards from where we had been frolicking.

I had my doubts and thought it may have been something less

harmful, maybe a dolphin, so I went up to the lifeguard, who hadn't signalled any sort of warning, and asked him what it was. 'A shark,' he said without a flicker of emotion.

It didn't improve in the evening when Bobby and I joined the television boys in a rather smart club to have a drink after dinner. Just after we took our seats the disco lights came on, dry ice billowed smoke out into the area where we sat and the volume turned up. We decided to make our exit and go back to our hotel. No taxis, so we walked and half way home the heavens opened and the rain came down in torrents. We were soaked by the time we ducked into the hotel lobby, too wet for a nightcap but able to laugh at the absurdity of it all.

Fools never learn, and we popped down to the sensational beach before our flight back to Mexico City and the final, though we looked long and hard into the distant horizon before we ventured into the water once more and asked the lifeguard to keep an eye open for us. There were no further dramas.

Maradona's failure to score in the final as Argentina beat West Germany 3-2 meant that Gary Lineker finished as the top scorer of the tournament with his six goals, not bad for a man playing with a tender wrist, and Bobby Robson left Mexico convinced that England could have won the World Cup away from home for the first time ever with just a smidgeon of luck, something he was seriously lacking throughout the entire process.

Reflecting on the tournament after the final Robson told me that he did not feel any bitterness towards Maradona for the handball but more towards FIFA for appointing officials who were not fit for the task of controlling a potentially explosive match, with opponents who had been at war just four years earlier, in front of 114,580 passionate fans. Robson would not have argued if a top South American official had been appointed and he believes Carlos Bilardo would have felt the same if a top European referee had been named instead of an inexperienced official who turned the game into a lottery for both teams.

He also said that the standard of refereeing throughout the tournament troubled him to, with too many brutal fouls ignored while minor indiscipline was punished and, of course, too much conning of the referees. In a final act of defiance as we finished the last chapter for the book we had written during the course of the competition he told me quite firmly that, looking back, there was nothing he would change that had been within his compass, only matters over which he had no control whatsoever.

12

*'I don't measure a man's success by how high he climbs
but how high he bounces when he hits the bottom.'*
General George Patton. US Five Star General: 7th Army; US 3rd Army.

BOBBY ROBSON CERTAINLY HIT ROCK BOTTOM IN 1988 after the European Championships in Germany. England had entered the tournament as one of the favourites but came away with their tails between their legs, without a win or even a point from their three matches.

The trouble was that no one saw it coming. Buoyed by their performances in the World Cup in Mexico, Bobby and his England team genuinely believed that they could challenge for the trophy.

'At the end of the World Cup in Mexico I wouldn't have put England any higher than eighth in the world rankings, exactly where we finished in the tournament,' he told me. 'We were top ten but nothing more, but two years when we set off for Germany and the finals of the 1988 European Championships I believed we had moved up the pecking order considerably because I had one of the best attacking forces in the world in Gary Lineker, John Barnes and Peter Beardsley.

'It all fell apart with Lineker suffering from hepatitis; Waddle hadn't fully recovered from a hernia operation and both Beardsley and Barnes were all in, exhausted after giving their all in their first successful year at Liverpool.

'We had qualified in style and didn't appear to have too many weaknesses and even the critical media said it was our best team for 22 years.'

It is true that the press generally thought that this could be England's best team to travel to a major tournament since the 1970 World Cup, and there were papers predicting England's first silverware since 1966. In the two years between the controversial defeat by Argentina in the Azteca Stadium in Mexico City and the European Championships, England lost just twice, the first time to Sweden in Stockholm on 10 September 1986 and the second to West Germany, 3-1 in Dusseldorf exactly a year later. Both of the defeats were friendlies. It was said that the first international in September of a new season was cursed and Bobby was beginning to believe it after six successive autumn openers without a victory, though it was not a worry he voiced in public for fear of a backlash.

He explained it to me by citing the fact that it was the first time the squad had gathered together for a new season and that they were finding their feet but, in truth, he felt he was jinxed, and it was not until a 1-0 win over Denmark in 1988 that he shook it off. He much preferred to point out that between Mexico and Germany he lost just those two non-competitive fixtures but put together unbeaten runs of seven and eight games either side of that. In qualifying for the European Championships, they had dropped just one point and conceded just one goal, scoring nineteen themselves.

The one goal conceded was in Yugoslavia against a talented side, but it was a game England won 4-1 as Peter Beardsley, Bryan Robson, John Barnes and Tony Adams scored in a 25-minute blitz. Robson's men had all but declared by the time Srecko Katanec scored. Perhaps the biggest disappointment in that all-conquering run was a goalless draw against the Turks at Wembley, provoking more boos and jeers aimed at the manager . Six months later Turkey came to Wembley full of themselves, only to be beaten 8-0 for a second time by England. Gary Lineker scored a hat-trick and John Barnes two, with further goals coming from Bryan Robson, Neil Webb and Peter Beardsley.

After the defeat in Stockholm England hit their straps, beating Northern Ireland 3-0, Yugoslavia 2-0, Spain 4-2 and Northern Ireland 2-0. The season ended with a more than creditable 1-1 draw with Brazil at Wembley and a goalless affair against the Scots in Glasgow, when avoiding defeat seemed to be the priority in front of a snarling, unfriendly crowd.

The most significant performance was the stunning 4-2 victory against the Spaniards in Madrid, when Lineker emphasised his world class credentials with four goals to annihilate one of the world's top sides. It was a timely performance by the intelligent, talented Lineker, who had moved to Spain after the World Cup and joined Barcelona.

The following season England, after their stumble in Dusseldorf, won four and drew four of their eight matches ahead of their next major tournament appearance, and their boss believed his side were ready to take on the best Europe could offer.

Robson was convinced that England had moved on and improved since the Mexican denouement, maintaining continuity but introducing just the right amount of fresh blood to keep the machine ticking over. Qualification was completed in style and it was widely agreed that Robson had an excellent pool of players to choose from.

Privately, he believed it was indeed the best chance since the Ramsey triumph at Wembley. Gary Lineker was in scintillating form and had scored twenty goals in his last seventeen international appearances, while Peter Beardsley and John Barnes had both come of age in their first season with Liverpool. Chris Waddle, another of England's bright young attacking sparks, had made rapid strides since joining Spurs in 1985.

There was also significant help from the clubs for a change. In direct contrast with Manchester United's refusal to allow Bryan Robson to have an operation on his shoulder in the run up to Mexico, Terry Venables at Tottenham had sent Waddle off for a hernia operation, telling him that the most important thing for him and his career was to be ready for the European Championships, even though it meant missing a two-month slice of Spurs' season.

It was the boost England needed, having lost the indomitable Terry Butcher, now with Glasgow Rangers, to a broken leg. They were limited to a squad of just twenty for the tournament, something Robson nor the other competing managers could understand when injuries and illness were almost inevitable after long, hard seasons in the various competitive European leagues.

Injury concerns had caused Robson to take his eye off the ball and it was only later that he realised he had not paid enough attention to the fact that heading into the tournament the goals had dried up for his dangerous forward line. In their last four matches before the competition, coming against Hungary, Scotland, Colombia and Switzerland, England found the net just twice. In the four prior to that the tally was fourteen.

Things were taking a turn for the worst at exactly the wrong time, and Jack Charlton's Republic of Ireland provided a nightmare opening to the competition and a horrendous experience for everyone involved.

A succession of errors in the defence led to Ray Houghton scoring after just five minutes. It was, at the time, nothing more than an inconvenience, a minor setback which grew and grew over the next 85 minutes as England wasted chance after chance, goalkeeper Pat Bonner made saves and shots rattled the goal frame. Lineker did everything but score, his partner Beardsley side-footed wide from in front of goal and an effort from substitute Glenn Hoddle slipped through Bonner's hands and rolled the wrong side of the post.

ENGLAND 0-1 REPUBLIC OF IRELAND, 12 JUNE 1988: *We respected Jack Charlton's Irish side but we certainly fancied that we would beat them. What we didn't expect was another defensive cock up to let in Ray Houghton to open the scoring after five minutes, leaving us chasing the game.*

We made enough chances to win it twice, but a combination of excellent goalkeeping by Pat Bonner, some bad luck and some awful finishing [resulted in the 1-0 scoreline]. There was no hint of the traumas to come and the players, cross with themselves, were still up for it.

At that stage the result was hugely frustrating rather than devastating, and a win against the Dutch, who had lost to the Soviet Union in their opening game, would put England back on track in a four-team group. A 2-2 friendly draw with Holland at Wembley in March of the same year had given Robson some tactical ideas to put into operation. In the centre of the park he wanted Bryan Robson wanted to take care of Jan Wouters, leaving the supremely talented but not so physical Hoddle to dominate Arnold Muhren in the creative department. However, there were few tactics that could have accounted for the genius of Marco van Basten. Only a substitute against the Soviets but coming off the back of a season which had seen him win his first league title with AC Milan, Van Basten lined up from the off against England and marked the occasion with a stunning hat-trick.

His first came shortly before half-time when his Milan teammate Ruud Gullit robbed Stevens and on the left and fed the ball to him on the edge of the box. With his back to goal there was still plenty of work for the striker to do and he did it in sublime fashion, swivelling his body 180 degrees to beat Tony Adams and then firing past Shilton with his left foot into the bottom corner.

It was a match high on quality and England did hit back through Robson not long after the break. They had also come within inches during other moments in the contest, hitting the post on two occasions in the first half, but those agonising misses opened the door for Van Basten, who was less forgiving when it mattered.

It was the same combination that did for Robson's side to make it 2-1, Gullit once again finding Van Basten on the edge of the area and Van Basten once again drilling the ball beyond Shilton with his left foot into the bottom corner, and when he added a volley from a corner just minutes later, England were on their way home.

ENGLAND 1-3 HOLLAND, 15 JUNE 1988:

We had drawn 2-2 with the Dutch at Wembley and felt we knew how to beat them. They had lost to the Soviet Union in their first match and looked ripe for the picking, and I matched up Glenn Hoddle with Arnold Muhren for a battle of their respective skills, while leaving the physical battle between Bryan Robson and Jan Wouters.

There is no doubt that we lacked our usual edge, especially in front of goal, but when Robson bundled the ball over the line to equalise the opener from Marco van Basten, the money was definitely on us. We reckoned without the superb Van Basten.

He was only used as a substitute against the Russians, but he played the full 90 minutes against us and scored a brilliant hat-trick, the sort of goals we had come to expect from the rapidly diminishing Lineker who, unknown to us at the time, was being consumed with illness.

We threw the kitchen sink at them as we searched for an equaliser and, inevitably, they hit us on the break with Van Basten showing his skills again by completing his hat-trick. We were out of the competition after two games, despondent with egg on our faces.

Robson himself was dreadfully disappointed in the result but hugely impressed by Van Basten, who was on his way to becoming one of the world's great strikers. He scored 300 career goals in a high profile career, including the winner in the semi-final against their bitter rivals West Germany and an iconic, angle-defying volley in the final against the Soviet Union. He was named player of the tournament, and as well as his winners medal that summer, he racked up three Eredivisie titles and the European Cup Winners' Cup with Ajax, followed by three Serie A titles and two European Cups with Milan in an astonishing career, which also saw him named FIFA World Player of the Year in 1992 and win the Ballon D'Or three times.

Robson could stomach falling short against such genius, but he wouldn't stand for anything less than total commitment to the cause. The only time I ever heard Robson slam his English players both in private and in public was after the 3-1 defeat to an ordinary USSR side in Frankfurt. He asked them to play with pride after their exit was confirmed, but felt they capitulated without a show of resistance and he told me afterwards that he was truly ashamed with the performance, adding that it was the worst in his six-year tenure, later extending that to his whole reign after he had left.

Hoddle disappeared from the game early on and Oleh Protasov took over the midfield as Russia added goals from Oleksiy Mykhaylychenko and Viktor Pasulko. As for the best forward line in European football – they never turned up. Lineker, the scourge of defences, was flat and uninspired and it was only after the tournament that it was discovered he was suffering from hepatitis, the condition eventually forcing him to hospital.

Waddle, despite the efforts of Spurs, had clearly not fully recovered from his hernia operation, while Barnes and Beardsley were left exhausted by their first season with Liverpool and had little left to offer. It all meant that in a period of less than a fortnight Robson had gone from being the manager of the best team to the manager who should be gone.

ENGLAND 1-3 USSR, 15 JUNE 1988:

We went from Dusseldorf to Frankfurt, hammered back at home and needing a win against the Russians to restore some pride and give the people back home something to cling to. Instead we were dreadful. We capitulated and at the end of the 3-1 defeat I was left wondering if I still had a job. According to the press I had not.

Certainly, in my years as England manager it was the worst performance by some measure and not one of my hotshot forward line had performed and Hoddle, brilliant in the second game, was awful, as the Russians swept past us in the second half. Two days later, Lineker was in hospital on a drip.

For the first and only time in his international managerial career he had his own doubts about his ability and his competence. The world, he felt, had turned against him and this time it was not just the *Mirror* and the *Sun* but also the more serious journals, including the *Daily Telegraph* and the *Guardian*, with the pundits on radio and television joining in the feeding frenzy.

The question he asked himself in the aftermath was whether he should pack it in and give someone else the opportunity. He knew they would inherit a talented side who had yet to reach their peak, although some thought they had reached their nadir in Germany that summer. He didn't ask my opinion, but I gave it anyway, telling him he had hit the bottom but should bounce back up. He hadn't become a bad manager over the course of seven summer days in Germany.

Fortunately, his regular supporter Bert Millichip felt exactly the same way and before the Football Association's Annual General Meeting in the summer, he brushed aside the offer to resign, telling Robson to get on with the job of taking England to the next World Cup Finals. He told his manager that he had the full backing of the International Committee. 'We can absorb the pressure – can you?' was the message, and indeed the question. It was a question that needed just a one-word answer, and the answer was exactly wanted Millichip wanted to hear. The meeting of two of the most powerful men in English football was over in less than a minute, two minutes shorter than the last time the subject was broached after Mexico.

But it didn't salve the wounds of the summer and Robson brooded over the whole affair, much to his wife's annoyance, as they took a holiday in Bermuda. Luckily for Bobby, his players did not seem to dwell on it as much.

'The remarkable thing was that the players took their humiliation in their stride as though the tournament had not happened,' he recalled. 'That was last season and there was a new season to look forward to.'

Two of the teams who beat England ended up meeting in the final of the competition, with the Dutch beating the Russians by two goals, including a fabulous Van Basten volley, but clearly that would not be enough for the English press back home.

Who was to blame? The manager, of course. One of Robson's apocryphal jokes on the dinner circuit was how his predecessor Ron Greenwood had left him three envelopes to open in case of emergency. He opened the first after losing to Denmark in the European qualifiers and it said simply blame the Football League for lack of cooperation. The second he opened after the defeat to Argentina and it said blame the clubs for their lack of cooperation. The third he opened after the three defeats in Germany, and it simply told him to prepare three envelopes.

The vitriol poured down as he sought to bounce back with the help of his trusty lieutenants Don Howe and Dave Sexton, and they began to put together a plan on how they were going to qualify for the World Cup Finals in Italy. They had just two years to repair the damage done in Germany, which had somewhat undone all the good work in Mexico two years before that.

They drew up a list of players that were in line to be included in future squads, which included Paul Parker, Stuart Pearce, Tony Dorigo, Gary Pallister, Paul Gascoigne, Brian Clough's son Nigel, David Rocastle and Michael Thomas. Older performers like the 38-year-old Peter Shilton and Terry Butcher would not be discarded until they showed frailties, while he was prepared to understand the failures of Lineker, Beardsley, Barnes and Waddle, who, he felt, all had legitimate excuses for their below-par performances in Germany. One of his major concerns was over Glenn Hoddle, a glorious, inventive player in full flow but something of a luxury when the chips were down.

These decisions were critical because he knew that, despite their resolve and good intentions, the International Committee would discard the management once their own jobs and reputations came under threat. Margins were fine and there was little room for error, as it showed when he began the new campaign with a single-goal victory over the Danes at Wembley thanks to Neil Webb and followed it up with a goalless draw at home to Sweden in the first qualifier in October. Had it been a new manager it would have been an acceptable start, but this was the man who had failed in Germany and not gone when he was told to by the media.

It was not looking good for Robson when the headline 'Desert Prats' greeted the 1-1 draw in Saudi Arabia just under a month later.

Following the European Championships the *Mirror* had ran with the headline 'In the name of God, Go!' and following the result in the Middle East, it was replaced with 'In the name of Allah, Go!' It was clever stuff if you were not on the end of it. Such headlines also caused some raised eyebrows in the pubs around Fleet Street – they were, after all, aimed at the man who on the same trip obliged the football writers by giving a midnight press conference. His team were travelling on a different flight to the British press, but he still found time to cater to us.

He had been hounded to bring in new faces, which is just what he did in Saudi Arabia, introducing goalkeeper David Seaman, Mel Sterland, Michael Thomas, Gary Pallister, David Rocastle, Paul Gascoigne, Alan Smith and Brian Marwood. It was not enough for the media and when the flight arrived at Heathrow it was the turn of the 'Rotters' and the 'Smudgers' to hassle him so badly and physically that he almost fell to the ground and had to be hurried away to a private room. There Don Howe told him if he had been exposed to that sort of treatment he would quit. It was left to Bert Millichip to front up the cameras and the news men to announce that he had no intention of sacking his manager in order to dampen down the volume.

To put that result into perspective, Saudi was not the friendliest of places to visit and around the time of England's draw Scotland and Argentina had also shared the spoils with this well-drilled side in 1988. I must confess that in all my travels round the world, I felt more intimidated in Saudi Arabia than anywhere else, even the Soviet Union at its worst during the cold war.

Colleague and friend Michael Hart from the Evening Standard and I looked around Riyadh after writing our pieces and felt distressed in Deera Square, the site where a recent execution had taken place. Also known as 'Justice Square' and 'Chop Chop Square' to reflect this ritual, it was like a must-see tourist spot. It was upsetting to find this square in such a public place, complete with drains for the blood to run off. We quickly moved onto the shopping area, but while looking at the goods on display in a smart jewellery shop for gifts, the door was flung open and two very large, fully-armed gentlemen dismissed us to the back of the shop to allow a 'Princess' to do her shopping in privacy. We scarpered back to the hotel as fast as we could. This was neither the moment nor the place to put up that typically offended British countenance.

Bobby was always a great sightseer and we often went out looking at markets and shops in the various countries, but he wisely decided that he didn't need to do any shopping around on this trip and he and the team sensibly stuck to the confines of the Western style hotel and the training ground.

Andy Roxburgh, who had taken Scotland to Riyadh, had warned Bobby when he discovered England were contemplating the trip, saying prophetically, 'Don't go. If you go and win you will get nothing and if you lose you will be decapitated (not literally). If you can do without the match don't play it. I warn you – you could lose there.'

Bobby was left with little choice because of government restrictions, weather and mid-season breaks. He needed to have a look at some of his youngsters and had he refused the fixture it would have meant that his team had a long stretch of almost four months between games, something he felt he could not afford.

England didn't win and the abuse ratcheted up. Bobby's old enemy Nigel Clarke from the *Daily Mirror* was interviewed by television on the flight on the way out to Athens for the next fixture and did not hide the intention of his trip to the viewers: 'We are here to fry Bobby Robson.' When England went a goal down Robson turned to Howe and said, 'Where's the frying pan? Clarke will be boiling the fat ready for me.' Clarke and his obnoxious sports editor were to be disappointed, however, as England hit back to win with goals from

Bryan Robson and John Barnes.

It was an interesting concept that international draws and international fixtures had been manipulated to keep the notorious English hooligans away from prospective battle grounds and supporters who fancied a scrap. In this period England travelled to places such as Cairo, Tel Aviv (twice), Tbilisi, Belfast, Belgrade, Riyadh, Athens and Tirana, all fascinating cities to visit but not conducive to the shaven-headed riot squad flying out to drink the place dry and do battle with the natives. They might not have come back and most of them were wise enough to know it. There certainly weren't too many of them in the capital of Albania, Tirana, which had only been opened to tourists and visitors just twelve months or so earlier.

While there I also made sure I went on the long coach trip to Shkodra for the Under-21 game, which England won 2-1 in front of a remarkably large crowd of 20,000. It was a 120-kilometre journey worth taking to this ancient city on the banks of the Skadar Lake with its narrow streets and quaint houses, overlooked by the Castle of Rozafa, built in the third century. It was an experience, and while not as fearsome as Saudi we were clearly the interlopers in a society which had been shut off from the rest of the world for a long time.

Tirana in those days was a fascinating place, notable because of a lack of motorised vehicles in the huge, oversized squares, surrounded by pastel buildings. The Skanderbeg Square, the main plaza in the centre of the city, was dominated by the statue of the military commander George Castriot – known as Skanderbeg, Lord of Albania – astride his horse.

The senior game saw Peter Shilton back to his best and a win with goals from Bryan Robson, who had been sick all the previous night, and John Barnes, supported by the classy David Rocastle, was enough for the points and a hasty retreat from a venue which even stressed out one or two of the press corps, one of whom wouldn't sleep on his own and instead curled up in a corner of another scribe's room, much to his amusement.

There was no substance to the perceived threat, just lingering thoughts probably caused by reading too many travel books, drinking too much Raki or eating the roast beef in fermented milk sauce.

The return fixture was under threat because it was scheduled just ten days after the Hillsborough disaster on 15 April when 96 Liverpool supporters died and 766 were injured due to police failings at the Leppings Lane end of the ground, leading to the biggest crush in English football history.

I was there to cover the FA Cup semi-final between Liverpool and Nottingham Forest and watched as the nightmare unfolded, seeing bodies carried away on advertising hoardings used as makeshift stretchers by their fellow supporters. My abiding nightmare was of the hundreds of shoes and trainers left behind after the disaster and picturing the young and old who had lost them in a needless disaster. No one has ever explained to me the physical reasons why, after any disaster like this and Heysel, or even a multi-vehicle pileup on a motorway, people lost their shoes.

Liverpool was closed down as Merseyside mourned its dead, led by the noble manager Kenny Dalglish and his dignified wife Marina. The Liverpool players had not trained since the trauma as they took counselling, attended funerals and comforted the grieving. By the time of the Albania game Peter Beardsley and Steve McMahon felt it was time for them to resume life, but John Barnes was unable to join the squad as he had already committed himself to attending one of the many funerals.

Beardsley was outstanding, with two goals in a 5-0 win. Lineker, Waddle and substitute Paul Gascoigne got the others. What an entrance Gazza made that night. Before he came on as substitute Robson instructed him to stay out on the right but within seconds he popped up on the left and enchanted the crowd with his skills and his ability, setting up a goal for Chris Waddle before scoring a beauty himself.

How Bobby loved the free-spirited Gazza. Given his inability to follow instructions and lack of defensive nous, he was not the sort of player you would expect the manager to embrace, but that night he put a smile on Bobby's troubled face and also sent the crowd home happy after the awful problems of just eleven days earlier.

The long season ended with a friendly in Denmark to celebrate its FA's centenary and ended in a draw. After three defeats in three in the summer of 1988, England were now undefeated in ten, with six victories. Bobby contented himself that the team was settled, looking confident and well on course for Italy. He wondered quietly what might lie ahead after the traumas of Heysel and Hillsborough, while also on his mind were the European bans England's clubs were serving, the ever-present threat of the lunatic fringe and, as ever, a domestic season not designed in any way to help the national team.

No one of an age and with any interest in football can forget the night England kicked off the new season against Sweden, in a crucial qualifier, in Stockholm, in the jinx month of September. There was no charismatic Bryan Robson, injured again, to lead the team and the honour fell to Terry Butcher, and how he loved it. They will not pass had always been his motto but as skipper that night he practiced what he preached in the extreme.

England weren't playing well against their main rivals in the group and on a bumpy pitch anything was possible – the last thing they needed was to lose yet another charismatic skipper after he clashed heads with centre-forward Johnny Ekstrom. Physios Norman Medhurst and Fred Street bandaged him up until half time, when Doc Crane whisked him into the treatment room, wiped off the blood and began inserting the ten stitches he told Robson Butcher needed.

When the bell rang for the resumption the Doc had completed only seven of the ten stitches but Butcher, backed by the Boss, couldn't wait and a bandage was hastily wrapped around the gash and his three lions shirt, stained blood red, replaced with a fresh white one.

Butcher resumed battle with the cut not totally sealed and it soon began seeping through and, he told Robson, every time he headed the ball he could hear a squelching noise.

Soon not only was Butcher looking like a butcher, everyone else on the pitch was splattered with his blood somewhere or another as they either came in contact with the ball or, indeed, with the towering centre-half himself. The biggest problem was for the goalkeepers as the slimy ball was difficult to hold onto, with Shilton becoming increasingly irate at his defender's carelessness in being injured.

Between them they held out for a well fought goalless draw – England, indeed, had not been passed – but the only story was Butcher. Not even poor Neil Webb, who had ruptured his Achilles, got a look in. The photographers went feral, with Butcher obliging them with a wild-eyed look he usually reserved for the 'Smudgers'. The iconic picture went ballistic, printed in newspapers across the globe, and later formed the cover of the autobiography I penned with him, aptly titled *Butcher*. I even have a signed copy of the photograph adorning the wall of my downstairs loo. It was too horrific for a more public display.

It wasn't even the end of the story, for Butcher had to see Doc Crane for the remaining stitches, missed in the hurry at the end of the half time break. This achieved, he had a plastic based bandage wrapped around his head so that he could shower and scrape off the matted blood from all over his hair and the rest of his body. The problem was that there was still fresh blood, which he discovered was coming from a separate wound over his eye sustained in another coming together with Ekstrom, and back he went to see the Doc for more stitches before eventually emerging to meet the anxiously awaiting press.

We had already tucked away the remarkable pictures and got our quote from the manager. 'People have been awarded Victoria Crosses for less,' was his take on the situation, much to the embarrassment of the injured man given his family's military background. We in the press were not convinced, for few were as dedicated as England's stand-in captain, but Butcher was also convinced that all of his teammates would have done the same.

There were more interviews at the airport and Butcher must have been light-headed, as he bought a round of drinks for the press, unheard of. There was more. As he was showing his wife Rita his bloodied kit upon his return home, the telephone rang: it was a company called Radion who made washing powder and they wanted the blood-stained kit for an advert. Both shirts came up spotless and one was hung in a display case at Ibrox, while there was a six-month supply of detergent from the delighted company supplied to the Butchers.

He has been signing the pictures of himself and his war wounds ever since, and his fame was so great that Baddiel and Skinner produced a skit of the event at Hendon FC, featuring Steve Hodge, with the two comedians dressed as Swedish commentators in woolly hats, along with a variety of lookalikes that included Elvis in his Las Vegas gear and the Pope in his robes, with everyone getting drenched in the fake blood that pumped out of a tube attached to Butcher's head by blood-soaked bandages.

He also came close to being immortalised in the famous 'Three Lions' anthem written by the same duo, with a verse along the lines of Butcher going to war, but the FA blocked it because it was considered politically incorrect.

The stalemate in Sweden, meanwhile, suited both teams and despite the lack of goals it was an end to end affair. It was much the same story against a remarkably attacking Polish side in October,

England's last qualifying match. Robson's men had beaten Poland 3-0 at home in June, but the hosts changed their team dramatically for the clash in Chorzow, a game England needed a result from to guarantee qualification. They were moments away from losing when a long-range shot from Ryszard Tarasiewicz rattled the crossbar, and it was another tough, nerve-wracking examination on the road. Shilton, fast approaching his 40th birthday, came off and joked to Robson that he could have put the effort over the bar but didn't want to give away a corner. He had just gone through an entire World Cup qualifying tournament without conceding a single goal.

He had backed up his manager's judgement of his fitness and continued form, while in turn Robson acknowledged his class as England's undisputed number one. He, the team and the ever-growing media army, returned from Poland that night with the memory of those three defeats in Germany firmly in the past, although not entirely forgotten.

Upon their return Robson made a plea to his bosses at Lancaster Gate for the toughest run in to Italia '90 they could give him, and they duly obliged with fixtures against Italy, Yugoslavia, Brazil, Czechoslovakia, Denmark and Uruguay, finishing off with an acclimatisation game in Africa against Tunisia. Five of those teams had qualified for Italy, with the hosts and Brazil among the favourites to win it outright.

Yet despite qualification, there was plenty of the usual sniping from the press. There was even an article that appeared in one newspaper which included a few sharp barbs towards the England manager from Sampdoria forward Gianluca Vialli. However, when the two teams did meet, Vialli made an effort to seek Bobby out in the dressing room, along with an interpreter, to explain that he hadn't said any of the things attributed to him and, in fact, had never spoken to the journalist who wrote the original 'exclusive' piece.

Butcher was not impressed and gave him that infamous long-range stare before the game and proceeded to put him in his pocket to such an extent that he was hooked and replaced by Roberto Baggio.

It was the start of a loss of form for Vialli, but England's forwards were having their own problems in front of goal, and went over five hours without finding the net, and so it was with some trepidation that they faced Yugoslavia at Wembley on 13 December 1989. They needn't have worried as Captain Marvel Bryan Robson – who else – popped up after 38 seconds to head home a Chris Waddle free-kick, the fastest ever goal scored at Wembley, paving the way to a 2-1 England victory, their hundredth at the famous old ground. This against a team who had whipped the Scots and topped their group ahead of the fancied French.

Soon afterwards England learned they had drawn the Republic of Ireland and the Netherlands for the second major tournament group stage in a row, along with Egypt. It was a chance for Robson and his side to prove that the results in Germany were a freak.

Hopes began to rise again as England continued their long unbeaten run by overcoming a strong Brazil side with a solitary goal from Gary Lineker; a near post header from a Peter Beardsley corner. Everyone hoped it was normal service resumed. In between the games against Denmark, a 1-0 victory, and Uruguay, a 2-1 defeat, Robson had to present his squad for the World Cup to the FA, the press and the players. He also had the dreadful task of telling four players they had not made it. By accidental irony, three of them were Arsenal players: Tony Adams, David Rocastle and Alan Smith. Robson wrestled over the decision to leave out the young leader of men Adams, but the best he could offer him was a standby place in case Mark Wright's damaged thigh continued to give him problems. The fourth player to miss out was goalkeeper Dave Beasant, who was also put on the reserve list and, indeed, joined the squad in Italy when David Seaman succumbed to injury.

Bobby was massively disappointed that the farewell game at Wembley was lost to their South American opponents, the first they had suffered at the venue for six years, especially after England had scored their finest goal in his reign, at least according to the press corps. Gazza hit a stunning 50-yard pass for Stuart Pearce to run onto, and the left-back crossed to the far post where John Barnes chested the ball down and volleyed it past goalkeeper Eduardo Pereira. Bobby also rated it as the best from one of his players. If that was the best scored under Robson, then one of Uruguay's goal was also the worst Robson's team conceded in his reign, as Peter Shilton of all people let a 35-yard free-kick squirm through his fingers to give the away side victory. There was no blood to blame this time.

All that remained was a 1-1 draw in Tunisia – prompting a further tirade of abuse from Sir Alf and some members of his World Cup-winning team. Some of his sniping was ridiculous and hard to understand, particularly when he wrote that the only time he saw Bobby Robson was when he was surrounded by the wrong sort of men in £1,000 suits. Bobby could only assume that he meant the dinners where they were both invited, where they were basically surrounded by strangers with little or no relevance to themselves or football, and certainly not at press conferences where entire wardrobes for the press pack were purchased for a lot less.

But for Bobby the very worst thing Alf did was to try and undermine the squad selected, writing about those who shouldn't be going to Italy, chipping away at their confidence. After all, they were being informed of their inadequacy by England's greatest manager.

Kevin Keegan, Emlyn Hughes, Malcolm MacDonald and Alan Ball all lined up for cheap shots as well, just when it appeared that Robson had persuaded most of the press and supporters that he was worth backing and was going to Italy with a puncher's chance of winning. Others like Steve Perryman and Terry Fenwick joined the chorus.

Other than Keegan, there were not too many successful managers in that list of players turned critics.

Robson had accepted that he had made a cardinal error when leaving Keegan out of his first ever England squad in 1982. Keegan had been captain of England for some time under Greenwood and Robson had not informed him of his omission personally before making it public. Strangely, Keegan had always been a Robson favourite; he used to tell his players at Portman Road what a great example he was to all of them for his commitment, energy and will to win. Robson had not made the decision lightly and spoke to all of the managers Keegan had played under and fully intended to bring him back at a later date if he could prove his form and fitness.

Keegan never allowed that to happen as he made his opinions on England, the manager and the players known, seemingly before every subsequent international. Robson even wrote to him through his manager Arthur Cox at Newcastle, offering to bury the hatchet. Keegan failed to respond, but did later say he would put himself up for Robson's job even though, at that stage, he had never managed and was living abroad.

The most surprising and downright bizarre critic was Rugby League manager and former player Alex Murphy, who questioned the manager's ability and told Chris Waddle how he should be performing. The players were playing for the wrong reasons according to Murphy, who claimed he knew how to handle professional sportsmen. Bobby's response was perfect, asking Mr Murphy what he would say if golfer Tony Jacklin had told him where he was going wrong with his rugby players.

He always claimed he could handle the day-to-day journalists, whether from the newspapers, radio or television, and I can vouch for that, but he couldn't stand those who sat inside and directed the troops in their continued assault. He told me that the most vitriolic of all of the sports editors offered him more than he made in a year to sit down with one of his lieutenants and spill the beans. It was so much that, for an instant, he considered it, but only for an instant. His mind quickly turned to how despicable the man he was speaking to was.

He had strong shoulders, but his mam and dad were now in their eighties, and his focus was protecting them, Elsie and his three sons – he did everything he could to keep them away from the circus.

He did enjoy the cut and thrust of David Lacey in the *Guardian*, who could be as scathing as any tabloid writer but never lied, and he enjoyed the company of Steve Curry, Jeff Powell, Michael Hart, Alex Montgomery, David Meek, Joe Melling and others, and we'd often take him out for lunch and dinner, especially on foreign tours.

He didn't read all the papers at home though, and when he finally quit and left for a new life in Holland, he told me that one of his great joys was that there were no investigative tabloids where he was going.

Peace at last, he sighed. But not for long.

13

*'So near is a falsehood to truth that a wise man
would not trust himself on the narrow edge.'*
Marcus Tullius Cicero, Roman statesman, orator, lawyer
and philosopher, assassinated December 7 43 BC.

ELSIE ROBSON HAS OLD-FASHIONED VALUES,
particularly about the sanctity of marriage, putting her family of three
sons above everything and warding off the marauding press contingent,
including myself. She kept her marriage and Bobby's all-consuming
passion for the beautiful game as far apart as she could. I am told she
rarely read the newspapers, though that could not save her from some
of the lurid tales, many of them based in the distant past, which she
dutifully ignored in public.

I liked Elsie but accepted she didn't like me, what I did for a living
or the time I shared with her husband when it could have been her by
his side. She was polite but vaguely distant when we were in company

together. She welcomed me into their home shortly before he passed away and said hello at the memorial service but, understandably, I have not heard from her since and she no longer returns the compliment of the annual exchange of Christmas cards, always written in Bobby's distinctive hand.

I was encouraged when, through a third party, one of the sons asked me to be involved in a television tribute to Bobby. I met up with the producers, directors and narrator, took a file of cuttings, photographs and a couple of books, but discovered that all they were really interested in was whether I still retained the many hours of tapes from our interviews for the several books we had written together. When I failed to produce them (I guess I recorded over them again for other interviews and other books) they lost interest and I have had no contact with the sons since then.

Not a problem. Bobby Robson was my friend and close confidant and we shared secrets that could not and would not be revealed in any public document. Nothing earth-shattering, of course, but just things men talk to each other about when you have a close relationship, certainly an unusual one for a journalist and an international football manager.

We both enjoyed sightseeing and shopping on our many trips abroad both for business and pleasure, and I used to watch impatiently as he would fuss for ages over Lapis Lazuli jewellery. He would study any number of the deep blue metamorphic rocks of the sort that were used in the funeral mask of Tutankhamun, before deciding on the one he wanted as a gift for Elsie.

We visited the pyramids in Mexico together and once took a private trip on our mutual friend Joe Sanchez's plane to the Basque country during a break in the season to take a rest and do a little more work on one of our books. He would confess to me that he found it therapeutic and, despite my prying and nosing into his past, he never lost patience and, indeed, he would make some revelations on the understanding that I would not use them. That promise remains intact because there was never any deadline and he knew as well as I did that I would never let him down. Perhaps it was fate that those tapes were recorded over, for we always left them running.

Joe Sanchez also used his aircraft to fly Bobby and I to view hotels and venues after the draw for Italia '90, a competition he always felt was his destiny. It so nearly was.

The rest and recuperation following another long domestic season ended on 1 June as the players – and the manager – said farewell to their wives and girlfriends, packed up their gear and prepared to move inland to the more isolated Is Molas Golf Hotel and briefly on to Tunisia for yet another friendly designed to keep them sharp. Elsie left with the rest of the ladies, heading home to Ipswich to do a little more packing before the move to Holland, then on to see her sister and mother, who had both been ill, in her native North East.

But for Bobby it was back to business and a 55-minute flight to Tunis where the sun beat down and the style of football played by the opposition was not a million miles from that played by England's World Cup opponents, Egypt. It also provided the opportunity to shake off a few of the cobwebs from the days spent sunbathing, swimming and relaxing.

It felt like nothing could go wrong this time, but with just an hour until kick-off our press bus whizzed past the team bus on the road. Worse still, they were headed in completely the opposite direction to the stadium. We were baffled until Bobby later explained that the local police had stopped their bus and the escort, claiming they had taken the wrong road. The local Bobbies refused to give an inch until a senior officer arrived and set them free to fulfil their fixture.

Bobby joked afterwards that he wished they had not let them into the ground for the game, because on a bumpy pitch and a hot and sticky day England could never get going. It was a ragged performance with mistakes all over. The players looked out of kilter, mentally still on the beach, and Steve Hodge got sunstroke. Wolves striker Steve Bull saved the blushes with a last-minute equaliser and the one thing Bobby took away from the game was that his surprise choice for the tournament was as deadly in front of goal as he suspected.

'Nowhere else,' said the manager with a smile, 'but a more than useful player to bring on when opponents legs are tiring.'

Gazza was also up to his usual nonsense with exaggerated celebrations in front of the Tunisian bench after the equaliser, before Bobby pulled him away and told him to grow up. However, alongside his antics he had also performed a lot better than some of his more experienced teammates. He was not the only one to behave childishly as well, as Terry Butcher was seen on television headbutting an opponent, leaving the centre-half with another cut, this time above his right ear and this time self-inflicted. Isolated in a television shot it was clearly a headbutt and, of course, the papers wanted and demanded action. The *Daily Star* insisted that Butcher be sent home instantly. Strange one that, as Butcher was 'writing' a column for them. Note the past tense.

Far worse was the news from home when Elsie telephoned Bobby to tell him that his brother Keith was in intensive care after suffering a heart attack, not helped by the fact that it soon became front-page news. It was not the right time for FIFA representative Heinz Maroski to give the England boss a lecture about on-field discipline. Bobby politely suggested he should look at his team's actual record and leave them alone.

Following the draw with Tunisia, Bobby felt the need for some more opposition before the tournament kicked into gear. They soon found it and ended up running in ten goals against the local side and then ingratiated themselves with the locals by doling out sweets and gifts to the kids and neighbours who had come along to watch.

Next up was the tournament itself that opened against Jack Charlton's Ireland, a team that liked nothing better than embarrassing their neighbours.

But Gazza was already managing that all on his own, tearing across the local golf course in an electric buggy, shirtless, shorts rolled up to his backside and wearing flip flops. Birmingham City director Jack Wiseman, the friendliest of men, took one look and flipped, hastening across to tell him to behave properly and get changed. Gazza came up at the next hole to apologise and Bobby ruminated that perhaps, at last, he was showing a bit of maturity. How forgetful he was. Earlier that day Gascoigne had emerged from his room screaming for physio Fred Street, swathed in what looked to be bandages. His left arm in a splint, a patch over an eye and the rest of his body covered in what turned out to be toilet paper, he had plunged head first into the hotel pool.

Italia '90 finally began on Friday 8 June, a day which started off with the news from England that Swindon Town, who had won promotion in May, were to be relegated instead because of illegal payments.

Far more interesting to the journalists, the manager and players was the opening game of the tournament which set the tone as Cameroon, despite having two players ejected with red cards, created one of the great World Cup upsets, perhaps the biggest since the USA beat England 1-0 forty years earlier, when they saw off Diego Maradona and his Argentina side, reigning champions. It was a clear warning that no team could be taken lightly, confirmed soon after when Costa Rica shocked a seemingly talented Scotland.

Robson had selected his team for their opener on 6 June, two days before that first game of the tournament, and told no one but his close staff. Peter Shilton kept his place in goal; Gary Stevens, Des Walker, Terry Butcher and Stuart Pearce were to line up across the back; the talented Chris Waddle and John Barnes on either wing; the reliable

Bryan Robson and prodigious Paul Gascoigne in the middle of the park with Gary Lineker and Peter Beardsley upfront. Mark Wright, meanwhile, was being kept wrapped in cotton wool for his important role against the Dutch.

The arrangements made by the organising committee had been almost too good for both England and the Republic of Ireland, with both teams turning up at the ground in Cagliari a full two hours before kick-off. The 40-mile stretch of road to the ground had been closed to all but official traffic and both teams and the media entourages swept through as if we were on the F1 track at Imola.

It left everyone feeling a bit twitchy, even more so when the warm evening anticipated dissolved into a storm. Temperatures plummeted, the wind gusted, and lightning flashed across the sullen sky. It was a bit like November in Eastbourne rather than a summer's evening in Italy. So much for the warm weather preparations.

It didn't seem to matter to England in the early stages as Chris Waddle played the ball into the area and Gary Lineker carried on where he left off four years earlier, sweeping the ball home from close range. But it was heavy going against the wind and the anticipated Irish long ball tactics, including their massive throw-ins, which saw Tony Cascarino and John Aldridge charging in at the fearless Peter Shilton, making his record-equalling 119th appearance for his country. Robson was looking forward to his team having the wind at their backs for the second half. Instead the heavens opened, the winds died down and the temperature plunged even further.

It should have been all over when Chris Waddle was upended in the penalty area by Kevin Moran, but West German referee Aron Schmidhuber waved play on, rubbing salt into the wound by indicating that he thought Chris had dived, whereas television later proved that it was a clear penalty. Irish manager Jack Charlton didn't agree, and he also thought that at no point were England in control of the game. He was proved right, as a mistake by Steve McMahon, brought on to shore up the defence seventeen minutes from time, let in Kevin Sheedy for an equaliser. It was a travesty of a goal and a very poor game in bad conditions that left everyone in the English squad, especially McMahon, shattered. Things didn't improve afterwards as everyone waited and waited in the bus for Gazza to provide a urine sample. It was in the early hours of the morning when their coach finally rolled up at the team hotel while we were ruminating, eating and drinking back at our state of the art press centre.

ENGLAND 1-1 REPUBLIC OF IRELAND, 11 JUNE 1990:

The build-up had been cruel – the usual injury worries, pressure from the British media, worries about possible hooliganism, but all paled in comparison with the news that my brother Keith was in hospital after suffering a heart attack. That was bad enough, but the media had besieged my Mum, who hadn't been told of Keith's fight. It was splashed across the front pages and although I should have been used to it, it was an intrusion as we prepared for our opening match, so often a stumbling block for us in major tournaments. I could look after myself, but the family shouldn't have been involved in the way they were.

The trip to the ground from our headquarters was 40 miles away and we judged our timing on previous trips and allowed a little extra for inevitable traffic. Wrong. The police had closed the road to all other traffic and we zipped through so quickly that we were at the ground far too early. Both we and the Irish had been misled and we were both at the ground a good two hours before the kick-off, with little to do other than worry.

The hot, balmy night we had planned and prepared for was also a fallacy as the skies filled in, lightening flashed, the temperatures dropped, the wind picked up to near gale force and the rain fell down in torrents.

Once again it was a war against the Irish and it couldn't have been a great game to watch, as we battled not only the expected Jack Charlton long ball game but also the elements. We struggled against the wind in the first half as the ball kept coming back at us as though it was on a piece of elastic.

The threatened storm swept in at half-time, killing the wind – which would have been to our benefit in the second half – with the rain now lashing down, which certainly wasn't to anyone's benefit.

I was beginning to wonder about my luck in these competitions as the German referee turned down a blatant penalty when Chris Waddle was upended by Kevin Moran, which would have given us the opportunity to go two up after Gary Lineker's eighth minute strike. Instead an error by substitute Steve McMahon let in the Irish for an equaliser 16 minutes from time scored by Kevin Sheedy. I guess it was partly my fault, for had Macca been playing for Liverpool the ball would have finished up in the top tier of the stand, but I had encouraged all the players to get the ball down and play it.

It left the dressing room flat and I could do little about it as I was whisked away to the compulsory press conferences, and by the time we had waited for Paul Gascoigne to provide a urine sample it was the early hours before we got back to our hotel. Gazza taking the piss as usual – but this time no one laughed.

The England coaching staff were far from satisfied with the performance and the subsequent result, but experience told them that poor starts were at least something to build on and while they had begun with just a single point, they were better off than Argentina, Scotland and the Soviet Union, who had all lost to teams they were expected to beat.

The frustrations bubbled over in Robson's press conference in our press centre at the Forte Village. You could tell he was piqued at the tone of the questioning, particularly from the studious *Times* correspondent David Miller, who wanted to know why Bobby hadn't been around the clubs to get some sort of conformity in their style of play so that the move into international football would be so much easier. It was a question that almost made Bobby laugh out loud, as he pondered what would be said to him if he went around telling Brian Clough, Kenny Dalglish, George Graham and the rest how they should play their football and what formations they should use to help England.

It was a barmy question from a guy who played football himself at a reasonable level, was cerebral in the extreme and who clearly knew his way round the game, or at least appeared to before that suggestion.

You could tell Bobby just wanted away as quickly as possible to catch the private flight to the Sicilian capital Palermo for the next game in the group between Egypt and Holland. He told fellow manager Ron Atkinson, who was co-commentating for the game, he thought Egypt might surprise a few and got the expected robust response from Big Ron who, as usual, took no prisoners, England manager or not.

Holland were England's next opponents and expected to be leading the group when they played Robson's side, but Egypt backed up the England manager's opinion and played really well to hold them to a frustrating 1-1 draw, leaving all four teams on the same points with the same goal difference. As you were.

The Dutch had been on Bobby's mind since the draw was made in Rome, and after conceding five goals against them in their previous two clashes he decided long before this one how he was going to tackle the problem of total football and some extremely skilful players. He had even told central defender Mark Wright, out injured for the first game against the Irish, that he would definitely play as sweeper if he was fit. He had to wait to make that decision – both Wright and Paul Parker had to prove their fitness in the lead up to the game.

The Dutch journalists were naturally excited at Bobby Robson's presence and wanted to know what he thought about the PSV players on show when, in truth, they had not even crossed his mind, only in regard to being amongst the opponents in an important game. He was certainly not ready to talk as PSV manager, at least for another couple of weeks.

When Wim Keift opened the scoring for the Dutch against Egypt, Bobby was ready to leave the ground and head back for his hotel, not believing that the Egyptians, despite their skill, would come back, but they did and equalised through a penalty scored by Abdel-Ghani eight minutes from time. Both teams had their chances to win it, but it finished all square. As they flew back to Sardinia at an ungodly hour, Robson confirmed in his own head how he was going to line up against the Dutch. He arrived back at his hotel at 3.20am, and was woken up five hours later by the alarm clock going off at the same time as his first call of the day. It was Elsie. She hadn't read the papers, but she had seen the headlines on breakfast television and warned her husband that he and McMahon had both been slaughtered in print, with the *Sun* hilariously demanding on their front page that they should all be sent home for drawing with the Irish. This was what he and his team were up against.

One thing that concerned Bobby about the Irish game was that his team had appeared somewhat timid, even the redoubtable 'Psycho', Stuart Pearce, who admitted his boss was right – nerves had played their part in the opening fixture of the World Cup. It didn't happen again.

The team relaxed in their quarters, listening to the virtuoso violin playing of football daft Nigel Kennedy and his American girlfriend Brix Smith Start, guitarist and lead singer for The Fall, both of them great fun and great company.

But that was as far as the entertainment went that night as Bobby took a call from the Italian speaking English liaison officer Jane Nottage, who coolly informed Robson that the *Sun* were going to carry a big splash on their front page on the coming Monday that several of the squad had misbehaved and taken to bed one of the glamorous Italia '90 hostesses who had been working at our resort.

Robson went away to check the facts but before he could get started John Jackson, the chief Rotter and vastly experienced news reporter for the *Daily Mirror,* had phoned press officer Glen Kirton and repeated the story, asking for a comment and confirmation. It needed nipping in the bud if it was true and, after dinner, he disappointed the players when he switched off the television, which was about to show the Argentina versus Soviet Union game, and told the players exactly what he had heard, watching faces to see if there was any giveaway. He was greeted with surprise, horror and finally indignation – they clearly did not believe the story at all.

The three players named were Peter Beardsley, John Barnes and Stuart Pearce, which caused some amusement and dark humour. One player was offended that he hadn't been invited to join in if it were true. Barnes was always smooth but polite with the ladies, while Beardsley and Pearce were an odd couple, indeed, to be named as Lotharios.

Pearce went back to his room to call his then wife Liz to tell her of the pending story. He was in a right huff about it as he had not even had a drink while he had been away, and fortunately his partner knew just how seriously he was taking this World Cup, having watched the previous one with him on his couch in the lounge.

Like the other players he was already aware that the news reporters had been sniffing their glasses after they left restaurants and cafes to see if they smelt of alcohol, and he was less than impressed, but this was a whole new ball game. Waitresses were constantly being offered money and Nottage, who was another secretly writing a book, claimed the girl in question had been paid £20,000 to spill the beans on the night of debauchery.

Bobby thought he had time for the FA to slap in an injunction as

Nottage had said that the paper were going to use the story on the Monday, but come Thursday morning it was splashed across the front of the *Daily Mirror* as the old tabloid war caught fire again. The players once again confirmed that the story was untrue and insisted that, in the climate, they didn't want to speak to any of the press, including the football writers, and they were hustled away on their coach before we were eventually let into the ground for the media conference attended by ten times the normal numbers.

There were denials all over the place, including one from the girl who had refused the *Sun* retirement plan and was suffering considerable humiliation amongst her peers and family, but it didn't stop worried wives ringing the players at all hours demanding to know what had been going on. Robson was eventually forced to ask the switchboard to block calls while they had their meeting to discuss the change of formation and to announce that David Seaman was to fly home and be replaced by Dave Beasant, not because of some naughty nightcap, but because he had fractured his thumb in practice.

Robson was not only juggling with the hostess story with one hand but also the flak from the papers about the Irish game with the other. *The Mirror*, whose sex story had been rubbished, tried to get their own back with a leader column hitting out at Robson for supporting his players, telling the world that he was a bad, inadequate manager. It could only have been written by someone who knew not the first thing about football or Bobby's record in management.

One or two of the players naughtily commented that it was their suggestion to play a sweeper against the Dutch and that Robson had taken their advice, but I can confirm personally through my daily diary pieces with him for our book that the decision was made long, long before Chris Waddle and one or two others even thought of it. Stuart Pearce was a little more succinct when he commented that one or two didn't agree with the plan, changing their minds and their comments after the game.

Robson described his team selection to me as the biggest gamble of his career, but for once the portents were good when the coach arrived at the ground moments before the FIFA set deadline of 7.30pm. Walking down the corridor Robson came face to face with the three PSV players in the Dutch squad, Gerald Vanenburg, Erwin Koeman and Hans van Breukelen, who greeted him most politely and told him they were looking forward to working with him. It was the first time he had met any of the players who were to be part of his immediate future.

For a while it looked as though the Dutch manager Leo Beenhakker had won the pre-match tactical battle when he switched his line up to play Hans Gillhaus at outside-left, supported by Richard Witschge at left-half. It was too late for Robson to change his team set up, and it meant the left-sided Butcher playing at right-back for the first time in his long career, with Wright still at sweeper behind Paul Parker and Des Walker. Butcher did the job so well that it wasn't long before John van't Schip went off to be replaced by Wim Kieft and the Dutch formation reverted to the one Robson had anticipated and planned for.

The other Robson, however, was a different story. He had torn the nail off a big toe messing around in Gascoigne's room in the early hours of the morning earlier in the trip and although the pain killing injection worked on his toe, his Achilles tendon trouble flared again during the game. The manager gambled again, sending on David Platt instead of Steve McMahon to keep an eye on Ruud Gullit, who was showing a return to form after a quiet start to the tournament. He did a fine job, helped by Butcher who, using swear words taught him by Ipswich teammates Arnold Muhren and Frank Thijssen, growled and cursed the brilliant Dutchman who, far from being intimidated, couldn't stop laughing, though gradually his form fell away.

ENGLAND 0-0 NETHERLANDS, 16 JUNE 1990:

It had not escaped the media's attention that several of the players in the Dutch squad played for PSV, the club I was joining directly after the World Cup, but that was not what I was there for.

We had been slaughtered again by the English papers, and they even suggested we should all be sent home. That was nothing compared with a story run by the Sun which claimed several of our players had bedded one of the Italia '90 hostesses. I fronted up the players, who were shocked and dismayed, except for one, who asked: 'If there was a gang bang why wasn't I invited?'

The story was rubbish, conjured up by a bar room whisper and turned into a story by a provincial journalist keen to make a few bob for himself and to hell with everyone else, including players, wives and the poor girl herself. As a consequence, the players decided to blank the media completely. I was attacked by one paper for backing my players, but I was more concerned with goalkeeper David Seaman – who fractured his thumb in training – with FIFA allowing us to replace him with standby goalkeeper Dave Beasant.

We didn't make the same mistake on the trip to Cagliari and arrived on the dot for the 7.30 deadline, where I soon learned I had misread the Dutch line-up, which meant I had to switch Terry Butcher to the right side of the defence to play right full-back for the first, and probably the last time, in his career. He was magnificent.

The curse of Bryan Robson fell again when I was told that his tendon trouble had flared up once more and I used David Platt to shadow Ruud Gullit, a role he had never been asked to play before. He was magnificent, too.

We were the better team and deserved to win, but I wasn't overly bothered with the goalless draw and another point, leaving us needing just draw against the Egyptians to be certain of qualifying. The boys deserved their glass of champagne on their return to the hotel.

Bobby had a lot to thank the itinerant Butcher for that evening. The pair had almost fallen out after the defenders' headbutt in the warm-up against Tunisia. Following the incident Robson had substituted him straight away to avoid any further trouble, and the player subsequently threw his shirt to the floor in frustration. He was angered at his own performance, not his manager's decision, but it didn't seem that way to Robson, who took umbrage. Butcher was adamant that there was no slight intended, adding, 'I respected the man so much I would never have dreamt of doing such a thing. Sure, I was cross, but only because I thought I had played myself out of the World Cup team.'

Everyone who knew Butcher loved him but there was no doubt he was a handful at times, and had Robson known the half of it he might well have sent his favourite player home. He was furious about him throwing an England shirt on the floor, for any reason, and emphasised his feelings when he saw his central defender hanging around unshaven later on. Butcher informed his boss that he wasn't getting rid of his new facial hair until England won, to which Robson's response was emphatic: 'Don't be so fucking stupid. Shave it off now.' As he strode away and offered a parting shot: 'What's more, you are fucking ugly, Butcher!'

Butcher's problem was basically boredom. He is an intelligent, restless sort of person and to break the monotony of the camp he and his roommate Chris Woods took a car ride to the local village of Pula, supposedly to buy shaving cream but, in truth, for a change of scenery and a couple of pints. They got so much pleasure out of their little trip that they soon did it again, and it wasn't long before some of their teammates heard about it and joined them, just three days before the Ireland game. Skipper Robson, who always enjoyed a drink, was with them along with Steve Bull, Steve McMahon, Chris Waddle and, inevitably, Paul Gascoigne. It all turned into a bit of a party as the locals welcomed them and the drinks flowed into the early hours of the morning, before they sneaked back into their ground floor rooms thinking they had got away with it.

Robson, though, had discovered they had gone AWOL and was then told about his namesake being injured in his frolicking with Gazza. He was understandably furious and demanded that the culprits report to him in the room next door, telling them they had let down him and their country. They trouped in one after another until Butcher walked in to a withering look from his former club manager.

'I thought it would be you, Butcher, I knew it!' he shouted. 'You were the first person on my list. You are a disgrace. You are always like this. I warned you back in 1982 about your safety valve and you continue to do it. You are a joke.' It didn't help that Gazza, out of the manager's line of sight, was pulling faces at Butcher who, in the end, couldn't stop a snigger, which raised the temperature with the manager another notch.

'What are you laughing at, Butcher?' he demanded. 'It's no laughing matter. You have let down your country. The captain of our team is in bed now and maybe out of the World Cup, thanks to you. Why is it always you, Butcher? Every time it is you! And another thing, Butcher, you are fucking ugly!' At this point both Waddle and Gascoigne curled up with laughter, unable to restrain themselves anymore and were promptly dismissed.

Luckily, this story did not surface. Butcher was confined to quarters for the rest of the World Cup, but it didn't put a halt to his antics. Before dinner one evening he somehow convinced his table mates, Chris Woods, Chris Waddle and Gary Stevens, to put their clothes on back to front and then persuaded the waiters to serve their meal from back to front, starting with coffee, followed by ice cream, the main course and the starter of soup. Robson and Howe looked on with open mouths and bewilderment while the rest of the team stood and applauded as the quartet exited the room at the conclusion of their meal, walking backwards.

It was such a success in Butcher's eyes that he took it all a stage further the night before the Egypt game when he, Waddle and Stevens (Woods declined the invitation) dressed in their England blazers, white shirt and official tie, gelled their hair into spikes and donned sunglasses, arriving early at the dining hall and seating themselves at a table with a long, overhanging table cloth which covered their legs. Ties askew and water filled wine bottles in ice buckets, the trio swigged the 'wine' and became more and more raucous as the private dining room filled up, shouting greetings to their mates and back room boys as they arrived.

Bobby was perplexed and wanted to know what Butcher was up to this time, asking Don Howe if it was wine they were drinking. The party – and the joke – was almost spoiled when the entire International Committee walked into the dining room to look on in amazement at three 'drunken' players, shouting and laughing. It was too late to back out and they ploughed on through the rest of their evening meal. When they finished they stood and toasted the players and Bobby Robson, before making a stately exit, displaying their trouser-less legs, stopping at the top of the flight of stairs, lifting their shirts and showing their backsides to the assembled audience, leaving Robson shaking his head in despair while the team rose to their feet again to applaud the bare cheek of their colleagues. That was Butcher.

The popular David Seaman went home on Monday along with Doctor Crane, who returned for a family funeral. Seaman would have liked to have stayed but it was thought it would not have been right for him to be around fit players and his replacement, Dave Beasant. One of my colleagues, the veteran Mike Langley from the *Sunday People*, deepened Seaman's depression when he telephoned to ask the goalkeeper if it was true that he had fractured his thumb separating two fighting teammates. That would have scooped all of us, except it didn't happen. There were lots of people around who witnessed David damage himself in a training incident with Paul Parker.

We were far more interested in the physical shape of England's two top players before the pivotal Egypt game, with Bryan Robson and Gary Lineker the big doubts. Robson had his ongoing Achilles difficulties, while Lineker's big toe was causing concern. The Doc had drilled the nail twice to drain the blood and, subsequently, Gary had not been training. Not that it bothered him – Gary was never that taken with pre-match preparations.

There was something of a communication problem between Robson and the players, with Peter Beardsley complaining that he had learned he had been dropped through the media, while his skipper suddenly informed his manager that he had telephoned faith-healer Olga Stringfellow and asked her to come over to see him and help if she could. Robson was clearly struggling to play, and it looked as though he was going to be wiped out of his second successive World Cup.

Robson was torn between giving his namesake a good old-fashioned bollocking for going behind his back and not even consulting the medical staff. On the other hand, he felt desperately sorry for his captain once more. They both needed each other, and he was prepared to allow what would normally have been seen as a serious indiscretion pass.

The skipper had kept his secret but Robson was forced to tell physio Fred Street, and eventually in such a closed environment it leaked out, although not immediately, as the manager and the press were more concerned about the ever-lengthening injury list, which also included Steve Hodge, who had hamstring trouble. When McMahon woke up with a stiff neck, there were three midfield players on the sick list. Robson also told them that he was abandoning the sweeper for the

Egypt game, to muted grumbles from some of the players.

After Beardsley's moans about not being told Robson made sure he informed Butcher he was leaving him out, explaining the reasons why, and although the big centre-half was naturally upset, he lifted his manager by telling him he was fortunate to have the caps he had. Bobby asked him how many and was told 74. To soften the blow, he assured Butcher that he would reach 75.

By now Olga had arrived and clearly it was going to be impossible to keep her presence secret. Bobby felt it prudent to tell Bert Millichip, but it wasn't long before he took a phone call from Graham Kelly. 'Guess what's on the front page of the *Sun*?' said the chief executive to the manager. They not only knew about it before Bobby did but had a journalist on the plane flying out with her.

Clearly Bryan was not going to play in this one and Bobby had concerns over John Barnes as well, who had been subject of a huge spread in the *Daily Mirror*, full of information culled from a Channel 4 documentary which had never seen the light of day. They traced his Jamaican background, his diplomat father and everything else they could about this intelligent young man. The 'investigative' report also contained a variety of interviews with people Barnes knew, hardly ideal ahead of such a defining match for the player. Once again, the timing was deliberate and far from helpful.

The manager, after a great deal of thought, decided to risk Lineker and his bad toe. After all, if they lost they would be on their way back home, which would give Lineker plenty of time to rest before the new season. He had yet another injection and more blood was drained.

There was an unusual occurrence at lunchtime on the day of the Egypt game – the written press' senior football writers gave a lunch to thank the manager for his help, cooperation and friendliness over his eight years. We had had a whip round and purchased an antique map of the island, which was presented to him at one of the many restaurants in the Forte Village. There were one or two among the gathering that he would rather have not been there, but he was as gracious as ever and seemed to enjoy the company and the craic. 'There were some there I liked, some I admired and some I respected, as well as a close friend, but there were one or two there who I wouldn't have accepted an individual invitation to lunch,' he later said.

It had been left to me to make the invitation, and once I asked he hesitated for only a brief moment before accepting. I would have been disappointed if he had refused as these were not the Rotters but the bread and butter football writers who had trailed the world from Australia to America and all points in between in his company for eight years. It was, ironically, the longest day of the year according to the calendar, 21 June, but it didn't feel that way to the manager as he made the short journey back to the team hotel, not regretting his decision to attend.

England won that evening with a single goal from Mark Wright, while the Netherlands and the Republic of Ireland again shared the spoils, with the two countries having to draw lots at the Hilton Hotel in Rome to decide who would finish second and who would finish third in the group. It was a remarkable way to settle such an important conclusion. It was Jack Charlton and his team who lucked out in the end, and so they slotted in behind leaders England and would face Romania at the next stage. The Netherlands still progressed as one of the four strongest third-place teams, but a draw they had no control over meant they ended up the team with the daunting task of facing West Germany. Group leaders England were unbeaten and scheduled to play Belgium.

The Egyptians had arrived for the game with England in Cagliari late and in something of a flap, and they were subsequently fined by FIFA for their indiscretion, but when it came to the match itself they were disciplined, keeping it as tight as they had done in their previous two matches. It wasn't until Mark Wright scored early in the second half with a header from a Gascoigne free-kick that they came out of their shell, but it was too little too late and when the final whistle blew there were tears all over the pitch. They couldn't believe they were out of the World Cup – they had fully expected another draw and to qualify. Thank goodness there was no Mohamed Salah around at that time.

ENGLAND 1-0 EGYPT, 21 JUNE 1990:

The build-up was chaotic: faith healer Olga Stringfellow, invited over without me being asked by my skipper Bryan Robson; three midfield players out injured; axing Terry Butcher for the first time in my life; Gazza messing about on boats and me flying at Mach 1 in a £27 million NATO aircraft. Flying at 800 miles an hour was one of the thrills of my life. It took a lot of arranging and I felt privileged. It also briefly took me away from my football problems.

According to my diary it was the longest day of the year and that was how it turned out, starting with the usual television interviews and checking on the fitness of both the inevitable Robson and Gary Lineker, whose damaged big toe looked ugly and needed yet more injections if he was going to play.

The Egyptians were well organised, played as we expected and didn't threaten us at all until after Mark Wright had put us in front early in the second half. They didn't have enough and were distraught when they went out, having believed they were going to beat us and qualify. Some of them were in tears and another went into hysterics and even needed medical assistance.

We were through but still not hitting our straps, notably John Barnes and Chris Waddle, while Lineker struggled with his poorly toe and Steve Bull was hardly in the game through no fault of his own. I finally hit the bed at 3am. It had certainly been the longest day.

Despite England's problems, they had still comfortably held out against the Egyptians after taking the lead, and headed back to their hotel to celebrate with dinner and a glass of champagne.

Meanwhile, the global press had quickly come to realise that there was a story a day as far as England were concerned and reporters from around the world gathered in ever greater numbers at the team's camp, waiting for the next revelation.

Naturally news and football writers alike were drawn into the Bryan Robson saga, and there were daily questions about him and Olga Stringfellow. Put simply the presence of a faith-healer wasn't working, and the evidence was there for all to see. In the absence of the England skipper from the training field there were sudden plans put in place to fly him back to the UK to see his own orthopaedic surgeon. Unfortunately, they could not smuggle him on the 3.30pm to Manchester on Saturday in time and so a flight was booked under an assumed name for the Sunday.

They need not have bothered as the plans quickly became known to the media, but it was decided that Bryan was a big boy and could look after it. A more important story was the consequence of a fatal crash, which sadly saw a young English supporter killed. To their credit John Barnes, Terry Butcher, Des Walker, Trevor Steven and Gary Stevens took the time and trouble to visit the injured boys who had survived the crash in hospital. They did it off their own bat, no publicity stunt, just decent blokes doing what they could. Meanwhile, Graham Kelly had invited the bereaved mother to the hotel for dinner. Bobby Robson had a quiet word of sympathy with her, as did Peter Beardsley, John Barnes and Steve McMahon, players who had all been so courageous in helping grieving families following the Hillsborough disaster.

Robson and England's media manager Glen Kirton had accompanied the skipper to the gate for his flight to Manchester via Milan, taking him through a back door to a private lounge with not a notebook, tape recorder or mic in sight. After smugly waving him off they made their way back through the public area to pick up their car, only to bump into Alex Montgomery from the *Sun*, Harry Harris from the *Mirror*, Bob Driscoll from the *Star* and Rob Shepherd from *Today*. This time it wasn't a question of another leak – the journalists were simply on their way to watch Holland play West Germany and were booked on the same flight. It was a surprise for Bryan, but one which he would have taken in his stride.

It was supposed to be a media-free day for the manager, with the squad due at the airport for their flight to Bologna ahead of the game against Belgium, but the local press chief, seizing his opportunity, set up a press conference for the rest of the media contingent, including head Rotter John Jackson of the *Daily Mirror*. Jackson was an ace reporter, and this was chicken feed to him after the various forms of tragedy and drama he had covered and uncovered in his career. He asked the first question: 'Is this the end of the two Robsons?'

Robson for his part had seen it all before and handled the question well. Bryan might not have been able to take any further part in Italia '90, but Bobby was far from throwing in the towel, as he plotted with his spies Dave Sexton and John Lyall on how to handle the young men from Belgium.

One of Bobby's most likeable assets was his approachability. He was never aloof, was always polite to strangers who treated him as if they knew him and, remarkably, he took phone calls to his rooms in hotels in Italy without ever asking the switchboard or the management to check them first. Naturally his family were frequent callers, but so too was an old age pensioner from Newcastle, who just wanted to wish him good luck and then didn't stop in case it changed England's luck whilst on a winning run. His only concern was how much it was costing her to call abroad.

Most callers were genuine well-wishers, with the sort of trolls that appear from the woodwork so frequently on social media these days few and far between. On the rare occasion any of them did make the effort, they would quickly get back what they were trying to give. There were strange calls, too, like the Aussie who phoned him at his hotel in Bologna on the day of the Belgium game, telling him he had a friend who worked for Belgian television who had told him that goalkeeper Michel Preud'homme was weak at the near post, on corners and for crosses. He thought Bobby should know as he wanted England to win.

Ironically the Belgian goalkeeper was magnificent that evening: solid at his near post, safe in handling set pieces, and brilliant in every other aspect. It made Bobby chuckle when he thought about it after the game, just as it did when the physio, Norman Medhurst, not fully hiding his embarrassment, asked his manager if he would mind giving his local reporter from a Devon newspaper a 'scoop' of a one–on–one interview. The journalist's very first question was, 'Can I have the team?' The answer was a firm no, of course, but the ever-obliging Bobby gave him the interview anyway. It was a measure of the man, even if it took too long for most people to realise that.

Robson changed his tactics again for Belgium, restoring Wright to his sweeper role, with Walker designated to be on the pacy Marc De Grijse and Terry Butcher on the more physical Jan Ceulemans. Steve McMahon had the important job of tracking their most skilful player Enzo Scifo, while Gazza had to keep an eye on Franky Van der Elst when the Belgians were attacking.

It was all stacking up nicely. With the players in bed away from the blazing hot sun, the team picked, the tactics sorted, what on earth could go wrong now? There was even time for the manager to have a dip in the hotel pool as he joined our mutual American friend, sports doctor Mike Shapow, and coach Mike Kelly. In a mad moment it almost seemed like a holiday until, hauling himself out of the water,

Robson slipped and fell on the edge of the pool and cracked a rib. A bruised rib is a pain like few others: it affects your sleep, your walking and even your eating. There was absolutely nothing Mike Shapow could do to help, despite his expertise in the field. Apart from Shapow and Kelly, no one was to know. It didn't do any good for people to know about the managers' problems when so many of the players, the skipper included, were already suffering.

I can only imagine how sore he was as he watched an excellent game unfold. The 40-year-old Peter Shilton, who had told Robson earlier in the week that he was going to retire from international football after the World Cup, was again in immaculate form, as was his counterpart. The Belgians hit the woodwork twice and John Barnes, declared fit on the lunchtime of the game, had what looked to be a good goal chalked off for offside in the days when VAR was a distant, improbable dream.

The game ebbed and flowed in remarkable fashion, a joy for the neutral but agony for those who nailed their flags to the masts of either team. McMahon was tiring having chased Scifo for more than an hour so Robson replaced significantly him with David Platt and, three minutes later, he sent on Steve Bull for John Barnes after the Liverpool winger indicated he was having problems with his groin. Gary Lineker was also suffering as the painkilling injection wore off, while Walker's injuries were catching up on him. Sensing this, the Belgians injected the pace of former Spurs striker Nico Claesen into their front line.

With all the niggles and worries the last thing England wanted or needed was extra time, but in the interval, Robson assured his players that the opponents were hurting every bit as much as they were and that he expected more from his substitutes Platt and Bull, who had been on the pitch for less than twenty minutes. There were those who claimed England were playing for the draw as extra time wore on, as players like Waddle and Gascoigne, who had both been exceptional, had started to walk rather than run with the ball.

The clock was ticking down when Belgian full-back Eric Gerets brought down Paul Gascoigne, a tired foul on a tired opponent. It looked as though Gazza was going to knock the ball off for England to keep possession and continue running down the clock, but Robson and the England bench were up en masse screaming for him to knock it into the penalty area, where Terry Butcher and Mark Wright had joined David Platt and Steve Bull. Gazza curled in a superb cross, and the only player to read its trajectory was Platt, who let the ball drift over his shoulder before hooking home a superb first-time volley. It was so good and so late that the England manager danced a jig, likely causing his ribs a great deal of pain. Not that he cared.

What he did care about was the thought of conceding in the dying seconds after battling so heroically for a late victory, and he was now roaring to Butcher to get his defence together and organised. He need not have worried. There was barely time to restart, and the final whistle heralded a second quarter-final appearance in successive World Cups for England and Robson, where this time their opponents would be tournament outsiders Cameroon. Bobby wanted to hug his players – particularly Platt – but there is etiquette in football and the first person he looked for was the thoroughly decent Belgian manager Guy Thys, who was even quicker than Bobby to offer his hand in friendship and congratulations. Both knew there was little or nothing between the two teams and either could have won, with the Belgians probably favourites had the game gone on for a minute longer and ended in penalties.

ENGLAND 1-0 BELGIUM (AET), 26 JUNE 1990:

The chaos continued with the players still at war with most of the media, the ongoing problems with Robson's Achilles tendon and other injury concerns, plus a quiet word from our legendary goalkeeper Peter Shilton telling me he was going to quit international football once England were out of the tournament. It wasn't going to be my problem and I asked him to keep it quiet until we were finished one way or another.

Relaxation came via Arsenal wheeler dealer David Dein and his sleek boat, with a late lunch and water sports which included water skiing, ski-biking and being hauled along at speed while sitting in a giant inflatable inner tube.

Gazza continued being the bane of my life, playing tennis and expending too much energy in the hot sun. I persuaded the hyperactive boy to have a good swim instead. On the eve of the game I had a long chat with my wife Elsie on my hotel room phone. It was our 35th wedding anniversary.

The match was so good I almost managed to forget about my own problems, until David Platt came on as a substitute and scored with a great volley in extra time. I jumped up, did a celebratory jog and paid the penalty… but that was infinitely less painful than the anxiety of a penalty shootout.

Following the victory Robson informed his players they could enjoy a beer before their early morning flight to Naples, where they would be travelling for their quarter-final encounter. When they returned to the hotel Butcher and co duly ordered a trolley of beer and wine, but no spirits. That was 'professional' in the eyes of Butcher, though he admitted that the second trolley they ordered was not. It was a tired and bleary-eyed lot who left for their plane the next day.

Sleep was almost impossible for Robson that night, but he only needed one look at the haggard faces of his players the next morning to realise what they had been up to themselves, and that they were in a far worse way than him. Robson and Howe were no fans of the drinking culture that was prevalent in English football and in his squad, but he had more important things to worry about. Cameroon awaited in Naples.

14

'Why don't we spread the games better to get a higher quality tournament, give the players time to recover from their injuries and give the public more exciting matches?'

West Germany manager Franz Beckenbauer, saying what every remaining manager was thinking at the quarter-final stage of Italia '90.

WITH THE QUARTER-FINAL SCHEDULED FOR SUNDAY

1 July, just five days after the gruelling encounter with Belgium, there was precious little time to assess the injuries. Robson barely had four hours of restless sleep before his bedside telephone started ringing early on Wednesday morning. He was in full agreement with Franz Beckenbauer's sentiments about the need for longer gaps between games, though nothing could be changed at this stage. Everything was done in a hurry, with FIFA demanding to know the requirements for Naples: hotel, stadium, training ground, timings and all the things that had to be sorted out in double quick time.

The phone didn't stop ringing, with a supporter calling from South

Africa to wish him well, while scouts Mick Wadsworth and Dave Sexton both reported to him with their findings. That was followed by an interview with BBC Radio, where a reporter in London asked him whether he would reconsider leaving the job and asked whether the FA had pleaded with him to stay, and if they did would he do so. The answer to both questions was a firm no.

The situation with the media was still bubbling unpleasantly, and I suggested to Bobby that as he got on well with the majority of the British press contingent, perhaps he should meet them on his own without the distraction of the foreign press. It gave both sides the opportunity to air their dirty linen in private without giving the world's media another stick to beat us with.

The manager tried to smooth the path, but the players were far more unforgiving. There had been an earlier incident when they had refused to speak to any of the press when boarding their bus following a training session, and had dragged the hapless Paul Parker back onto the bus when he tried to have a conversation with the *London Evening Standard* football writer Michael Hart, a journalist who had not been involved in any of the earlier skirmishes.

A polystyrene cup of water was thrown over one or two of the journalists standing by the coach, and they immediately claimed the high ground while the rest of their colleagues could scarcely conceal their giggles behind their hands. A splash of water? Had they never stood on the Spurs car park in the pouring rain after a game in the hope of talking to Jimmy Greaves?

It did not help that the *Mirror* and the *Star* described the players as yobs after the affair and, as if feeling left out, the BBC and ITV teams were handbags drawn after Jim Rosenthal mistakenly thought it was Gazza's birthday through a misprint in the FA brochure. The commentator presented him with a big, gooey chocolate cake. It didn't need a genius to forecast where it would finish up, especially with the unpredictable Gazza involved, and sure enough it was soon all over his face. Rob Bonnet's BBC crew saw what was happening and tried to muscle in, resulting with some unseemly pushing and jostling between the two crews.

No one enjoyed the unusual sight more than Bobby Robson, who wasn't slow in asking who the media were calling hooligans and yobs now.

A special charter flight whisked the England squad off to Naples and then into the hills above the bay, where they were ensconced in their superb hotel, which seemingly hung off the cliff itself. The players refused to entertain the idea of talking to a subcommittee of journalists and instead decided that they would talk to the reporters they trusted and not to the ones who had let them down.

There were also the arrangements to make to bring the wives and girlfriends out to Italy, which had to be set up before the game against Cameroon. The Africans had the luxury of eight days' preparation compared to England's five, which also included a travelling day. Robson put his foot down and insisted there would be no tennis, no golf, no sightseeing to Vesuvius or visit to see the erotic drawings in Pompeii, no shopping trips and definitely no sunbathing.

It was a question of counting heads when training resumed, with Des Walker, Gary Lineker, John Barnes and Steve Hodge all absent and Bryan Robson back home. Remarkably, Terry Butcher declared himself fit after his injury and was ready to go. The management kept it light and frothy as the fission began to evaporate, and the players spoke to their mates among the press which was, I thought, fair enough.

I also light-heartedly accused Bobby of selling his soul when he agreed with Andrew Croker, son of former FA secretary Ted, to do a television advert for Hamlet cigars for an eye-opening amount of cash. To be fair, Bobby did enjoy the very occasional cigar just as he enjoyed a very occasional drink and he could never, ever, be accused of chasing a payout.

The negative vibes from some of the media had fallen on deaf ears back home. It is funny, but when you are away with the team you don't really know what the reaction is. Bobby found out about the growing fervour in the football cities of England when he telephoned his wounded warrior Bryan Robson at breakfast time, who remarked that the whole country seemed to be singing and waving the red and white cross of St George.

Bryan himself had been away for three World Cups and had never been fully aware of the response of the ordinary punter back home, but he would be spending the remainder of this tournament on British shores. He had now undergone his operation, and the surgeons had discovered something which would not have cleared up without surgery. In short, there would have been no chance of him playing had he stayed in Italy.

The only remaining doubt was over John Barnes, and the word among the press was that he was facing the axe. It was simple: Barnes needed to prove himself fit and ready. Fred Street put him through the fiercest of tests – sprinting, twisting, turning, shooting, and crossing. He did everything that was asked of him, and once he had done so there was never any doubt in the mind of the man picking the team. He would start.

He would need to be fit to face the Cameroonians – the reports coming through from the scouts and the footage available showed they were a physical outfit unafraid of mixing it. They had been filmed and every free-kick they had taken and defended had been monitored. They were, without doubt, a very good team who deserved to be where they were, but confidence was high, with Wilkinson telling the manager he thought they had drawn as good as a bye into the semi-finals. All they had to do was replicate their form against the Belgians to be guaranteed a place in the last four.

Wilkinson knows more about football than most people I know, but he had this one wrong, putting too much emphasis on their four-goal beating by the Soviets in a group game when they had already qualified for the next stage. The reports did single out the talents of the semi-retired 38-year-old striker Roger Milla, who had been arriving into games as a substitute after an hour or so, lifting the team to ever greater heights in the closing stages. England were keeping their goalscoring hero David Platt in for the unlucky Steve McMahon in an otherwise unchanged team, chasing a semi-final spot at a major tournament abroad for the first time in their long and not so illustrious international history.

Before the team left they were able to watch West Germany squeeze past Czechoslovakia in their quarter-final thanks to a Lothar Matthäus penalty after 24 minutes, thereby confirming their opponent at the next stage if they did their job against Cameroon.

Any chances of a late Czech assault were halted when Lubomir Moravcik was sent off by experienced Austrian referee Helmut Kohl, and throughout the match the official seemed to take a harder line with the Eastern Europeans, showing them five yellow cards to Germany's one, which was shown to the scarcely belligerent Jürgen Klinsmann.

It was clear from their solid performance in front of 73,347 fans in the San Siro Stadium in Milan that Beckenbauer's side were going to be no pushover, especially if referees were favouring them.

Back home everyone was fully behind Robson's men, but in Italy – and certainly in Scotland – they were all on the side of the under-dog, who responded in some style. Cameroon thrilled their multitude of fans around the globe in two hours of excitement which dripped with tension and uncertainty. England were cast as the villains, with Robson describing his side as the most disliked team in the world on that day, 1 July 1990.

Cameroon were giants that evening, and even Terry Butcher found himself looking up to some of his rivals in the tunnel. It didn't bother him in the slightest, and he continued with his routine of trying to intimidate his adversaries prior to kick-off with a wide-eyed stare and a battle cry, but it had little effect. The Cameroon players came bouncing into the tunnel, chanting in unison. They were ready for battle as well.

Bobby must have caught the tremor that rippled through the team, for he turned to his players and said: 'Don't worry lads. They might be able to sing, but they can't play.' One of their players overheard and promptly passed the word down the line. Stares suddenly became barbed and threatening. 'We had been out-Butchered,' said Butcher afterwards. 'Suddenly we didn't have a quarter-final on our hands, we had a war.'

England were up for it as well though, and they went in front through David Platt, who swooped in on a Stuart Pearce cross to the far post. Everyone thought that was it. Cameroon would surely crumble, and England would march on. It didn't happen that way at all.

Cameroon came back strongly and were pounding England, and for a while only Peter Shilton stood between them and a fairytale. They were the better side right up until the break and Robson told his team exactly that in an uncharacteristically raging half-time address. Worse was to come as John Barnes held up his hand in the locker room to tell the boss that the groin strain had returned, and he couldn't carry on.

It might have all been so different had Mexican referee Edgardo Codesal Méndez given a penalty when goalkeeper Thomas N'Kono whipped away the legs of goalscorer Platt early in the second half, but he waved play on and Cameroon swept jubilantly upfield to claim a penalty of their own, when Gascoigne waved a leg at Milla and the shrewd old campaigner threw himself over it. Emmanuel Kundé converted from the spot.

Gazza had been awful in the first half and this was a shattering blow, sucked in against an experienced and very clever centre-forward. It deflated England and encouraged the Cameroonians, who had taken off their smallest player, Louis-Paul M'fede, and brought on another colossus in Eugène Ekéké. Just three minutes after the penalty, the substitute took a superb pass from Milla and beat Shilton to put the underdogs in front.

At that point Robson could see the game slipping away. England were busy trying to sort themselves out, while Cameroon's confidence continued to grow. It could have been a lot worse when François Omam-Biyik should have added a third. Robson told me that as he watched the match slipping away his thoughts strangely turned to the flight they had organised to bring the families out, not just the players' wives and girlfriends but Bobby's dad Philip, his wife Elsie and his boys. He didn't want to let all these people down, but he wasn't the one on the park.

The first signs of a spark of life came when Gazza, who had suffered a poor hour, began to get on the ball in the right areas and the pendulum slowly began to swing. To help it swing further, Robson pulled off his lucky charm Butcher and sent on the neat and compact Trevor Steven, someone who rarely gave the ball away and was never flustered no matter the pressure.

It was a brave decision by the manager, particularly in view of the physical stature of the rivals. It soon looked to have backfired: just five minutes later, Mark Wright suffered a gash above his eye and Fred Street was quick to tell the bench he didn't think the defender would be able to play on. Big problem. Both substitutes had been used and by the time Wright walked round the pitch the eye had closed, and he looked in no shape to play any more part. To compound the problem Des Walker was limping again, and so the diminutive Paul Parker had to revert to centre-half against opponents far bigger in stature.

Despite all of that, Gazza soon missed an opportunity to equalise. He then made up for it with a world class pass to put Platt through, only to see his midfield partner's shot to graze the wrong side of the post. Meanwhile, Wright had insisted he would go back on once he was strapped up. It would not have been allowed nowadays with the protocols for head injuries, but Robson hurried him back on with one eye covered and a bandage round his head.

It was a timely and brave gesture and suddenly English fists were clenched and, even above the frenzied 55,000 crowd, you could almost hear the English players shouting encouragement at each other and demanding one last gigantic effort. Time was running out fast when an inch perfect through ball from Gazza found the ideal recipient: Gary Lineker. Before he could pull the trigger he was hacked down, and England had their first international penalty in competitive football for five years. That is how long it had taken for a referee to decide in their favour, and it came as they stood eight minutes from going out of the World Cup to a team of rank outsiders. Up stepped Lineker – bad toe or not, he was not going to miss this one.

The lift of the spirits was huge, even though it should have been a shattering experience for these eleven tired men to drag themselves through another period of extra time. How much had that equaliser taken out of the Cameroon players who thought they were standing on the very edge of a semi-final? When play resumed it looked as though it was they who were fighting for breath. Every one of the English players worked their socks off with the quiet, inoffensive Trevor Steven showing he had the intelligence and nous to play in almost any position.

Just like London buses, you wait all that time for one penalty and then two come along together. It was the third of the match and the most critical, as punch bag Lineker was again upended by the goalkeeper. Penalty again? No doubt. Lineker was as cool as you could be in such circumstances, drilling the ball straight as N'Kono dived in the direction the first penalty had gone. 3-2. Was it enough? If anyone was going to score another it was England, and they almost had that fourth when Steven sped forward and fired in a cross which should have been converted. Thankfully three proved to be enough, and for the first time in a World Cup outside of their own country, England had qualified for the last four.

ENGLAND 3-2 CAMEROON (AET), 1 JULY 1990:

We were strict with the players. Cameroon were blessed with eight days preparation the way the fixtures dropped, and England only five. The orders were to stick to the hotel and the shade. Rest and recoverery were the two words I tried to impress on the players.

It was so hot it was too much to sunbathe, never mind train, but the players were talking to the journalists again, at least the ones they wanted to talk to according to the agreement that was reached. I even made a few pounds by agreeing to do an advert for Hamlet cigars at the request of Andrew Croker, the son of former FA Secretary Ted.

We were besieged by pressmen from the world over on the day before the game and still the phone calls rolled in, with the inevitable Mrs Porter still spending her pension on long distance calls and, incredibly, a call from the coach of Albania who told me how much he loved our team and the way we played and hoped that we were going to win the tournament outright. Cameroon first.

On the morning of the game we impressed on the team how physically tough and strong the men from Africa were, with a special mention to beware the 38-year-old Roger Milla, but everyone was confident of winning a place in the last four, especially after reports from our scouts, who wrongly wrote our opponents off.

It turned out to be nail-biting and heart-rending as it ebbed and flowed with everyone, except the massed ranks of the English fans, firmly on the side of the underdogs. For two hours, we were the most disliked team in the world as we found ourselves playing a team of inspired giants. Frankly they were the better side in the first half despite us going a goal ahead through David Platt. I was furious at half-time and let the players know what I thought of their performance in the first 45 minutes.

In finality, the game turned on two penalty decisions that could have put us back on a plane home. Platt was brought down by goalkeeper N'Kono but referee Codesal Mendez of Mexico waved play on. Seconds later Gazza hung out a leg, half time substitute Milla spotted the chance and over he went. Kunde scored past Shilton from the spot and suddenly it was all tied up at 1-1. There was worse to come as Ekeke, another sub, put them ahead three minutes later.

I was furious for I warned them all about Milla, but Gazza had walked straight into the trap. What is more they were still the better side, and my thoughts slipped away to all the people and family who were getting ready to fly over for a semi-final we might not make.

Maybe the penalty woke him up but suddenly Gazza, who had seen the game pass him by, got us going. It still looked unlikely when Mark Wright was helped off with a badly gashed eyebrow. We had used all our subs and the medical men were telling me there was no chance of Wright going back on.

It would have meant playing out the game with ten men, plus having Des Walker limping badly. But Wright insisted on being bandaged up and going back on, and you could see the spirits lift amongst the rest of the team as they were back up to a full compliment.

We still needed some help and it came when Lineker was upended as he ran onto a Gazza through ball. This time the referee had no alternative but to point to the penalty spot. Sure enough, Gary slid the penalty home and we were back in the game. Extra time came and it was now down to fitness and character. As we turned around for extra time I asked my *players if they wanted to play in a World Cup semi-final because, if they did, this was their chance.*

They took it and, once again, it was my talisman Gary Lineker who put us through. All this time as England manager waiting for a penalty and two came along together. Again it was the darting Lineker, who always came alive in the box, who was chopped down and again he got himself to his feet, shook himself down and scored once more and England were in the last four and due to play West Germany in just three days' time. It was around three in the morning when we finally got to bed.

Bobby was as proud as punch and told his players it was their character and spirit which had carried them through and that their bottle was better than their opponents. There were no crazy celebrations, they were simply too tired, too whacked, to dance around. It was Chris Waddle who lightened the atmosphere when he looked up at his manager and said: 'Some fucking bye that was! Don't get us another bye like that one, boss.'

Robson was soon storming into the television studios to pull Gazza and Wright away in the middle of their interviews, with the boss especially angry at Wright, who needed immediate medical attention to his damaged dome if he was going to be able to play against the Germans in just three days' time.

Gradually the realisation of what they had achieved began to sink in, and Robson quietly shed a few tears when we met up just outside the tent after the interviews with the world press were completed. There would have been more had he been aware of the hysteria back home where, we soon learned, the population had gone wild, in the nicest possible way.

The team arrived back at their Positano hotel in the early hours of the morning, and discovered for a second time in the competition that in their absence several of their rooms had been ransacked. Shirts, jewellery and money had been lost. A couple of beers was all the boys could manage before dragging their exhausted bodies to bed.

Robson got his own back on Howard Wilkinson with his first phone call of the next day, telling him to watch out for angry England players attacking him when the season resumed. He was suitably bemused until Bobby explained that they were far from impressed with his idea of a bye. He hadn't realised that the manager had passed on his message to the players.

There was also an apology from Jim Rosenthal over the Mark Wright business and the usual round of interviews with the various factions of the media before he made his way down to the pool, which was positioned between the hotel and the seashore. It was there he found his captain Terry Butcher reading a book. Bobby put his towel down in the warm sunshine and asked Terry what he thought of the shape of the team and other tactical matters. Butcher launched off on a diatribe he had obviously been storing up during the tournament and only hesitated when he heard a light snore. Robson had dropped off and Butcher didn't know whether it was because he was so boring or because his boss had suffered another late night. Revenge was in the air and he walked to the far end of the pool, turned, ran and bombed into the water, sending a spray over his surprised and suddenly fully awake manager who was too slow to spot the culprit, now swimming serenely away.

Robson was at least grateful to one of his other senior players, the goal happy Lineker, who was helping his boss share the post-match media demands following the exhilarating but energy-sapping victory. I have no doubt that Gary Lineker's assent into becoming a success-ful broadcaster began with his many interviews on international duty, usually after another goal or two.

The spirit in the camp was boosted even further with the news that the flight bringing the families to Italy had been confirmed, and they would all be joining the team in Turin. They were also learning further news of how the nation had gone absolutely barmy over their comeback victory, with flags waving, cars honking their horns and drivers and passengers behaving more like South American fans in the aftermath of success rather than the usually reserved English. They almost all admitted England had enjoyed their fair share of luck, but hadn't it been due? Especially those penalties.

Bobby was never a vindictive man, but he took enormous pleasure from seeing the small clutch of journalists who had disrespected him all along finally having their bad judgement rubbed in their faces. He was particularly overjoyed at one writer, who had described the team as a disgrace to the world game, looking very foolish and having to change his opinions in tune with his excited readers. In my pleasure at the result, alongside the mountain of work for my newspaper and for the book we were writing, I never did discover who this person was. A black mark for poor research by me, but it was perhaps a good thing in the long run.

The adrenalin was bubbling and suddenly it appeared that England were the centre of the sporting universe. Only four of the 24 teams remained: England, West Germany, Argentina and the hosts Italy, and so all media converged on them. When it came to the neutrals in the media, England were the most popular, simply because more stories had emerged from their camp than from the three other competing nations put together.

It was a good thing they didn't discover the many pranks Paul Gascoigne, Terry Butcher and others had perpetrated behind the back of their manager, who remained blissfully ignorant of how some of his squad were passing the time – or so he claimed.

There was nothing wrong with the spirit, the character or the commitment of those remaining in the camp, with the regular players being fully backed up by those on the fringes. Though they were rarely getting a look in on match days, they gave everything in training and were unflinching in their support for their teammates.

The feeling of success was growing as Bobby met up with his spies, Dave Sexton and Mick Wadsworth, who joined with Don Howe and Mike Kelly to plot a way to the final. The general feeling among everyone, including the players, was that the game against the Germans was as good as the final. Argentina, even with Maradona, were not the team they were four years earlier and their surprise victory over Italy in the semi-final took a huge amount out of them, with injuries and suspensions finally taking their toll. Put simply, they looked to be ready for the taking.

The big question Robson and his trusted advisors asked themselves was whether they could afford to play just two in midfield against Franz Beckenbauer's three. Bobby decided that he would stick with a sweeper regardless of whether Mark Wright was fit or not, but he was still in turmoil. He couldn't leave out either Paul Gascoigne or David Platt because of the way they played in Bologna, but the alternative was to drop Chris Waddle. Robson described Waddle's form as like the curate's egg: good in parts, poor in others and absolutely brilliant against Belgium.

In the end Robson took Waddle off to the empty team room to explain his dilemma, asking the player if he was responsible enough to switch to midfield from the wing in order to look after Pierre Littbarski. The winger, who must have guessed he was on the verge of being axed for the biggest game of his career, couldn't convince his manager quickly enough that he was his man and would confidently follow team instructions. Trevor Steven had made a strong claim for a starting berth, and I know he was disappointed he did not make it, but he took the decision like the gentleman he was and still is. McMahon did not take his omission so well and sought out the manager for an explanation. Even that was appreciated, though, as Robson much preferred a face-to-face confrontation to a player running to the newspapers with his story.

For the only time to my knowledge – and I saw the manager most days either for press conferences or on his own for our book – Robson was riddled with self-doubts over whether he had chosen the right England team. It was his decision, no one else's and he was prepared to hang his much-improved reputation on it.

In the end it was Beckenbauer who sprung a surprise before the kick-off, leaving out Littbarski – the player Waddle had been tasked to deal with – and Uwe Bein, bringing in Olaf Thon and Thomas Häßler in their place. It was only then, 50 minutes before the kick-off, that Robson shared his fears on selection with his close mate Don Howe who, with typical earthly Midlands mindset, looked at him and said: 'It's too late to worry about that now, Bob.' He was right.

Any doubts disappeared in the opening 35 minutes as England played as well as they had in the entire tournament. Waddle was doing a fine job, particularly with his long range passing, while Gazza tested goalkeeper Bodo Illgner and set up Stuart Pearce, who hit his powerful shot wide.

By contrast it was the West German team who were faltering, with Jürgen Klinsmann and Rudi Völler being firmly held by Des Walker and Mark Wright. The injured Völler lasted until just before half time when he was replaced by Karl-Heinz Riedle, and it was while Völler was off receiving treatment that the Germans had their best chance when Peter Shilton saved from Olaf Thon, a sign of things to come as the new boy drove the Germans forward as half-time approached.

It had been a tremendous first half, full of quality and excitement, and Robson told his players in the dressing room how they could go on and win the World Cup if they were unafraid of taking the Germans on. England continued to control proceedings in the opening exchanges of the second period until the Brazilian referee

José Roberto Wright upset everyone when Stuart Pearce was harshly penalised for a foul on the limping Thomas Häßler just outside the penalty area. Andreas Brehme drove the ball goalwards, it struck Paul Parker on his outstretched boot and spun crazily over the head of Peter Shilton and into the net. It was a cruel blow and here they were again, a goal behind and playing with a sweeper.

With his side visibly tiring after two successive games involving extra time and all the attendant emotion involved, Robson gambled once more, bringing off his skipper Terry Butcher for the second time to go to a conventional 4-4-2. He sent on the reliable and classy Steven and moved Waddle onto the wing. It took a little over 20 minutes for them to get back on terms with Paul Parker making up for his unfortunate error with a superb ball into the box which put the German defence into a state of confusion. Who do you want in a situation like that? Gary Lineker, of course, and Robson's lucky charm duly beat goalkeeper Bodo Illgner with a fierce left footed shot.

The major problem now was tiredness as England entered into a third period of extra time in the space of just eight days and with all substitutes used. It was asking an awful lot and the manager could only hope that the goal would give them all a lift. There was no lowering of the intensity and, indeed, England might well have taken a decisive lead when the unlucky Chris Waddle hit the inside of an upright and watched as the ball came straight back out into play instead of going in-off. The Germans also struck the woodwork through Guido Buchwald, while Shilton did his usual business to keep out efforts from both Lothar Matthäus and Jürgen Klinsmann.

Nine minutes into extra time there was a moment which went down in football folklore. It was not a great goal nor a save, not a miss or an horrendous foul. It was that jovial young character Paul Gascoigne who had delighted his manager, his fellow players and the England fans with his ebullient spirit, his approach to life and his skill on the ball. He had run his heart out for his team once again and the legs were beginning to go when he raised one more gallop as he chased Thomas Berthold by the touchline, mistiming a challenge right in front of the German bench. They leapt to their feet as one, screaming for retribution and the referee capitulated. Gazza was given his second yellow of the tournament, meaning he would miss the final if England were to get through.

Gascoigne knew the consequences immediately and, with tears streaming down his face, he begged and pleaded with the Brazilian official to change his mind, not something that was ever going to happen.

Robson's heart bled for him. It had been such a sporting, well contested semi-final and he truly believed that it was Berthold's reaction to the challenge and the orchestrated complaints from the German bench which persuaded the referee to take action, totally out of character with what had gone before in the game.

Lineker was aware of how broken up his teammate was and ran over to the bench, where he warned Robson that Gazza had gone. Robson acknowledged that Lineker knew the youngster as well as anyone in the squad and subsequently kept a close eye on his player, though steadfastly refused to take him off. At the break he told him that though he was out of the final, he could still get his country there.

'I can do it,' Gazza responded, choking back a fresh wave of tears. But the fairytale didn't happen, and it was almost destiny that England were to play out their third bout of extra time without being able to find a resolution. Penalty kicks loomed.

That night Bobby told me that he hated those cruel penalty shootouts, but accepted at the same time that it was a far, far better solution than tossing a coin or drawing lots. His choice, he said, would have been an extra period of extra time, even though the legs had gone and there was only the character left with which to combat the

Germans, who had enjoyed an easier, less demanding, less time-consuming ride to the last four.

England had naturally talked about the possibility of penalties in the approach to the game, and there had been a good response when the manager asked who would take them if it came to that. Unfortunately, they were already without two of their five designated takers, with both Bryan Robson and John Barnes out of action, but the English were sure they had the best goalkeeper in Peter Shilton, while the distraught Gazza lifted the spirits when he bravely volunteered for the sixth spot kick if it was all square after ten.

Lineker was, of course, the best and had already scored two from two in the competition, and the next best was the Master Blaster himself, Stuart Pearce. He would take the crucial fourth.

England's toss win was good as it allowed them to take the first kick and exert pressure on their opponents, and the first three takers all did exactly that: Lineker, Beardsley and a nervous Platt all found the net. How close Shilton came to giving his team the edge – three times he chose the right way, but on all three occasions Brehme, Matthäus and Riedle beat his fingertips with fierce shots. No problem. Pearce, ice cool and with a shot to frighten any goalkeeper from twelve yards, was next up and he sent Illgner the wrong way. Yet somehow the FC Köln goalkeeper managed to save the effort anyway, deflecting the ball with his leg despite diving away from the ball.

The world caved in on Pearce, Robson, his staff and the players standing in line waiting for their turn. Not Pearce, of all people. The sporting Lothar Matthäus was the first to him and put a consoling arm around him. Thon subsequently put his penalty away to make it 4-3, and when Waddle blazed over the bar, it was all over. England were out, and the Germans did not even have to take their fifth spot kick. It was they who were going forward to play Argentina in Rome, leaving England to play the hosts Italy in Bari in a third-place play-off.

Robson was struggling to keep it all together as his players sank to the ground in tears.

ENGLAND 1-1 WEST GERMANY
(GERMANY WIN ON PENALTIES), 4 JULY 1990:

The Italians thought we were lucky to have reached the last four, but phone calls from home told us that the nation was jumping for joy and full of World Cup fever. We watched Italy lose to Argentina on penalties in the other semi-final, undefeated but still out of their own tournament. It suited me because Argentina were not the side they were and I was sure that if we met in the final we would triumph. But first we had to face the favourites, West Germany.

The phone was red hot on the morning of the match with all the usual suspects including my wife Elsie, Mrs Porter, Mike Shapow and Uncle Tom Cobbley and all. We were carrying a lot of hope on our shoulders and I confess I was concerned whether I had picked the right team for the job. I guess it was natural as I had made some close decisions, disappointing some and thrilling others. If it went wrong there was only one person to blame. Me.

It all ended in bitter defeat and the fact that everyone, particularly the neutrals, described it as the match of the tournament meant little when you lost. There was nothing to choose between us, the teams were so well matched and it was no surprise that yet another Lineker goal took us to extra time. It was cruel because this was the third time in three games we had to play that extra half an hour, draining at the best of times, but strength and energy sapping in a World Cup.

With a sliver of luck we would have been in the final as Chris Waddle hit the inside of an upright while Buchwald hit the outside of the post.

But the moment that captivated the hearts of the watching world came eight minutes into extra time when Gazza, who had become the hero of the neutrals as well as the English fans, mistimed a challenge against

Berthold right in front of the German bench. They rose as one and referee Jose Ramiz Wright responded by giving the Spurs player his second card of the tournament. He was out of the final whether we made it or not. Tears were streaming down his face and Lineker was signalling for me to get Gazza off but I stayed with him and at half time of extra time I told him simply to get us into the final.

But try as we might, it was all down to another bloody shootout. They are great when you win them but so depressing when you go out to them, especially for the players who miss, in this instance Stuart Pearce and Chris Waddle. Strange, isn't it? If there was one player in our entire team I would have backed in this situation it was 'Psycho' but goalkeeper Illgner, going the wrong way, saved with his outstretched leg. No player deserves that in the biggest day of his sporting life.

We were out and facing a meaningless play-off game for third place against Italy, while the lucky old Argies had done it again and were to face the now odds on favourites West Germany for the title.

The German manager Franz Beckenbauer, heading for his fourth final as a player and manager, said to me: 'What a pity it has come to this. They were two fine teams and you played so well.' Choking back the tears I told him to go and win it for us.

The dressing room was awash with tears. Words were not needed from me nor anyone else and, anyway, I had to prepare myself for the grilling from the world's press.

There was no hiding place for Robson, who had to face the torture of the usual series of media interviews under the bright lights and the probing gaze of the television cameras. I managed a brief word of sympathy as he went from the cameras into the written press conference and I could see he had switched on to automatic to get through what must have been an ordeal.

Outside the two team buses were parked together side by side in the stadium car park. The Germans were naturally celebrating, giving interviews and generally doing what winning teams do, while the English boys sat silently – for a while. Suddenly someone began singing 'Blaydon Races', and gradually they all joined in and followed up the Geordie anthem with a good old Cockney style rendition of 'Knees Up Mother Brown'. The Germans looked from the windows of their coach totally bemused. The English bus was rocking and so were the players.

But not all of them. Certainly not Stuart Pearce – he was still in a daze at having missed from twelve yards out. He had been taking penalties all his footballing life and he couldn't believe he had missed the most important one of them all. He remembers hitting the ball straight and true, with Illgner diving to his right, but the goalkeeper was aware enough to know he had been suckered and instinctively threw out a leg to make the save.

We talked about it long afterwards and Pearce shouldered the responsibility entirely, taking the blame that England were not in the World Cup Final. When we were writing his book *Psycho* together, he told me: 'I felt the tears prickling my eyes as I took the long walk back from the penalty spot to the centre circle where I was immediately surrounded by friends – special friends – including Des Walker along with my other Nottingham Forest teammates Steve Hodge and Neil Webb, quickly followed by Mark Wright and Terry Butcher. I couldn't speak.

'I saw the other players going over to applaud the fans who were still backing us, and while I am from a working-class background and knew it meant a lot to the fans when the players go over to them and thank them, I just couldn't do it because I felt so guilty at letting them down.

'Webby threw me a towel so I could hide my tears beneath it like a criminal leaving a court of law. It was the first time I had cried on a football pitch and I didn't want anyone to see my shame and as soon as Chris missed his penalty I was off, not because I wanted to hide, I just didn't want to shed my tears in front of the cameras and the fans.

'As I walked off Bobby Robson was waiting. I had let him down, too. He was gutted like the rest of us because we were convinced that had we won this one, we could win the World Cup.

'Don't anyone blame Chris Waddle for his miss because it was all over once I missed mine. His was irrelevant. Credit to the Germans, they always showed that mental strength and to this day I admire everyone who takes a penalty in those circumstances.'

He cried all the way back to the Hasta Hotel in Asti, with only big Terry Butcher brave enough to go and sit beside him and chatter because he thought that was the right thing to do. Both knew it was probably their last chance to win the World Cup.

Robson reminded his players they still had another game to play, the appalling third place play-off against the Italians, and told them to respect their fitness and to see if they could retain their unbeaten record in the competition, true if you didn't count penalties.

+++

COME THURSDAY BOBBY WAS EVEN UP FOR A LITTLE joke, telling me that for the first time he had lost a match and no one was demanding his head, which would have been a little pointless as he was off to Holland after the game in Bari. The manager of the hotel wished him well and told him that the staff would miss us and that we were in a different class to their previous guests from Brazil, who left a lot to be desired with their behaviour and their demands. Having confirmation of the stories that had circulated throughout the World Cup, it was no surprise that they had gone out, losing to their bitter neighbours, the ordinary Argentina, in the last sixteen.

Despite the fact they were going to be playing the local Italian heroes in the play-off, a big crowd were out to greet them when they arrived in the village of Truli. Everyone could have done without the burden of the meaningless game but tickets had been sold and television schedules had been sorted. England had to play their part. It was an ordeal for both teams, yet it was a game of more than decent quality and both sides were competitive enough to make it watchable for the fans in the stadium and the viewers at home.

The English supporters played their part and that was a relief to all of us; they seemed to get on with the Italians and enjoyed the visit to this then largely unexplored area of Italy. It was a good advert for the game at a good time, with English clubs due back in European competition the following season.

The only thing that jarred with Bobby, apart from the result, was the officiating of Frenchman Joël Quiniou and one of his linesmen Mohammed Hansal. Robson was so disappointed with them that he refused to even discuss them for our book. Baggio should have been awarded a penalty when Shilton brought him down after a lapse of concentration in his final appearance for his country – cap number 125 – but the referee subsequently allowed the forward to go on and score when clearly in an offside position after receiving Toto Schillaci's pass.

The character England had shown throughout the tournament emerged again and they came roaring back, and they looked to be in control when David Platt headed in from a perfect Tony Dorigo centre. England went in search of the winner, only for the effort to founder against the rocks.

In the end, it was the referee Quiniou who decided the outcome of the contest, It seemed to be something of nothing when the weary Schillaci lost control of the ball and tumbled over Parker's outstretched leg, but it was enough to earn a penalty, a penalty which the same player stuck away. Robson described it as 'weak and unfortunate' and then went on to project the theory that it came five minutes from time and no one wanted what was almost an exhibition match to go to yet another period of extra time. There was nothing for it but for England to pile forward to look for an equaliser and maintain their unbeaten record in the competition. With everyone up the Italians broke away to score a brilliant goal which lit up the game. Inter midfielder Nicola Berti broke and ran half the length of the pitch to head home a picture goal only for it to be disallowed for offside, a ludicrous decision which, according to your affiliations, was either the referee compensating for an earlier poor decision or showing that he was just a poor referee with equally poor officials exposed on the big stage.

It ended without the usual whimper as players of both sides joined the departing manager Robson in celebrating what had been a roller coaster of a tournament, with everyone agreeing that the game was so good it could have been the final. Unfortunately, it wasn't. Despite defeat the England fans were determined to celebrate, or to have a disco as they called it, and they stayed in the new stadium chanting for the retiring manager to appear until he poked his head down the tunnel after his media duties were complete. He was immediately greeted by the same supporters chanting and cheering his name.

It was all very emotional as he shook hands with the Italian coach Azeglio Vicini, who agreed that these were the best two teams left in the competition, regardless of the fact that West Germany were to play Argentina in the final the next day in Rome's Olympic Stadium. It was turning into a party in the dressing rooms as well, as players from the two teams mingled, exchanged shirts, shook hands and patted each other's backs.

ITALY 2-1 ENGLAND, 7 JULY 1990:

I was sad for me, sad for the players and sad for their families who had flown over for the final. No one had come to watch a play-off for third place between two teams whose chins were on the ground. It was to all intents and purposes a meaningless match and naturally I would have much preferred that my final game as England manager was against the Germans in the final.

But it was an England international, a World Cup game and a challenge to finish third rather than fourth.

It was the ultimate leaving party for the England manager when the squad returned to the Trulli Hotel as Dick Wragg and Jack Wiseman called the group to order and presented him with a painting, while Terry Butcher handed over a Wedgwood Dinner Service. FIFA had awarded England an extra seven medals for finishing a creditable fourth in the world's most important cup and he handed them over to Don Howe, Dave Sexton, Mike Kelly, Doc Crane, Norman Medhurst and Fred Street. Naturally he kept the last one for himself and not a single person objected.

Robson had still not revealed to the squad his own injury complications – the cracked rib nor the pain it gave him. He soon wished he had, as the players surrounded him, lifted him high into the air and dumped him unceremoniously into the hotel swimming pool. He just had time to take off his watch and hand it and his medal to Fred Street, before being hurled into the water, just missing the diving board but having the satisfaction of taking Butcher, Barnes and Walker into the water with him.

In keeping with the trip, and his entire eight years as England boss, he cut his foot on the way out of the pool. Everyone was in great spirits as he slipped away to put on an Elastoplast and a dry set of clothes. He left the players singing and dancing and then left them to it entirely, giving himself time to reflect. He soon came to the conclusion that other than winning the trophy itself, this was the most glorious way to depart the job he had loved so much.

No one saw, but tears flowed again.

On Sunday morning Bobby was at the airport at Bari not just to catch his flight to Rome for the final, but to wave off the players, their wives, the officials and all the staff who were flying direct to Luton in their private charter. The two flights were within minutes of each other and airport officials were happy to let their celebrity have unusual access.

It was only later we learned that more than 100,000 people had turned up in Luton, both at the airport and in the streets, to welcome back the players who had become heroes. Bobby was looking forward to the final, but a large part of him was missing the emotional welcome home. The hero at last and he wasn't there to appreciate and accept it.

He wasn't just at the Olympic Stadium as an observer for the final, he was also present in an official capacity to receive the Fair Play Trophy. England had committed fewer fouls and had received fewer bookings than any other team, remarkable when you consider they had reached the semi-final and played three lots of extra time. Robson and his team had every right to be proud.

The team had been lectured how important it was for the future of the game not to foul, not to try and get an opponent sent off by feigning injury after a tackle, not to retaliate, to be hard but fair in their tackling and to leave the referees alone, regardless of provocation. This at a time when FIFA had instructed a clampdown by their officials, resulting in more bookings and sendings off than ever before. England were shown no red cards and just five yellows, three of which Robson disputed.

In terms of gamesmanship defending champions Argentina were as bad as it got, and by the time they reached Rome they had lost four players through suspension. Maradona, who in fairness had been kicked from pillar to post himself throughout, was a shadow of the player who knocked England out four years earlier. Predictably they were totally negative in their approach to the final against West Germany: they didn't have a shot at goal in 90 minutes and German goalkeeper Bodo Illgner could have left for his summer holidays.

The Germans were left to do all the creative work against a wall of defenders and it eventually took yet another disputed penalty as Rudi Völler fell over a tackle from Roberto Sensini. Andreas Brehme dispatched the penalty, beating the goalkeeper to his right.

The game was rightly described as cynical and ugly, and that was all down to the defending champions, who were a disgrace to the beautiful game. Pedro Monzón had the distinction of becoming the first player to be sent off in a World Cup final for a studs up challenge on Klinsmann who, this time, had no cause for one of his spectacular dives. Gustavo Dezotti became the second South American to be dismissed by Mexican referee Edgardo Codesal Méndez for a straight red card, following his earlier yellow, for a tackle which would have earned a dismissal in a rugby international.

A tearful Maradona unequivocally blamed the referee for the result, a remark which made Bobby Robson laugh out loud.

It was the West Germans' third successive final and avenged defeat by Argentina four years earlier. Franz Beckenbauer became the only footballer in history to finish as a runner-up and a champion in a World Cup both as a player and a manager, but remarkably it was Bobby Robson who was feted and congratulated at the farewell party in Rome's Hilton Hotel that night, with everyone saying that the third place play-off was far, far better than the final itself.

As Robson left Rome for Heathrow he was greeted by the usual barrage of photographers and a young lady who not only wanted his autograph, but also asked if she could walk with him so that she would be in the newspapers the next day. 'Certainly,' said the smiling and now ex-England manager, 'if you fancy being on the front page of the

Sun tomorrow.' She didn't. She was off like a startled rabbit.

Robson was further surprised when people and staff applauded him all the way through the terminal to the baggage reclaim carousel, and when he emerged from customs control, the people waiting for friends and relatives burst into a further round of spontaneous applause.

He found it both embarrassing and touching. He was sad to leave his dream job but looking forward to the challenge that lay ahead in Holland. He had just two days to clear out his office at Lancaster Gate and to prepare himself for his new adventure.

During eight years as England manager he had changed in the public's estimation of him from idiot to icon, and his only sadness was not being able to bring home a trophy for his country.

15

DESPITE EIGHT YEARS OF INTENSE PRESSURE, stress, abuse and the rest of the baggage that came with being manager of England, Bobby Robson would still have gone back to the FA at the drop of a hat – any position and any time. He was not just a patriot, he was far more than that, and walking away after the experiences of two World Cups hurt him deeply.

When he heard that the man who replaced him, Graham Taylor, might be on the verge of leaving the job in 1993, with England struggling to qualify for the World Cup in America the following summer, Robson let it be known to me and everyone else with any vague connection with the FA that he was prepared to drop everything and return. England still had three games left against his old adversaries Holland and Poland and minnows San Marino and needed to win all of them to qualify.

Everybody told him he was crazy to even contemplate going back, but he was serious and wouldn't have even asked what the salary was. It never happened. Taylor stayed on, Robson remained in Portugal and England failed to qualify for football's showpiece, only four years after going so close in Italy. It hurt Robson to the quick, but despite offers that would have bolstered his pension, there was no possibility of him breaking his word and attacking any England manager, be it Taylor or anyone else.

By this point Robson had already established himself on the continent: after two successful seasons at PSV Eindhoven, he was now in his second year at Sporting Lisbon. From Lisbon he would move north to Porto and then east to Barcelona, before finishing his voyage across Europe with another spell at PSV. In 1999, after nearly ten years away from his country of birth, he returned to manage his home town club of Newcastle United. How proud that would have made his father Philip, who had passed away during Bobby's years overseas, the man who kindled his interest in football when he took him to soak up the atmosphere of the ground in the middle of the Toon, St James' Park.

There were some who knew him well who doubted his ability to manage a club abroad when he first took the PSV job, considering he had no grasp of the language and little experience of the league he was to manage in. How wrong they were. Bobby had been a regular visitor to nearby Holland to watch games and scout players when he was manager at Ipswich and was one of the first English bosses to bring in foreign players when he signed Arnold Mühren followed by Frans Thijssen. He had also spent a large part of the previous eight years abroad, and although he picked up bits and pieces of the local language, he was always sure that English was the language of football, just as it was with the pilots who flew him over to Eindhoven and other places around the globe.

He arrived in the central Netherlands city as Robert William Robson CBE, having been honoured by the Queen for his services to English football.

A city with a population twice the size of Ipswich, Eindhoven was dominated at the time by Philips Electronics, and that company was the main backer of the football team, with PSV playing their home games in the Philips Stadion to this day. Despite the most popular form of transport being the bicycle, Eindhoven was by no means the back of beyond, as some of Robson's critics made out. The city is home to the second largest airport in the Netherlands, serving 75 destinations and just 90 minutes away from Antwerp, Amsterdam and Dusseldorf. I also quickly discovered I could be over in a trice from London's splendid little City Airport on a direct flight.

Bobby was still managing England when PSV made their first approach. He was in Eindhoven to watch a match which involved a number of international players who figured in his dossiers for Italia '90 when he bumped into agent Tom van Dalen, who he had built up a good relationship with when he took Mühren and Thijssen to England, and he wanted to know what he had planned after the World Cup.

Robson hadn't a clue and was still hoping at that stage that he may be offered another contract by the FA, but nothing was certain. Tom explained that he was asking because he knew that PSV were looking for a new coach and he, and they, thought Robson fitted the bill.

He appreciated it was not idle chatter as he knew Tom was close with the general manager of PSV, Kees Ploegsma, and sure enough Ploegsma contacted him officially towards the end of the 1989/90 with the next campaign in mind. It was not a temptation as long as he had the England job, but he still felt obliged to tell FA chairman

Bert Millichip and chief executive Graham Kelly about the approach, giving him the opportunity to ask where he stood with them as far as his future was concerned.

Bobby was hoping, of course, they would refuse to grant permission for the Dutch club to speak to him and offer him a new contract. They didn't, instead telling him that if he received a good offer they would not seek to stop him taking it. He asked if he could talk to interested clubs and they told him he could, providing it was kept quiet until after the World Cup had finished.

That suited Bobby nicely, although he was a bit miffed about their enthusiasm at the prospect and the lack of argument to persuade him to remain. Still, he retained his trust and his liking for the two men who, in effect, controlled his future alongside the chairman of the International Committee Dick Wragg and his assistant, Peter Swales, the chairman of Manchester City. Robson, who always looked for the best in people, had an enemy in Swales, even if he didn't yet know it. Swales wanted him out and someone of his own choice in, and though he was pleasant enough to Bobby's face, behind his back he was completely different, demonstrated by his later admission that it was a good job England did not win in Italy as they would have then been stuck with him.

It was clear that Robson had to protect his future. International management paid the bills, but it didn't assure his long-term financial future and he knew he would need to find work. Even if he had saved enough for retirement he would not have taken it. He was far too active, far too involved, to divorce himself from the game he loved so much.

It was necessary because of the circumstances that any discussions he had with PSV were conducted in secrecy, but because he was so well known at home and abroad it was difficult, and it was hardly helped when Ploegsma and president Jacques Ruts flew in from Eindhoven on a Philips private jet to a secluded airport in Cambridge, where they met in an equally secluded restaurant to open their discussions. There are no secrets in football and it was soon widely known that PSV were in town and talking to Bobby Robson. The jet had been a bit of a giveaway, despite the location of their meeting. They explained to him the background of the club, their ambitions, the players they had and the players they would like to bring in. These initial talks did not extend as far as salary and they weren't, at that stage, rushing him for a decision.

But it stirred his interest. The prospect of returning to management in England was a little daunting after his experiences with the national team, but the prospect of returning to work with players on a daily basis at a big European club was an exciting one. He was wise in the ways of Dutch football not only through his interaction with Thijssen and Mühren, but also because of England's regular meetings with the Netherlands – they had played each other at the European Championships in 1988 and two years later in Italy. Robson liked the people and he liked the way they played their football. He knew he could slot in easily with his broad palette of experience.

Money was certainly not going to be an issue. He had taken a cut from his Ipswich income to become manager of England at just £65,000 a year, and by the time he left eight years later it had risen to only £80,000. His accountant John Hazell flew to Eindhoven for further talks and came back with an offer which doubled his salary. Top managers in England at the time were earning a great deal more than that, but Robson told me that if the FA had offered him a further four years on the same salary, he would have taken it, because he genuinely believed he could bring the World Cup back from America.

To this end he even delayed signing his contract with PSV until after the World Cup just in case he won it and the FA had a change of heart and asked him to stay on. Yet nothing was ever said or offered, even in the euphoria of reaching the semi-finals abroad for the first time in their history. It didn't happen and it was never going to.

Despite all the precautions the news was leaked, and Bobby was never sure whether it came from Holland or from Lancaster Gate. It broke immediately after a meeting with minister of sport Colin Moynihan at the House of Commons. The meeting had focused on the importance of England's behaviour and how the needed to represent their country in a positive manner overseas. It was a complete waste of time in Robson's eyes, who knew how disciplined his side were on the field. It was the fans Moynihan should have been targeting.

Afterwards he went straight to the Great Western Hotel to report on the meeting to Millichip and Kelly. There were journalists around, as it was the venue for the FA's AGM, and one of them came up with the fantasy that the manager was seen handing brown envelopes to every member of the international committee, offering his resignation in a handwritten letter. The response was brief and brilliant: Robson immediately offered a million pounds to be paid to a chosen charity if anyone could produce any one of those supposed batch of letters. You can be sure had it been true in any shape or form that one of those on the International Committee would have been only too happy to produce a copy.

An assault on his character followed, though this time the FA were firmly in his corner, as they were when he took the unprecedented action of suing *Today* for calling him a traitor. They settled out of court and he left it at that, instead of trying to take on the rest of the powerful – although somewhat weakening – British newspaper industry. As far as he was concerned, he had made his point. The only people the revelation helped were PSV, who were able to make their announcement of their new manager public. In the meantime, Robson had the full support of Don Howe and his players – who knew all about the uncertainty of a manager's position – going into the World Cup.

+++

FOLLOWING THE CONCLUSION OF THE WORLD CUP, Bobby had one night at home before catching the night boat from Harwich to the Hook of Holland with his wife Elsie. From there he drove to Eindhoven, arriving at the palatial training ground in the suburbs at around ten in the morning to be welcomed by president Jacques Ruts, who was to be an almost permanent fixture at the training ground during his tenure.

They wanted Bobby because their reign as undisputed Eredivisie Champions had been disrupted after four unbroken years by bitter rivals Ajax. They wanted their title back and, even more, they wanted success in Europe again, and that was why they had brought in the England manager. There was no plan B.

PSV were the last winners of the European Cup before AC Milan took over, beating Benfica 6-5 on penalties in the 1988 final in Stuttgart. The Italians themselves, guided by three Dutch players – Frank Rijkaard, Marco van Basten and Ruud Gullit – had subsequently beat Steaua Bucharest and Benfica in successive years and were considered the most powerful force in European football, but PSV now wanted a second success of their own in Europe's biggest club competition. It was a trophy Robson craved as well.

'Look at my career,' he said, 'What's missing? The European Cup!'

He knew that to win it he first had to reclaim the Dutch title and he also knew that was why PSV had appointed him – to win the Eredivisie in his first season and the big one in his second. He would receive £500,000 plus bonuses over those two years, and though it wasn't necessarily break the bank time, it was enough for him and his way of life, built around the family and football.

He was thrilled to show me around the town and the superb training ground, and he was energised by the day-today involvement he had missed in his eight years with England. He was in charge of the playing side of the club with nothing else to distract him. It was a stark contrast to his Ipswich days, where he did everything but mop the dressing room floors.

Bobby's Dutch assistant Hans Dorjee had already informed him that the club were desperate for a top quality libero – a defensive sweeper – and while Robson was in Italy he had looked hard and long before coming up with a player: the Romanian Gheorghe Popescu. Having had his qualities confirmed by Howard Wilkinson, he was ready to bring him in. At Ipswich Bobby had done everything, but here at PSV he had to quickly get used to a new routine. He would tell Ploegsma who he wanted, and it was up to the general manager to sort the deal and then negotiate the players' contract.

There was plenty of immediate movement: Wim Kieft and Flemming Poulsen were both on their way out, while Ivan Nielsen and Søren Lerby were both retiring. Jean-Marc Bosman, who subsequently found fame for winning freedom of movement for players on the expiry of their contract, and the talented Dutch international Erwin Koeman had arrived.

Because of the comparative success in Italy, the English media retained an interest in what their ex-national manager was up to in the land of the tulips and windmills, sniffing out anything that looked remotely like a story for the folks back home. The Dutch press, having been well aware of what was happening in Italy, were still amazed at the number of English journalists who turned up to watch the games and the sharp criticism which followed, particularly after Robson's first league loss in his eighth game, a 3-1 defeat to reigning champions Ajax.

One journalist even had the temerity to ask the surprised Ploegsma how safe Bobby's job was after that defeat. They were able to feast further when PSV went out of both Europe and the main domestic cup competition early on, and while the Dutch press were more interested in the tactical side of the game, they often reprinted what was being said in our tabloids. They were particularly fascinated to see whether Bobby would introduce the long ball game that was being played by many teams back in England, but it had never been his preferred mode of football. Given he had a skilful midfield and Romário at his disposal, it would have been pretty self-defeating to employ such a one-dimensional method anyway.

Romário de Souza Faria, to give him his full name, was a phenomenal goalscorer who netted 679 times in 886 matches, including 55 international goals for Brazil in just 70 games. He missed out at Italia '90 as he slowly recovered from a broken leg, but he was back in his usual scoring mode four years later in the USA where he scored five times to help Brazil to their record-breaking fourth World Cup victory. He eventually left PSV for Barcelona where he became part of their dream team and scored at a rate of more than a goal every other game.

Bobby knew he had a gem, but he lost him to injury from September 1990 to January 1991 and, needless to say, they missed a player who scored 127 goals for the club in five years. His lengthy absence meant that PSV huffed and puffed to keep up with Ajax and it wasn't until the last day of the season that they clinched the title, pipping Leo Beenhakker's side to the post.

Having lost two English titles with Ipswich on the final day of the campaign, Bobby was fearful of missing out for a third time and was riven with doubt. No one could claim any advantage as the Dutch ensured that both games kicked off at precisely the same moment by stationing an official with a walkie-talkie to signal to the match official. With the two teams going into the final day level on points, nothing could be left to chance. It looked as though his opportunity of a first ever domestic title had hit the wall when his side crashed to a shock 4-1 defeat to third placed Gronigen on the penultimate weekend of the season. They remained top going into their final game with Volendam, but only with a slender two-goal advantage. No points separated the top two.

Exactly a year earlier Bobby and Leo had been face-to-face in the World Cup as England drew with Holland, but this time Ajax were playing Vitesse in the National Stadium to accommodate the big crowd, while PSV were at home.

Spectators were linked to both games by thousands of transistor radios, and Bobby couldn't help but hear how the other game was going. PSV went one up and then Ajax went two up to claw the deficit down to a single goal. PSV eventually scored three, and it was those two second half strikes that sealed the deal. Robson's men had lost 3-1 to Ajax away from home but beaten them 4-1 in the return fixture. Fine margins.

There was no waiting about for the celebrations, which began straight after the game in a downpour. They were soon aboard an open top bus, travelling through the streets packed with supporters to the Town Hall, where the players threw their saturated jackets to fans as they piled off.

There was no immediate holiday for Robson as the club were contracted to a tour of India. I didn't need to find out if it had been successful as he telephoned me while out there, describing his fascination at such a diverse country and waxing lyrical about the huge crowds at the three games, including 100,000 at Salt Lake Stadium in Calcutta. There was no Romário, who had controversially gone home to Brazil, but PSV scarcely needed him as they scored 19 goals and conceded just one against their three opponents, who did not match the enthusiasm of their fans.

In the meantime, Robson's assistant Dorjee had left PSV to manage

Feyenoord and was subsequently replaced by Frank Arnesen. Wim Kieft was brought back to the club to replace the Anderlecht-bound Bosman, but apart from that things remained very much as they were at the end of the season. 1991/92 was a much calmer campaign – Feyenoord drifted off the pace at the halfway stage, and PSV dropped only ten points. They lost just once in the league all campaign, 1-0 to Ajax in January, but this time they were able to finish above their rivals on points rather than goal difference, three points the margin.

The big test this time around was the European Cup, but after squeezing past Beşiktaş in the first round, they were drawn with Anderlecht in the second, and following a goalless draw in Eindhoven they lost 2-0 in Belgium. They were without the services of injured internationals Gerald Vanenburg, Romário, Juul Ellerman, Kieft and Eric Gerets, but because of this defeat , despite the two domestic successes, Robson was not offered an extension to his contract.

It was no big deal on the continent, and Bobby had told me he would be leaving at the end of the season anyway – he already knew that his club had approached and secured the services of Hans Westerhof for the next season. Not that it helped: Ajax took the title back and PSV again missed out in Europe.

It was rumoured back home that he had fallen out with the powerful Ploegsma, who was always looking over his shoulder and did many of the jobs Bobby had done at Portman Road, including arranging the Friday night travel and sorting out players' contracts. But despite the rumours, they got on well enough and never once fell out. Both shared the disappointment of failure in Europe, although they knew it was because of a lack of depth in the squad, meaning they were unable to cover for an unusual glut of injuries.

Bobby had a good relationship with the Dutch people in general, and there was no animosity at his departure. In fact, I am still in touch with a couple who looked after him during his stay, Cor and Marjan

Sprengers, who made me as welcome as they did the famous coach. It was a quality club and he also formed a lasting friendship with Frank Arnesen, who he promoted from the junior ranks as a coach, though he couldn't leave him in charge of training until he passed his coaching diploma.

Another good friend to Bobby was the towering central defender Stan Valckx, who was to follow him to Portugal, and the veteran Belgian full-back Eric Gerets, a strong and respected captain who eventually moved into coaching. Goalkeeper Hans van Breukelen was another character who enjoyed a jape and led the press, particularly the English, into believing he was going to walk out on Bobby at the end of the season, and then signed a new two-year contract. It had never been in doubt.

The player Bobby really admired was the mercurial Romário, who he said could turn a game in an instant with his sublime skills around the penalty area but couldn't take any responsibility either on or off the pitch. He liked parties, dancing and late nights, and wouldn't stop for anything, no matter how important the upcoming game was.

His goals were his salvation and Bobby admitted he couldn't stay cross with him for long because of his angelic face and even temperament, but mostly because of his goals. They were his currency and because of them he could do as he pleased, flying home to Brazil when he wished, refusing the summer tour to India and rarely offering his help on or off the field.

He was on a six-year contract, earning a lot more than a manager who was never going to go to war with him for that exact reason. Robson knew there would only be one winner, and it wasn't the man who picked the team. The one man who would take him on was his skipper Gerets, who earned Robson's lasting admiration when he stood up in the dressing room and told the Brazilian that he expected him to give as much as everyone else in the team, especially those who needed success to earn their bonuses to support their families. Gerets himself was on a low basic wage and got his point across by telling Romário that he didn't begrudge him his salary because he was a better player, but that he needed to give a little more effort.

Knowing he was going to depart at the end of the season, Robson fully intended to return home to Blighty to resume his career, but he was also enjoying the continental lifestyle and when Sporting Lisbon came knocking on his door in the spring of 1992 he accepted the challenge. He let his PSV players know what was happening before knuckling down to win his second title.

PSV were excellent and even allowed Bobby two trips to Portugal so he could look over the vibrant city of Lisbon and see what his new club had to offer him, which in terms of salary alone was a lot more than the Dutch. They had a good stadium, a good team, and wined and dined him very well, demonstrating how much they wanted him. Bobby liked to feel wanted both in and out of football and accepted a contract from the start of the 1992/93 season.

16

'In victory, you deserve port. In defeat, you need it.'
Napoleon Bonaparte, one of history's great military leaders.

ONE OF THE VERY FIRST PEOPLE BOBBY ROBSON MET
in Portugal, indeed at the airport when he first arrived, was a young
man he had never heard of, a former local schoolteacher by the name
of José Mario dos Santos Mourinho Felix, who was in the delegation alongside new club President Sousa Cintra, the bottled water
magnate. Their new manager described Mourinho upon introduction
as a personable young chap, keen to help and with good English.

José was delegated to look after him because of his linguistic
skills and his strong background in football – his father had been a
goalkeeper at Vitória Setubal, before becoming the general manager of
the same club. He was intelligent and, like his father, he was passion-

ate about the game.

Bobby had nothing but good to say about José, who watched his back as well as translated for him. He was so enthusiastic about football he lapped up every word, learned from every coaching session and showed an appetite for the game that Robson had rarely come across.

Mourinho later learnt from Robson at FC Porto and Barcelona too, and he put the wisdom gained in these years to good use, eventually becoming one of Europe's most successful and controversial coaches, achieving worldwide fame at Benfica, Porto, Inter Milan, Real Madrid, Chelsea, Manchester United before linking up with Spurs. I came across him personally at Bobby's home in Sitges in Spain before he became a manager, and I always found him charming and polite. That aspect of his character somewhat disappeared when I was asking him questions at press conferences at Stamford Bridge as a journalist rather than speaking to him in my capacity as Bobby's trusted friend, but that wasn't a problem. However, I was deeply disappointed one day at the Bridge when he left Bobby sitting in his outer office after he had popped in to say hello and was asked to wait for a long time. Bobby didn't mind but I was furious, and that day this outstanding manager slipped slightly in my estimation. To me it was deeply disrespectful.

Still, it could not take away what he did for Bobby in Portugal. Never a great linguist – as he displayed in Holland – Bobby relied on him to get his message across to players and media alike. That required a lot of understanding on Mourinho's part, who had to translate not just Robson's words but his nuanced takes on the game to a host of others. It's not something many can get right, even with a deep understanding of football.

José, it has to be admitted, was no great shakes as a player but always he had a thirst for knowledge and received the coaching bug when given staff jobs at lower league clubs Vitória Setubal, Estrela da Amadora and Ovarense. There is little doubt he would have made the grade eventually – he had already held the post as assistant coach at Amadora – but there is equally no doubt that his future was accelerated and improved by his connections with Bobby.

He was a sponge, taking it all in and learning the trade at the knee of one of the giants. That's not to say he would always agree with his coach, and the two would discuss rather than argue the various merits of their approach: Robson with his pure football outlook, and Mourinho with a rather more modern, scientific and psychological approach. Where Bobby scored highly was man management, and his pupil was only too aware of this aspect, where he didn't always hit the mark.

The pair didn't fall out, far from it – they revelled in each other's company and both learned from the other, with Mourinho showing his worth on the practical side with intelligent, in-depth dossiers, which Robson described to me as outstanding and enormously helpful.

In his official biography, *Jose Mourinho: Made in Portugal*, he admitted: 'I was a nobody in football when he [Bobby] came to Portugal. He helped me to work in two clubs here and he took me to one of the biggest clubs in the world.' Yes, it was said, or rather whispered in Barcelona and Sitges, that there was something more between these two men. That was either the biggest joke or the biggest libel of them all.

+++

THERE WAS A STRONG PRO-BRITISH FEELING permeating around Sporting when Bobby arrived, as he was following in the footsteps of larger than life Malcolm Allison, big John Toshack, tactical expert Keith Burkinshaw and the stern Jimmy Hagan, who had all been part of the large British expatriate community in Lisbon at some time or another. It was the Brits who not only invented football but also introduced the alcoholic drink of port to the country, when they added the local brandy to the unpalatable, almost undrinkable rough red wine of the time. Both the red wine and the port wine have continued to grow in stature over the years, although a little strong for Bobby, who preferred something sparkling and white and preferably a little on the sweet side.

Mourinho wasn't ready or well versed enough to become Bobby's assistant when he took over and so the club called in Manuel Fernandes, a veteran Sporting player with a dozen years of service behind him and a former Portuguese international, who was coaching a team in the lower divisions. He proved to be a good choice – trustworthy with enough English, and also friendly with Mourinho, which all helped.

It was looking good. It was a sound club with strong support, friendly people and a nice climate. It was a bit like a sunny Eindhoven, with great potential. He was able to take the squad to France to the national training headquarters, where he swiftly got to know his players and discovered what he needed to strengthen the side. To this end he signed Stan Valckx from his previous club for half a million pounds and talented youngster Sergei Cherbakov from the Ukraine for pennies. They joined players like Luís Figo, Jorge Cadete, Krasimir Balakov and future Aston Villa player Fernando Nélson, while Fernandes used his local knowledge and brought in Portuguese players Carlos Jorge from Marítimo and Barny from Boa Vista.

They expected a lot from their new manager. They had won nothing for more than a decade and there was clearly a lot to do. Robson discovered this for himself when, while still at PSV, he watched his next club play Aston Villa in a friendly. He even used loan player Andrzej Juskowiak, who had just competed in the 1992 Olympics for Poland, and told the club to sign him at the end of a match which they won 2-0.

It was all to no avail. They simply weren't good enough and won nothing in that first season, finishing third in the league behind Porto and Benfica and losing in the semi-final of the domestic cup. On the plus side they had played good, attractive football, had brought the crowds back and had finished close up on their main rivals, nine points off the pace.

Bobby was comfortable with a nice apartment set between Benfica's Stadium of Light and the Alvalade stadium, which meant his travelling time was cut to a minimum, but the second season saw him and Elsie move to the seaside, taking a house in São João in the resort of Estoril, complete with a garden and swimming pool and next door to the golf club.

He looked set for a good two years and brought in fitness coach Roger Spry, while the president snapped up António Pacheco and Paulo Sousa, who had both come to the end of their contracts with Benfica. Bobby had absolutely nothing to do with the double deal, which was totally conducted by Cintra. It was fortunate for everybody they were two quality players, and Robson posed the question of what would have happened if they hadn't been. Who would have taken the blame?

He was soon to find out, as Cintra also brought in a young goalkeeper to the club, Paulo Costinha – signed from Boa Vista despite never having played in the league for them – and he would soon play a huge part in Robson's departure from the club and showed that the president wasn't always as good a judge of a player as he thought.

There was no hint of what was to come at the start of the new season, 1993/94, as Sporting went straight to the top of the table and looked capable of staying there. Progress was also being made in the UEFA Cup, where they put out Celtic and then beat Salzburg 2-0 at home in front of 70,000, a performance which left both Robson and Cintra purring.

Away in Austria for the return leg, all looked secure at 0-0 with 45 minutes of the second period remaining. That was until Cintra's new signing intervened. Shortly after the break the young goalkeeper let one through his hands from 35 yards, and in added time at the end of the contest the 19-year-old repeated the trick, diving over a 30-yard effort. Suddenly the game was headed to extra time.

Figo hit a post and Sporting did everything but take their chances, and with the tie heading for penalties, the Austrian side scored with a header from a corner and Sporting were out of Europe.

The flight back to Portugal was sensational. Cintra took the mic at the front of the plane and spoke at length in an angry tone to his captive audience. Robson could not follow what was being said, but he told me he could sense the tension amongst the players as they went quiet and their heads dropped. He turned to Mourinho to ask what was going on, and his man translated the president's words. In short, the performance was a disgrace and he would be speaking to his boss as soon as the plane landed.

As it transpired he didn't. Instead he waited until the next morning when the team went out to train, pulled his manager to one side and told him he was dismissed. Robson was stunned. He was expecting him to talk about the goalkeeper he had brought in and maybe even apologise. How could he be sacked on the back of one bad result brought about by two disastrous goalkeeping errors from a player he had nothing to do with signing?

It was the first time Robson had been sacked in 25 years in football and in his deep distrust of the man, he asked what would happen about his wages. Cintra responded that he would be paid monthly, not in one lump sum. Robson was suspicious that he was up to something dishonourable, and was soon proved right – the club were pocketing the tax deducted from his salary and he was duly presented with a bill for £80,000 from the Inland Revenue.

He cleared his locker and headed out for Estoril, only to discover Cintra had tipped off the press about what he was going to do. When he arrived home they, along with a number of fans, had gathered at his residence – not to jeer and boo, but to commiserate with the man who had taken Sporting Lisbon back to the top of the table. He simply could not understand the decision, but the president's agenda soon became clear. Cintra's close friend, former school teacher Carlos Queiroz, had just quit his job as Portugal's manager, and was duly appointed in his place.

The great irony was that just a week before the president's hissy fit, Robson had been offered a return to the top level of English football with Everton. It came about via a telephone call from his friend David Dein, who was far more to Arsenal than his title of vice-chairman suggested. He had been asked to pass on a message to call Everton chairman Dr David Marsh, who was looking for a new manager.

It was flattering but Robson was adamant that he had a good, young and developing team in Lisbon and he was enjoying the sunshine and the life offered in Portugal. He also believed in honouring contracts. He told Dr Marsh that his team were top of the league and believed he could win his third title in as many years but thanked him for his offer anyway.

This was the third time a big club had come knocking on his door and, due to varying circumstances, he had to turn each one down. He was also invited to join Wales when he was between jobs, but the offer was for £40,000 a year against the £250,000 he had been paid by Sporting. His bonus would have arrived if Wales had achieved World Cup glory, something unlikely to happen. John Toshack took the job when Bobby turned it down and quit after one game.

Instead of rushing into a job Robson took his time in Lisbon and spoke to his lawyer, and was regularly greeted by disgruntled fans who had not wanted to see him leave at a time when he had turned round the club's league fortunes. The players felt exactly the same and threw a farewell dinner for Bobby and Elsie in the resort of Cascais, where they presented him with all manner of gifts.

The happy night morphed into a nightmare morning when a

telephone call from José Mourinho woke him to say that Sergei Cherbakov had crashed his car after he had continued the celebrations late into the night and the news was that, if he survived, he would never walk again. He had jumped a set of traffic lights, been hit side on and was not wearing a seat belt.

Bobby immediately dressed and went to the hospital where a surgeon, recognising him, took him to one side and told him that the player he had signed had broken his spinal cord, was paraplegic and had no hope of making an even partial recovery. Life was put in perspective when Robson was taken to his bedside where the player was awake, aware, feeling totally numb, with no idea as to the extent of his injuries and the ending of his dream of being a top professional footballer.

Sporting Lisbon immediately stopped Cherbakov's salary and it needed the largesse of the former manager and his teammates to have a whip round to keep him going. Sporting arranged a testimonial for him but made little effort to promote the game and raised little money. Later, when Robson was in charge of rivals Porto, he arranged for the player to join the club for dinner before the game against their old club, and when they reached the cup final and beat Sporting in Lisbon, they shared the mutual joy of retribution. The 21-year-old, confined to a wheelchair for life, returned home with his parents at the end of the season.

+++

WITH PLENTY OF TIME ON THEIR HANDS, BOBBY and Elsie returned home to England for Christmas and decided that as they had a lovely house, a monthly pay cheque coming in and a nice standard of living, they would continue to winter in Cascais. In fact, Bobby did better, for he also fulfilled a lifelong wish of watching England play cricket away against the West Indies. The opportunity arose for him to accompany a group of *Daily Telegraph* readers to the Caribbean in February 1994. It was his first ever winter break in a life in football that now extended to 44 years and he spent a month working on his golf in the Algarve and then a month away in the West Indies with Elsie, talking to like-minded people about cricket and football. 'It was,' he remarked, 'better than managing Wales.'

Better still, when he returned to Portugal he was contacted by Porto, who offered him the job of coaching their team. They met within twelve hours of their initial telephone conversation, but not before they promised him that former coach Tomislav Ivić had been properly looked after and was leaving in happier circumstances than he had left Sporting. Robson was offered a two-and-a-half-year contract at considerably more money again.

He spoke to José Mourinho about the deal in confidence, and the young coach soon stoked the fire. He was quick to point out what a big club it was, how good the technical staff were, and how they had a stronger president than Sporting. José also spoke of the plentiful beaches and golf courses in the region, no bad thing in Bobby's eyes. He was bowled over when Robson told him that the club had already agreed he could take Mourinho with him, if he accepted the job. He didn't need the 24 hours thinking time he had asked for and immediately drove north to accept the contract that January day.

Under Ivić the gates had slumped and the football was boring. Robson changed to a more attacking system and found immediate success, with Porto soon developing a pleasing taste for a 5-0 victory. In February they won two league games by that scoreline in succession, and at the end of the March they travelled to Germany and beat Werder Bremen by the same margin in their own backyard. It was a remarkable result given the stage, the Champions League, and earned Robson a new nickname among the fans: 'Bobby Five-O.'

Yet it wasn't long after his arrival that off-field disaster struck in the form of an £800,000 unpaid tax bill by the club. It meant that Porto's Estádio das Antas was closed down and padlocked with iron chains for a time, forcing the squad to train in the car park. It was another rich moment in his never boring life as a manager and one that was, fortunately, soon resolved. Porto continued their charge up the table, pulling in crowds of 35,000 to 40,000, four times the number before he took over. They and Benfica successfully caught Sporting and both ended up ahead of Robson's former side, but the nine-point lead Benfica already had over Porto at the start of Bobby's reign proved too much too overcome, with only two points awarded for a victory. They got close, but two points separated the two teams at the end of the campaign.

In Porto, Robson soon met another bright young footballing mind, and it wasn't long before he was guiding him into the upper echelons of the footballing world as well. This young man was Luís André de Pina Cabral e Villas-Boas, better known simply as André Villas-Boas. André was another, like Mourinho, whose playing career amounted to little and, indeed, he never played professionally at any level. But like his fellow countryman, he also had a deep passion for the game and when he discovered the famous Bobby Robson had moved into the same apartment block in which he was living, he was overjoyed.

Never a shy boy, he decided he must inform the new Porto manager about a player, Domingos Paciência, who he felt was wrongly being ignored, and he left a note in the Robson post box explaining his hypothesis. He had no problem with his English as his grandmother, Margaret Kendall, whose mother moved from Cheadle to start a wine business in Portugal, taught him to speak the language fluently from childhood.

Unaware that this 'expert' was just 16 years of age, Robson invited Villas-Boas to join training next day and there asked him to write a report backing up his theory. A complete dossier followed almost by return, complete with statistics and diagrams, and certainly enough for the Porto manager to offer him some work alongside the youth team staff.

Villas-Boas later said that Robson was decisive in his career, allowing him to talk seriously about tactics and inviting him to training sessions despite his age. His experiences and his admiration of Mourinho's knowledge had made Robson realise that a star-studded career as a professional was not crucial for an enthusiast to become a top coach.

Robson arranged for the Villas-Boas to take his UEFA C coaching licence in Scotland – he was a year too young to have gone to Lilleshall – and also to watch and study Ipswich and their training methods.

He proved to be a natural and neither age nor his lack of professional experience could halt his climb up the coaching ladder. He earned his C licence at 17; his B licence at 18 and his A licence at 19, before going on to pick up his UEFA Pro Licence. By the age of 21, he was technical director to the British Virgin Islands, although he didn't tell the team he coached how young he was until his last day before leaving the position. Not only was he proving to be a damned good coach, he was also a quick learner, attentive and polite.

It was because of Robson's further influence that Villas-Boas returned to his hometown club of Porto and by the time José Mourinho returned as manager in 2002, he was Under-19 coach. Mourinho had remembered how astute he was, and therefore asked him to create an Opponent Observation Department, compiling information on Porto's rivals. His work was attentive in the extreme and he followed his new boss to Chelsea and Inter Milan, where they won trophy after trophy, although Mourinho's decision to never appoint him officially as his number two eventually led to their break up.

Villa-Boas went on to have a successful managerial career, but never forgot what Bobby Robson had done for him. 'I see myself more in the image of Bobby Robson than José Mourinho. Like him I have an

English heritage, I've got a big nose and I like red wine,' he joked in a later interview.

Robson for his part was incredibly proud of what both of them went on to achieve, rather like a headmaster with two successful pupils.

That was all in the future. Back at the end of the 1993/94 campaign, Robson had the opportunity to write the perfect script as his new side met his old side in the Portuguese cup final. After a 0-0 draw in the first game, they won the replay 2-1 to give the manager one of his most pleasurable moments in his long career in the game.

It was even better a year later when Bobby and his attacking team returned to Lisbon to play Sporting in a game which decided the title at the beginning of May. They won 1-0, which meant Sporting could not catch them, and the players celebrated by throwing their manager in the air to the cheers of not only the away fans but the home fans as well, who were still only too aware of how he had been thoroughly shafted by their president.

There was still a little black cloud which followed Robson around, and tragedy struck again in August of 1994 when local boy Rui Filipe tragically died in a car crash after going out for dinner with his family. Filipe had been academy graduate at the club and had re-signed in 1991 after spells at Espinho and Gil Vicente. He had become an important part of Robson's midfield, scoring in the opening league game of the season, while he also had started and been sent off in the 1-1 draw with Benfica in the first leg of the Portuguese Super Cup just four days before his death.

It was after his death that the president, anxious to lift a depressed club, came to Robson with a contract extension and another considerable raise in his salary. Bobby agreed, but only if the president in turn would agree to allow him to walk away if a another major job came up. They shook hands on it in front of the ever-present José Mourinho. Robson, as honest and trustworthy as the day was long, didn't bother to ask for it in writing and was to regret that decision not long afterwards when one of his dream clubs came knocking on his door.

This time David Dein was not asking on behalf of another club but for his own, Arsenal. It was May 1995 and George Graham had left Highbury under a cloud three months earlier following a bung scandal. Only Newcastle United and perhaps Ipswich were held dearer to him, for he always thought that Arsenal were the quintessential English club and he had always dreamed of coaching or managing them.

They didn't just offer him one job but the choice of two – he could decide to be either coach or technical director. Bobby told him about the deal he had with the president and the two promptly arranged a meeting in Portugal to discuss the deal. Dein assumed that Bobby would like the senior job, and even asked him who he would suggest as coach. That one was easy. He named himself. He didn't want to sit in an office, he wanted to be amongst the players doing what he had always done.

Dein agreed, and the next meeting was in London, where Robson met the rest of the board and was convinced that this was his destiny. He already knew Chairman Peter Hill-Wood and the knowledgeable managing director Ken Friar, while he took an instant liking to the money man Danny Fiszman and the Carr brothers, although his mind was made up even before they met together and, indeed, before he knew what salary he was being offered. Football transcended the money.

That night he and I met up to attend a pre-arranged dinner at the English branch of the Porto Supporters Club in London and Bobby couldn't wait to tell me he had agreed to be the new manager of Arsenal, even giving me the go ahead to write the story for the back page of the *Sunday Mirror*. I have rarely seen him so excited and animated, though he couldn't tell any of the Porto supporters around him, who were so delighted to have him at their own club. After all, they had arranged a special themed dinner for him that night.

All that was left was for Bobby to confirm his deal with Jorge Nuno Pinto da Costa, and once he had, to sign the contract which was being prepared. He would never have dreamed of signing the contract first, despite his verbal agreement. But when he returned to Porto it was to find a message from his president asking him to meet in Switzerland the next day at the Swiss Cup Final. They watched the game and Bobby was able to advise him that the players he was watching were not good enough to improve Porto and to save his money.

He waited until after the game to reveal his news and, subject to their earlier agreement, was exercising his right to leave. Da Costa and his wife Philomena fell silent. It was Philomena who was doing the translating, telling him that her husband could not possibly let him go and was relying on him taking the club into the European Champions League. It would be a terrible blow to the club, the supporters and the players if he left.

Bobby reminded him of their conversation and handshake when he signed the new contract, but Da Costa responded that he could only remember the conversation vaguely and, anyway, would not give his permission for Bobby to leave, whatever offer he had received. It left Robson with the option of walking out on his contract with Porto to join Arsenal or staying, and neither he nor Dein were prepared to tarnish the move. Instead he said he would do what he could, but when Robson spoke again to Da Costa and asked him if a compensation deal from Arsenal would change his mind, the president dug his heels in and told him to get on with his job at Porto.

It was natural that after the George Graham scandal, Arsenal would want and need the deal to be pristine so they would not be accused of poaching someone else's coach. After a couple of nights tossing and turning in bed he came up with the only solution he could. He would stay and do his best for Porto while Arsenal appointed Bruce Rioch in his stead. He held no grudges as Da Costa rewarded him with another increase to compensate for his forgetful mind and then backed Robson fully and comprehensively when, just three months later, he was diagnosed with cancer, a malignant melanoma which needed instant action.

He was back in the saddle by November, just six weeks after the operation, with the scars on his face healing but still showing. He didn't care as he threw himself back into the task of retaining the title, backed by the players who were delighted to see his quick return. José Mourinho, rapidly learning at the feet of the master, had taken charge in the intervening period with coach Enancio and returned Porto to his boss in good shape, though Robson would be without the services of international goalkeeper Vitor Baía for a time, who had been suspended by the club for two months for a punch up at the training ground.

But lack of success in Europe continued to dog Robson despite finishing top again, 11 points ahead of Benfica and 17 ahead of Sporting. Defeat to Sporting in the Cup semi-final was a disappointment offset by their return to the Champions League for another next season. He had given the president the extra year he had asked for, and when Barcelona called in the spring to offer him the job for the third time he told him he was leaving. Da Costa didn't like it and withheld around a quarter of a million pounds in salary and bonuses, despite Robson having the documents which proved the debt was owed.

There was a distinct lack of honesty and integrity in Portuguese football at the time, a fact confirmed when, once more, he received another tax bill for £110,000, Porto having pulled the same stunt as Sporting Lisbon.

17

*'I had this perfect dream; this dream was me
and you; I want the entire world to see; a miracle
sensation; now my dream is slowly coming true.'*
Barcelona by Freddie Mercury and Montserrat Caballé

BOBBY ROBSON HAD ALWAYS DREAMT OF MANAGING
Barcelona, the biggest club in the world as far as he was concerned.
Twice he was forced through circumstances to turn them down, but
this time, no matter what Porto or their owners had to say, that was
not going to be the case. It meant he plunged himself into a political
battle with Porto he did not deserve and could not win, while he also
ignored warnings from his surgeons that he should not put himself
under the undue pressure the job would bring with his lingering
cancer problems.

He signed a spurious two-year contract with the Barcelona board,
who knew full well that his replacement had already been lined up

and would be in place within the year, whatever Bobby did with the Catalan team – and he did more than should have ever been expected, giving them their second best season in a hundred years in terms of trophies won. He won the Spanish Cup, the Spanish Super Cup and the European Cup Winners' Cup and was subsequently voted European Manager of the Year.

He always wondered what would have happened had he accepted the job when it was first offered. In those days he was still at Ipswich and during that golden spell they twice drew the Catalan side in European competition. The first time was in the 1977/78 UEFA Cup, when the Tractor Boys thumped a surprised Barça 3-0 at Portman Road, losing the second leg at Camp Nou by the same score before going out on penalties. Fifteen months later they were paired together again, this time in the Cup Winners' Cup, and this time Robson's side lost out on away goals after a 2-1 win at home and a 1-0 reverse away.

He built a strong rapport with both the president Josep Lluís Núñez and the man behind the throne, Joan Gaspart, both of whom were impressed with his success against the odds at Ipswich. Gaspart had trained as a hotelier at the Connaught in London and knew his English football as well as the next man. In 1980/81 it was Gaspart who telephoned Robson personally to offer him the job he dreamed of taking some time in his life. Despite his love affair with Ipswich, he was ready to say yes and pack his bags, but he was in the middle of a ten-year contract and John Cobbold, not as daft as some might have believed, said he would agree for the payment of suitable compensation. Barcelona, as much as they wanted the Englishman, believed at the time that they were too big a club to pay a fee for hiring their coach and the deal collapsed.

Robson thought Ipswich should have released him for all he had done for the club, but he could also see it from their perspective and carried on doing his job as though nothing had happened, never once falling out with his chairman.

Gaspart and Robson maintained their contact, however, and he would often ask Robson's opinion about all matters football, even asking for his thoughts on players they were planning to sign. In 1984 he knocked on the door again when Robson was having all sorts of trouble in his tempestuous role of England manager. He was, in fact, at the team hotel in Troon about to take the players out training as they prepared for the usual war against Scotland at Hampden Park. Gaspart told him they needed someone straight away and they decided he was the man they wanted, top of their list of one.

This time he didn't even consider it because managing England was his pinnacle, above any club side, not matter how glamorous or how rich. Gaspart was even more respectful than he had been before when the man he wanted responded with an unequivocal no.

To give a glimpse of Bobby Robson's character, he never once used these offers from other clubs to boost his salary, not even mentioning it to his employers in most cases. When he took the call in Scotland, there were journalists standing a few yards away, but he gave away nothing, keeping this sensational offer to himself.

It shows the stature Barcelona held Robson in, for when he turned them down they asked him who he would recommend, and he told them about Terry Venables – a young, bright, forward-thinking English coach who was going to go a long way in the game. He, said Robson, would be the perfect choice.

Gaspart, in truth, had never heard of Venables, but rather than dismissing his friend's opinion he made further enquiries. He liked what he heard and soon appointed Venables to the role, who in turn led Barcelona to the league title in 1985 and to the European Cup Final in 1986. Barcelona were more than grateful and let Bobby know it, regularly repeating that they would like him in charge of Barcelona one day in the not too distant future.

When he did eventually agree to join them, the entire deal was totally Machiavellian. Barcelona wheeled and dealed to get rid of their revered manager Johan Cruyff, and Robson found himself in a whirl of controversy over when he was first approached – was it March or April? It was significant as Cruyff had supposedly not been under any pressure in March, but a month later was suddenly on his way out.

It was typical of the dealings Barça got themselves involved in as they desperately tried to protect their image which, at the time, was about as shaky as their manager's future. Of all the times Robson could and should have taken the manager/coach title at Barcelona, this was certainly the worst, for he was to replace the most influential man in the club's history: Johan Cruyff, the man almost single-handedly responsible for Barcelona's modern identity.

A stunning and innovative attacking midfielder who brought Total Football to the world with Ajax, Barcelona and the Netherlands, Cruyff had also proved a revelation as a coach, first with Ajax and then Barcelona, where he had famously created the Dream Team, featuring Romário – who Robson had nurtured at PSV – Michael Laudrup and Hristo Stoichkov, among many others.

As a player he won the Ballon D'Or three times, and also won the Golden Ball as player of the tournament when Holland finished as runners-up to West Germany in the 1974 World Cup. While he won everything an individual could in a team game (apart from on the international stage), he was also an inspirational leader, taking the Netherlands from obscurity and Ajax to eight league titles, three European Cups and the Intercontinental Cup. After a world record transfer to Barça he had won La Liga in his first season, a year when he was also named European Footballer of the Year.

He would go on to become the club's most significant coach, influencing the likes of Sir Alex Ferguson, Arsené Wenger, Pep Guardiola and Frank Rijkaard, while clubs from far and wide developed youth academies based on his philosophies and his teachings.

He turned Barca from a near bankrupt shadow of a side into a team that dominated their rivals Real Madrid, and gave the entire club from first team down to the kids in the youth team an identity and a meaning.

However, in his final two years he failed to win a trophy and had fallen out with Núñez. Cruyff's popularity with the fans did not wane in the slightest, though, and that was the situation Robson walked into, acting as a bridge between the Dutch giant's departure and Louis van Gaal's arrival. He had grasped the real dirty end of the stick.

The shadow of Cruyff was always there, and in truth it was far more than that – Cruyff still attended the Camp Nou for games while his son Jordi, a Catalan name, was in the Barcelona squad. Robson had to get all of this detritus out of his mind to concentrate on taking Barça back to the top, while his employers would be happy just for him to steady the ship and leave the club in good shape for their new man.

Bobby Robson had been in tough spots before and no one was going to deny him this great opportunity to manage the club he had admired and dreamed of managing all of his football life.

He could always spot talent on or off the pitch and he had seen something in José Mourinho which excited him in Portugal, and he told Gaspart he would be taking the young Portuguese lad with him. It was agreed and both of them went in to see Porto's president to tell him the news. He told the perplexed president that he was going because of the promise he had made and broken and because of the club defaulting on his payments.

This time Da Costa had stymied himself because there was a rule in Portuguese football stating that if a player or coach had not been paid for three months, they were entitled to leave the club for no fee. Some of the money his manager was due dated way back to the start of the season. Robson was as sympathetic as he could be, saying that everything Da Costa did was for the club, and that included trying to keep him, but everything at Porto seemed to be spiralling out of control.

Players were also owed their bonuses and in the end he had to sell one of his greatest assets, the Brazilian Emerson, to Middlesbrough for almost £4 million, just to pay off the players before they too walked out.

In a little over two years Robson had won two Super Cups, two league titles and the Portuguese Cup, as well as taking them to the semi-finals of the Champions League. He brought the crowds and the good times back to a club that was perishing. It was all taking its toll on Robson, who was in remission from his cancer. He knew that whatever happened at Barcelona, they would definitely pay everyone's wages, bonuses and their taxes on time and in full.

What he wasn't aware of was the politicking going on behind closed doors at the club he had always respected. The war had divided the club in half with those who still supported Núñez, who was trying to hold onto his presidency – which was voted on by the members – and those who were firmly on the side of the ever popular, God-like figure of Cruyff. Those who belonged in the latter category would never accept Robson in his place. He was quickly rubbished by those in the media who supported the Dutchman, and so had a point to prove.

He did that on plenty of occasions across the 1996/97 campaign, but the day where he showcased all his craft and skill as a manager arrived in March in the second leg of the Copa del Rey quarter-final against Atlético Madrid, as he engineered a comeback that to this day remains one Barcelona's greatest. Atlético were the somewhat cocky reigning champions of La Liga and had taken a three-goal lead at the Camp Nou after the first leg finished 2-2.

The Barcelona fans had thought that draw in Madrid a good result, but by half-time they had their white handkerchiefs in their hands, waving them above their heads in disdain at their team and its manager. Serbian midfielder Milinko Pantić had scored an unanswered hat-trick and Barcelona were on their way out. A subway strike had kept the crowd down to a miserly 80,000, but it sounded like more as they screamed for the manager's blood.

Robson's response was to take off superstar defenders, skipper Gheorge Popescu of Romania and French captain Laurent Blanc, five minutes before the break. In their place he sent on attackers Hristo Stoichkov and Juan Antonio Pizzi to further the anger of the Barca faithful. But it was his half time team talk which changed the match and indeed history. It must have had the watching Louis van Gaal wondering how he was going to top this as he watched from his seat in the stand.

Robson's key was Ronaldo, who responded to his boss with two goals early in the second half before Pantić scored his fourth. Back came the Catalan Kings, with Figo hitting a screamer from the edge of the box in the 67th minute and Ronaldo completing his hat-trick five minutes later to put the teams level.

With less than ten minutes to play Pizzi scored the fifth and Robson, keeping his head as all around him lost theirs, sent on Miguel Ángel Nadal for hero Figo in the dying minutes to keep Atlético at arm's length.

For all Robson did for Barcelona in that one season, restoring their pride and refilling their trophy cabinet, this was the result that endeared him to the Barcelona hearts – even the sniffy *Mundo Deportivo*, who the next day described it as 'the most vibrant, emotional and spectacular match of recent years'.

If he had not been such a trusting soul Bobby would have known there were troubles ahead, as his lawyer had pointed out that there was a codicil in his contract which stated that after twelve months the club could move him from his position as coach to a job upstairs. He had known all along that if he failed he would be on his way out anyway, but thought that if he was successful they would surely keep him. He should have read Keir Radnedge, the well-versed *World Soccer* writer, who actually spelled out in print that Louis van Gaal was to come in and that Robson was to be moved to technical director, which is exactly what happened in the end despite Robson's huge success on the playing side.

Bobby loved the bustling, busy city of Barcelona, loved the people and loved his little retreat on the Mediterranean coast at Sitges. He was delighted to manage a proud club with its magnificent 120,000 capacity stadium and its 'Mini Estadi' of 25,000 next door, used by the B and Junior teams.

He always said it was more like managing an international team than a club side, particularly when they played their great rivals Real Madrid at the Bernabéu. When they travelled thousands would turn up at the airport to watch them leave and thousands more would be on duty when they landed at the other end. He related the time when they played Real Sociedad in San Sebastián and couldn't get to the hotel doors because there were 3,000 people outside waiting to catch a glimpse of the superstars, especially Ronaldo, the other great Brazilian signing from PSV. There were another 5,000 waiting to watch them train in Majorca.

Bobby loved it but was always hounded by the shadow of Cruyff and his supporters. It also meant Robson had to pick up the tactical pieces. Cruyff had naturally played the Ajax way, and had instilled quick, one-touch football into his players. It was magic to watch and also incredibly successful, with Barcelona winning trophies for six years until they eventually ran out of steam. Cruyff won his first trophy in the 1989/90 season, a Copa del Rey triumph, and then went on to win four straight league titles. After that fourth successive league crown they were beaten 4-0 in the European Cup final by Fabio

Capello's rampant AC Milan side, signalling the beginning of the end, and no trophies were won under his watch from that point on.

Barcelona were in turmoil and the only oasis was the green field in the middle of the imposing concrete towers of Camp Nou. That was certainly where Bobby concentrated his attentions as he let the politics fly over his head, while everyone else was taking sides on who should be the next president, never mind the next manager. Núñez was not going to give it up easily.

If anyone had bothered to notice, the 1996/97 season was going rather well with Robson at the helm, with the club enjoying its best start for 33 years. It was not until November they lost their first match when they were beaten by Athletic Bilbao in a packed San Mamés Stadium, just two matches short of the record set by his recommendation Terry Venables. Still the factions fought.

By late January the point should have been made when they put six past Rayo Vallecano at the Camp Nou to take their goals tally for the season to sixty, twenty more than at the same time the previous season and with seven points more. They were five to the good at half time in front of 85,000 fans, but the next day the headline on the local paper read: 'Barcelona wins 6-0 – but don't play any football.' All the time Johan Cruyff was at the back of the stand giving out soundbites to anyone who wanted them.

To be fair he was not hard on Bobby, and Bobby respected him for that. In truth Robson was full of admiration for the man, putting him up there with Pelé, Platini and Maradona as one of the great players of his generation. He also acknowledged him as one of the outstanding, innovative coaches and refused to criticise him in any way.

However, he would have appreciated it if Cruyff was not always there in the background when he was trying to run a football team. Cruyff had a good excuse, though – not only was he there to watch a team he loved, but he was also there to watch his son, who he loved even more.

Jordi desperately wanted to stay at the club, but with his dad in the stands it was an untenable situation as far as Robson was concerned. The only solution was a move and Robson managed to find him a place at another of the great clubs, Manchester United.

In summer 1996 Robson had also brought in Ronaldo from PSV for a world record fee of $19.5million to give the fans someone else to adore, and he was convinced as he could be that they were heading in the right direction, if only he had the help he needed. The pitch was a quagmire, so bad that they had to move out and briefly play at the nearby Olympic Stadium in Montjuïc. The recently relaid pitch there was not much better, and when the players ran and turned, huge sods of turf would be uprooted, littering the pitch and affecting their pass and run style.

At least they had Ronaldo, who was fast developing into another Brazilian icon, an absolute natural goalscorer who popped in 42 goals in 46 Eredivisie games and followed it up with 34 in 37 for Barcelona in La Liga.

Bobby still had his battles with some of the journalists from *AS* and *Sport* but was treated with respect by the national paper *Marca*. Football coverage in Spain had been completely over the top for many years and it took a long time for the English national newspapers to catch up, starting with a newspaper I was asked to launch as its editor-in-chief. It was called *Sport First*, and we spent around two years designing and redesigning it from a couple of different offices, but there were always delays and financial problems. I had spent a lot of time being interviewed by newspapers, magazines, radio and television, explaining the vision of a British version of the famous French sports paper *L'Equipe*, and gave so much away that virtually every national newspaper eventually produced a sports supplement and the dream was withered, if not quite dead.

Bobby, of course, was very supportive, loving the idea of a serious sports newspaper rather than the blatant, in your face coverage of the tabloid media at home and even publicly took a named role in the venture. He did not suffer the worst excesses of the Spanish newsprint by dint of the fact that he could not read them, although Mourinho, who was to understand his boss's problems when he moved to England, would occasionally translate when he thought it necessary.

Mourinho was also useful at press conferences, which were held three times a week and conducted by press officer Miguel Terres, who Robson also found to be a huge help. Whereas in England managers had to have their arms twisted to talk about upcoming opposition, never mind a club who weren't in their immediate sights, in Spain, they would regularly fire questions about Real Madrid or the controversial president of Atlético Madrid, Jesús Gil.

Gil, who sacked his coaches as regularly as taking wine with his dinner, was in charge for the famous fight back game after which Bobby, for once in his life, was smug and told the reporters to go away and enjoy what they had just seen. But their response outdid even the *Sun* and the *Mirror* and their worst excesses – they said that Robson had lost the first half and the players had won it for him in the second, infuriating him by claiming it was his stars who had demanded the changes.

Pep Guardiola, who has gone on to even greater things as a manager than he did as a dazzling player, and knows full well these days how to handle the media not only in Spain but Germany and England as well, made a statement saying that people could not blame the coach when they lost and then say it had nothing to do with him when they won, adding that Robson made changes in the way he always did and it was the manager who told the players where to play and what to do and not the other way round. 'It is his job to decide the tactics. It is simply not true that we rode roughshod over his instructions,' he added, 'Robson is in charge, we limit ourselves to playing football.'

For once Robson fought back on the training ground and asked the offending journalists to produce the players who had given them the quotes. The only name they could come up with was Stoichkov, who laughed in their faces and denied the allegations totally. They didn't have another name to offer.

The other suggestion from the press desks was that the team who had won the game in the second half should have been the team Robson selected every game. He picked it almost out of devilment in the next league game, and they struggled to beat Logroñés 1-0. He made his point even at the risk of losing a game in a bid to shut up the detractors and let them get on with their season. Robson was deeply hurt by the comments after the Atlético win and while he fell out with the news reporters in England, these were football writers who he felt he should be able to trust. He had discovered he could not.

One thing he did appreciate in Holland, Portugal and Spain was the lack of 'pub' culture among his squad, and even after a big win there were no wild celebrations, with the players preferring mineral water to pints. If he knew half the truth about some of his English players, he would have had a fit. In 1996, not long after Robson's move to Arsenal fell through, club captain Tony Adams attended his first Alcoholics Anonymous meeting. Though he ended up suffering more than others, Adams was far from alone – many of the stars of that era at Arsenal spent their afternoons after training binging in pubs and hotels until the arrival of Arsène Wenger.

The one player Robson would hold up as thoroughly professional was Pep Guardiola, who played in 53 of the 58 games in the 1996/97 season. He showed the traits that were to lead him into such an astral coaching career, possessing a powerful personality and an ability to influence players. He was helped in keeping the dressing room happy by Guillermo Amor, Sergi, Figo and even the supposedly fiery Stoichkov, who were all outspoken but backed their manager Robson. It was hardly surprising given they lost only eight of 58 in all competitions that season.

Still, there were growing stories about the soon to arrive Louis van Gaal, aided and abetted by the man himself when he made comments on Dutch television early in February indicating that he was heading to the Catalan capital. Robson assumed it would die a natural death as they made a strong bid to add the league title to the two cups they had already won. It was, he said, never mentioned in his regular meetings with Gaspart and Núñez.

It was only later in the season when Van Gaal announced that he would be leaving Ajax to join Barcelona that Robson took it up with his bosses, and when he did they told him to carry on – he had another year on his contract – but it soon became obvious that the clause in this contract was going to be taken up to 'promote' Bobby out of the coaches' job, and what is more the contract further stipulated that if he were to walk out he would owe them double what they were paying him, costing him in the region of £2 million. The thrill and privilege of managing such a great club and bringing them a basket full of trophies was dissipating fast, to such an extent that he had his contract, half in Spanish and half in English, carefully translated, notarised and stamped by lawyers.

With that all done, he returned to concentrate on winning as many matches and trophies as he could. Despite the uncertainty Barcelona's form did not dip, and the players showed what they thought of him on his birthday, opening a rare bottle of champagne and unfurling a banner which read: 'Happy Birthday dear Mister,' in English. This was the very day *AS* had forecast that Robson would be sacked by the club.

There was just one really bad day in the run in for the title when Barça were leading Valladolid 1-0, while rivals Real Madrid were losing by two goals at Bilbao. If those scores had remained Barça would have been favourites to sweep the board, but in the second half they slumped to a shock 3-1 defeat while Real came back to win 4-2. What really clinched the title for Real was when Barça inexplicably collapsed to already relegated Hercules, losing 2-1, which meant Real went ahead by two points with just two games left to play. Barça had won more games and had scored 17 more goals than their rivals. It was not enough.

But as well as the two domestic cups Barca went on to triumph in Europe, winning the now defunct European Cup Winners' Cup, beating Paris Saint-Germain in the final in Rotterdam in May, a Ronaldo penalty enough to clinch victory. They had beaten AEK Larnaca, Red Star Belgrade, AIK of Sweden and Fiorentina on the way to the final. The Italian fans had gone berserk in Florence following Barcelona's 2-0 second leg win – they had fully expected to progress after holding Robson's men to a 1-1 draw in front of a packed house in the Camp Nou, and when they didn't they began hurling missiles on to the pitch and at players. Iván de la Peña was hit on the head and needed medical treatment and the reaction to defeat was so bad that UEFA hit Fiorentina with a two-match ban.

The latest cup success made many view Robson in a different light, though the change of heart was somewhat belated. Supportive newspaper *La Vanguardia* said that Robson deserved nothing but praise after being the victim of fierce, unjustified and indiscriminate criticism, while even *Sport* admitted that Robson has set high standards for the incoming Van Gaal and that it was a triumph for a man who had never lost faith with himself. Three trophies was not a bad return for a first season in Spain.

The pusillanimous Barcelona board waited until the end of the season before finally coming clean and telling Robson officially that his time was up and Louis van Gaal would, as expected, be the new boss. Bobby was to take the new role of Technical Director.

Robson believed right up until that meeting that he would be kept on after his successful season and that it would be the Dutchman who would be asked to wait in the wings for another campaign. It was smart business bringing in a talented coach sixteen years Robson's junior while honouring the Englishman's large contract for what Robson himself described as a sabbatical year, travelling around the world watching top players who may or may not be wanted by Van Gaal.

Belatedly Barcelona were trying to make it right for the man they had successfully duped, the man who had returned them not only three cups but a more than honourable runners-up finish in the league, so close to their great rivals. For all of Cruyff's success, Robson had added ten points to Barcelona's final league tally from the season before. Perhaps embarrassed by their decision, they informed him that if the right offer came along during that second year they would not only release him but would even be prepared to make up his salary if the new club's wages fell short.

Typically, Robson kept his distance from the new man and made sure he did not rock the boat. In truth he loved his year in the sun, and his main regret was not being able to guide the team in the Champions League.

The footnote to this chapter is that Louis van Gaal took Bobby's team to two La Liga titles and the Copa del Rey, but he also discovered a sample of what his predecessor faced. Van Gaal was constantly at loggerheads with the local media and even his own players at times, notably the Brazilian Rivaldo, who he wanted to play on the left-wing instead of through the middle. He eventually left the Catalan side on 20 May 2000, uttering the immortal words: 'Amigos de la pensa. Yo me voy. Felicidades,' translating as, 'Friends of the press. I am leaving. Congratulations.' Bobby sent me a copy of his quote without further comment.

Whilst at Barcelona Bobby acknowledged he had played his part in the dramatic increase in transfer fees. For a man who treated Ipswich Town's money like his own and who never displayed any overt greed in his own rewards, it seemed totally out of character when he pushed through the transfer of the Brazilian Ronaldo.

Having allowed Jordi Cruyff to go to Manchester United, Barça needed a replacement and Robson made a strong case for the Brazilian prodigy. Barcelona made their offers and reached $17 million dollars before impatiently asking the Dutch club what it would take for them to change their minds. They came back with the then stunning figure of $20 million dollars, a blatant attempt to frighten the Catalan club away.

Núñez was horrified but signing Ronaldo had become something of a badge of honour and it was left to lie for a few days, with no one else likely to come in and pay the cash for a 20-year-old who had been out injured for three months. Then Barca produced the cheque for the full amount – $19.5 million – and the Dutch side could do little after stating their price – they had to let the player go.

Robson was explicit about the kid he had watched grow up. He was, said this excellent judge of footballing talent, the best player in the world, a statement agreed by any number of clubs as he moved for ever increasing fees to Inter Milan, Real Madrid and AC Milan, who spent the money knowing they were buying goals.

He knew he needed a top striker if Barça were to challenge for the top honours and he whittled his shortlist down to Alan Shearer and Ronaldo, eventually identifying the Brazilian as the player of his choice and informing Núñez of his wishes.

He was so right. Ronaldo, despite his youth and immaturity, scored 47 goals in all competitions, including 34 in the league and five in the successful European campaign. Barcelona's hesitation was not just over the inflated fee but the word from the Netherlands that he was a difficult boy to handle. That was no longer in Bobby Robson's remit as a coach and his only dealings with him were on the pitch and the training ground, and the most trouble he caused his 'Meester' was his reluctance to leave the training pitch begging: 'Please Meester, just a little longer, just a few more shots.'

He was always his manager's sunshine boy from the beaches of Brazil, a player who learned his trade – and his physical strength and mental toughness – on the streets and the waste grounds of Bento Ribeiro, a poor suburb of Rio de Janeiro. His family did not even have the money for his bus fare for a trial at Flamengo who, to their eternal regret, refused to buy his ticket for him. Their problem, not his.

He wasn't long at Second Division São Cristóvão before superstar Jairzinho recommended him to Cruzeiro of Belo Horizonte, where he scored virtually at a rate of a goal a game, attracting a flock of European clubs to Brazil all keen on signing him. PSV won the battle and watched him score thirty league goals in his first season despite a debilitating knee injury, which kept him sidelined for a long while.

While PSV kept upping the ante, Robson's need became more urgent. Ray Harford had told him that he could keep his money because Shearer was staying at Blackburn Rovers. While keeping an eye on the Ronaldo situation, Robson looked at João Pinto at Benfica; Alen Bokšić at Lazio; Argentinean Gabriel Batistuta and even studied the option of bringing back the crowd favourite Romário, but it eventually always came back to Ronaldo.

The offers kept on going up and up and up, and it was Gaspart who eventually persuaded Núñez to pay PSV's final asking price, saying that it was no use them dying and leaving the money for someone else to squander, better to squander it themselves.

Robson always maintained he was a tremendous lad to work with and a very fine player who grafted hard to improve his game, always with a smile on his face. If he was trouble, it was with the men in the shadows who controlled his career and his moves, with one of his agents commenting that the whole world deserved to see him play, without mentioning the whole world would also have to fill the agent's account with every transfer move he made.

Bobby was so enamoured with him that he not only described him as the best player he had ever coached but also put him in the same bracket as the best ever, Pelé.

Robson believed Barça had signed him on an eight-year contract, but as the goals went in and his fame grew, and clubs every bit as big as the Catalans cast covetous eyes on him, they decided to change his contract to protect their investment, as they were allowed to do. The release clause in the contract was upped from $20 million to £20 million and when this didn't put off the likes of Manchester United and Inter Milan, they upped it even further, taking Ronaldo's salary past a million pounds, after taxes, and then doubled the release clause to guarantee a transfer fee of £40 million.

They might have kept him – although that was unlikely as one of his agents, Giovanni Branchini, had already started negotiations with Inter Milan – until the Spanish Government decided they didn't like the tax percentages the top players were paying because of their lowly taxed image rights. The barriers were brought down and Barça found themselves having to find more and more money for the young player, even going to sponsors for financial assistance.

It was a mess, with the three agents demanding more to sell off their rights and even when he went to Inter there were massive complications as Barcelona turned Robson's $20million investment into £20 million, plus an extra $2million awarded to them by FIFA, who had been called in to arbitrate.

Bobby's only problem with the player at this time was the number of trips he would make back home to Brazil, not just to play for his country but for other things like buying an island off the coast. It still tickled him all the while, and he commented that the last time he went home he bought himself a new tie. His away day trips had an effect in the end, and although he scored the winner against PSG in the Cup Winners' Cup final in Rotterdam, he missed the Spanish Cup final and, more importantly, the loss to Hercules, where his presence could have made that critical difference.

Ronaldo was never moody with Robson and always showed him the greatest respect, admitting that he wanted to stay but his agents wanted to make money. His job, sadly, was to play football where they told him.

18

'As a trainer without doubt Robson is one of the greatest in the world,'
Ronaldo, who played under Bobby at both PSV and Barcelona, after
Robson had been named European Manager of the Year for 1996/97.

WITH THE BRITISH PRESS STILL GAGGING ON EVERY
hint, rumour and gossip surrounding a manager who had been
elevated to the world of superstars, there was never any shortage of
the problems he faced coaching – not managing – such a high-profile
club as Barcelona. Yet throughout it all he remained content, enjoying
the victories on the pitch and the relatively tranquil life in Sitges off it.

Needless to say, other clubs keen to lift their profile had him on their
most wanted list, including his hometown club of Newcastle United,
who he had supported as a kid growing up in County Durham.

It was 7 January 1997 when he received a telephone call, completely
out of the blue, from Toon's chief executive Freddie Fletcher. It was

a total surprise as there had been no whispers anywhere that current Newcastle incumbent Kevin Keegan was anything but delirious with his job back at St. James' Park.

Bobby, like all Newcastle United fans, was thrilled at the brand of football the former England captain had introduced and the way they were pursuing honours in front of sell-out crowds for every home match.

Robson was, to put it politely, gobsmacked, when Fletcher told him that Keegan was wanting out of Newcastle and they wanted him as a replacement. He was just six months into a massive two-year contract with Barça. At that moment Robson yearned for home, back to the club where his father Philip had introduced him to the beautiful game.

On the other hand, he had waited a long time to get the job at Barcelona and now he had it he was expecting to win major trophies in that first season. He didn't mention the clause in the contract which would have meant any club poaching him would have to pay back double his salary. There was also the morality of it all, with Robson always strongly on the side of honouring contracts, even though he had been let down so often on that very subject and was about to be let down again.

But this time he didn't say no and within a few days of the telephone call, he was meeting with Fletcher, Sir John Hall's son Douglas, a director, and Mark Corbridge, the man from the city, who was looking after Newcastle's stock market flotation. After all, he thought, he was only going to listen to what they had to say.

They arrived at their designated meeting place, a hotel in the middle of Barcelona, and immediately offered him a five-year contract with a two-year option. The money was more or less the same as at Camp Nou and to back up their bid and confirm the details, the club owner Sir John Hall himself turned up the next day. It was through his instigation that the deal was offered.

With the irony only football can offer, Kevin Keegan departed Newcastle as forecast and five days later Barcelona lost to bottom club Hercules, a result which cost them their place at the top of La Liga and eventually the title. It was probably not the best time for Robson to lay out his cards in front of Gaspart and Núñez, after being jeered off the field by white handkerchief waving Barca fans, but instead of saying on you go, they told him he was contracted and didn't expect him to leave.

He told me that had he known exactly what lay in wait around the corner, he would have snapped the hand off for the offer to return home as he felt he had been well and truly conned.

Newcastle were not the first nor the last to make a move for the man who was leading Barça to multiple honours. Everton, desperate to regain their toehold on top of English football's greased ladder, came in for him for a third time. He had actually shaken hands on a deal with the Toffees when he was still at Ipswich in January 1977 and travelled to Merseyside to meet the president Sir John Moores and chairman Philip Carter. They agreed a ten-year deal which would have made him the highest paid manager in the country and what was more Sir John Moores had presented him with a rather large cheque there and then – worth more than his house and several times more than his Ipswich salary – as a gesture of goodwill and intent.

He asked for 24 hours to tell his chairman John Cobbold at Portman Road and to talk to Elsie, who described it as the best day's work of his life. But he ripped up the cheque and turned down the job the very next morning when he opened the *Daily Express* and read the banner headlines: 'Robson goes to Everton.' He felt he couldn't work for a club who had let him down on the very first day, for the story could have come from nowhere else but Goodison Park.

He immediately went around to John Cobbold to apologise, told him the details, showed him the cheque and ripped it up and threw it on the fire in front of him. John was thrilled he still had the manager he wanted and, according to Bobby, Elsie thought he was barmy.

Twenty years later Everton had returned with their chairman Peter Johnson, calling Robson to say he had heard things weren't as they should be for him at Barcelona and they were looking to replace Joe Royle, who had just left. Everton did everything properly and visited Robson in Barcelona, discussing the essence of the deal, about how much they were able to spend on new players, the prospect of moving to a new stadium (still waiting) and that they felt he had the perfect gravitas for such an important job.

Salary was never discussed. Robson thought Everton needed a long-term appointment and that there was too much to do and, as much as he admired the club and could see their potential, it was not for him.

The next in line were Celtic via a letter sent to the Camp Nou from their president Fergus McCann at the end of May. It was an unusual approach and contained a job description which was followed up by a visit from former Barça player Steve Archibald, who tried to persuade him. Although he never met face to face with McCann, there were any number of phone calls and Robson himself made calls to friends in Scotland, who all told him what a good job it was. Clearly word went around in typical football fashion and before he knew it he was, according to *The Times*, attending a press conference the very next day when the club would make a formal announcement. This wasn't a red top trying to jump the gun but much respected writer and broadcaster Roddy Forsyth, a man really in the know north of the border, who submitted the copy.

Bobby never mentioned it to Barcelona and they didn't ask him about the headlines in the establishment broadsheet. He turned down the Scottish giants, saying he was enjoying the Barça run-in at the end of his first season, despite the distraction of Louis van Gaal. They kept coming back and he kept putting them off until they eventually appointed Dutchman Wim Jansen instead. Another time and another day and he might well have followed his former Ipswich captain Terry Butcher to Scotland.

Coaching a top club certainly wasn't hurting the Robson reputation. Interest came from Turkey in the shape of the wealthy Beşiktaş, who had tried to get him while he was at Porto, and, to his surprise, from his old club in Portugal, Sporting Lisbon, and their bigger, better off neighbours Benfica, who really stirred not only his interest but his ego as well. To have been able to say he had managed the three top clubs in a country he loved was a serious temptation. The only real comparison was the late and much loved Radi Antic who managed all three top clubs in Madrid.

Their offer came at the end of June 1997 as Robson wrestled with the political infighting and turmoil in the Catalan capital, waiting for Barça to spell out the deal that was on offer to him for the next season, when he would be playing second fiddle to a new coach who had been approached and appointed behind his back. Still, he was on the same salary and was now in a job where he could fly anywhere in the world to identify young talent he could bring to the club. It was the equivalent of being offered a year's sabbatical on a huge income, and he was streetwise enough to know that when he eventually did leave to join a new club he would have huge amounts of information on some of the finest talents available on all four continents.

The least likely destination seemed to be his old club in Lisbon, Sporting. The old regime had been removed and the new man in charge José Roquette, a banker by trade, had invited Bobby to Lisbon while he was at Porto, not to offer him a job, but to sort out the money problems which had left the Englishman short and having to pay his tax bill twice. It was sorted and Bobby was paid what he was owed.

Then, in November 1997, their coach Octávio Machado resigned and Robson immediately became the new target. The Portuguese newspapers jumped the gun and announced he was on his way back and, sure enough, the banker approached him while he was on a visit to England. By the time he returned to Sitges there were newsmen on his doorstep. Soon contact was made and Robson's accountant John Hazell was asked what figures had they in mind. They were written down on a piece of paper, which surprisingly didn't curl up and burn.

However, for a public company the deal was too big and was dropped when Robson refused permission for the two club presidents to speak – clearly they could not compete in terms of his monthly income.

As his final year in Barcelona drew to a close the offers started coming in again, with both Nigeria and Saudi Arabia showing an interest and contacting him with a view to managing their teams in the 1998 World Cup finals in France. Saudi, with their huge budget for wages and preparations, attracted him but friends and contacts put him off taking the Nigeria position, despite the quality of their players.

19

'Bobby made my career what it was. For some reason he stuck with me and I'll be eternally grateful to him for that. My life would have been nowhere near as good without that.'
Gary Lineker, Bobby Robson's go to striker.

BOBBY ROBSON ALWAYS HAD A GOOD EYE FOR A striker: he signed Paul Mariner at Ipswich, made Gary Lineker the focal point of his England team and nurtured the talents of Romário at PSV and Ronaldo at Barcelona. He then did it again when he unexpectedly returned to Eindhoven, more or less as a favour to his old captain Eric Gerets, unearthing a young man from Heerenveen named Ruud van Nistelrooy.

It took everyone by surprise ahead of the 1998/99 season when Robson opted for a return to the club he had led to two Eredivisie titles at the start of the decade. He seemed to have the world of football at his feet, and could have stuck a pin in any European country and found a top club who would have broken the bank to get his name on a contract. The same thing had happened when he had taken the PSV job the first time around in 1990 – he had spent eight years at the helm of one of the biggest international jobs in the world, and a whole host of elite European clubs would have loved his signature.

Upon leaving Barcelona, he had contemplated all sorts of options, even picking up his pension and his bus pass as he had reached the ripe old age of 65. I think it was Elsie who made it clear that that wasn't an option, not terribly impressed with the idea of having him moping about the house all day when it was too wet to play golf.

He also considered watching a few test matches, with South Africa visiting England that summer and the Ashes in Australia the following year. But the passion for the game he loved most burned as fiercely as ever, stoked by the sheer number of offers coming his way. It surely meant he was still rated as a leading coach.

Sir John Hall was amongst the first callers in March 1998, towards the end of his season travelling around the globe on behalf of Barcelona. Newcastle United had been ripped apart by scandal when two of their directors, chairman Freddy Shepherd and Douglas Hall, were forced to resign after making disparaging remarks about their players, fans and the local women. As the team struggled against relegation, the pair allegedly described Newcastle women as 'dogs' and star striker Alan Shearer as 'Mary Poppins'. They even mocked their own fans for the price they paid for replica shirts and regularly jetted off to a Spanish house of ill repute after watching home matches.

The switchboard at BBC Radio Newcastle was deluged with complaints about the pair and more than 1,000 fans demonstrated outside St. James' Park after the team slumped to defeat against the bottom club, Crystal Palace. More than £6 million was wiped off the stock market value of Newcastle United the day after the allegations were published in the now defunct *News of the World*. Sir John told

Robson the board needed a stabilising figure at the club which meant not only a return to England but a return home.

A month earlier, in his new role at Barcelona, he was in Yugoslavia to watch Red Star play Partizan in the Belgrade derby as the season reopened after the mid-winter break, fully expecting to be on his own. Fat chance. He was joined by representatives from Inter Milan, Olympique Marseilles, AS Roma, Valencia, Bayern Munich, Celta Vigo, Oviedo, Ajax and his old mate from PSV, Frank Arnesen. He searched in vain for a compatriot from an English club but not one was to be found.

Bobby was chatting away to the former Spanish star Luis Suárez who, he discovered, was doing the same job as him for Inter Milan. They were waiting for the sell-out 70,000 crowd to make their exit when he spotted Arnesen in another part of the stand, talking to the former Yugoslavia national coach Miljan Miljanić.

By coincidence Robson and Arnesen were staying in the same hotel and when they returned after the game, Arnesen urgently pulled his friend away from the rest of the football fraternity and explained that he had been trying to get in touch because their current coach Dick Advocaat was set to leave to take over the reins at Glasgow Rangers. They had identified Bobby's former skipper, Belgian international Eric Gerets, as the replacement, but had come upon a stumbling block when the team he was already managing, Club Brugge, insisted on him seeing out the remaining year of his contract.

They wanted someone to come in, keep the seat warm and keep PSV at the top of the table until Gerets was ready to take over. He said that Robson's was the first name mentioned because they were aware he was due to leave Barcelona at the end of the season and that, as he knew the club so well, he would be the perfect fit.

Robson, however, was far more interested on developments in England and the chance to return home, but something kept niggling away at the back of his mind at the thought of another year coaching at a club and a city he loved. After all, he would only be away an extra nine months.

He had almost talked himself into giving Arnesen a call when PSV got in touch with him directly and offered him the chance to coach, which no other club had actually done so far. Most of the others who had signalled an interest were keen on him becoming their director of football, a role becoming increasingly popular among Europe's biggest clubs, especially given his knowledge of the top players around the continent.

The rewards on offer from PSV were massive, more than he could have earned at any of the top English clubs, with bonuses if he could help them keep pace with Ajax and if he could help them into a money-spinning place in the Champions League. He knew he'd also be welcomed back to a club where he was popular and successful, and a couple of the older players called him to express their hopes that he would return to their club. Another factor was that chairman Harry van Raaij was still around, a man he liked and, more importantly, trusted.

After a great deal of thought Robson telephoned Arnesen and told him he would accept the challenge, providing his brief was to coach, train, motivate and select the team. Most of all he wanted to take on Ajax again.

In the middle of his negotiations Barcelona asked him if he would stay with them, while his old club Ipswich wanted to know what his plans were when he quit Camp Nou. He even met up with the chairman David Sheepshanks, who wanted him to assist their bright young manager George Burley. Robson had even spoken to Burley on a couple of occasions to assure him that if did join them for a second time he would not be treading on his toes.

He was impressed enough to file it away at the back of his mind for his return to England. After all, his old house was a short walk away from Portman Road and he knew he would get job satisfaction, even if the big bucks weren't there. There were further links with East Anglia when, in October 1997, the University of East Anglia bestowed an honorary Master of Arts degree on him, specifically for the contribution he had made to training and encouraging young people during his time at Portman Road.

Eventually the lure of getting out on the practice pitch proved too strong, and he agreed to a short deal to take him back to the Philips Stadion for the one season. That same day a top English club – he would never name them having promised the chairman – offered him the coaching position he craved. It was too late. He had given his word and that was a binding contract as far as he was concerned.

He was honourable, too, with his old club Barcelona. He had established a worldwide scouting set-up, watched hundreds of players in scores of competitions and had built up a solid rapport with the man who replaced him, Louis Van Gaal, disappointing those who claimed the two hated each other and didn't talk. It wasn't a job he originally wanted but he loved every minute of it and blazed a trail for other top clubs in Europe to follow.

They must have liked what he did for them as he was called to a meeting with Van Gaal and Josep Lluis Núñez. Both the coaches thought it was a final farewell and a handshake, but Núñez was delighted with the way the year had gone and wanted Robson to stay on for as long as he wished, with a lower but still very healthy wage.

Yet Robson wanted to be back working with players and it was PSV who had offered him the opportunity. He would be returning to coaching feeling that he was a better, more rounded personality because of all the travel he had undertaken and the people he had met. He also knew that his advice and judgement on key decisions with high quality players earned Barça far more than the seven-figure salary they paid him.

One of the major problems he had when he rejoined PSV was that they had sold top players, including Jaap Stam to Manchester United and Wim Jonk to Sheffield Wednesday, while Barcelona had taken both Boudewijn Zenden and Phillip Cocu. Robson knew that he needed a striker and, using his contacts, he zeroed in on a 22-year-old who was scoring goals for fun at Heerenveen. That striker was Ruud van Nistelrooy, signed for just £4.2 million, rising to £6.3 million, and they ended up making a huge profit on their investment when he was sold to Manchester United in 2001 for £25.65 million.

Van Nistelrooy would become a star under Sir Alex Ferguson, scoring 150 league goals in just 219 games, while he also still sits high up on the list of all-time Champions League leading scorers with 56 to his name. He might have been a superstar, but he failed to realise that there was only one person who called the shots at Old Trafford and that was Fergie, no matter how good you were or how many goals you scored.

The Flying Dutchman never achieved his dream of winning the Champions League, mainly because of a fallout with Sir Alex Ferguson in 2006. It was rumoured that Van Nistelrooy had called his boss a 'Scottish Pig' after being left on the bench for the League Cup final against Wigan Athletic, and though he never confirmed that he admitted to flying into a 'blind rage', an outburst that saw him sold to Real Madrid for only half of what United themselves had originally paid. He would have gone in a similar fashion, if not quicker, if he had spoken to Bobby Robson the same way, as would any player.

There was a time at Newcastle United when Craig Bellamy was furious with Robson for substituting him, although he was doing so to save the fiery Welshman's legs for things to come. Bellamy, not known for his gentle manners, unleashed an angry volley at Bobby, with the manager telling him to shut up in return. When he didn't comply, Robson said: 'Who are you? Ronaldo, Romário, Stoichkov, Hagi, Guardiola, Luis Enrique, Gascoigne – these are the people I deal with. And who are you?' There was no answer to that.

There were no problems for Bobby on his return to Eindhoven, however, and although he was only in the job for a year, it was a busy time. Having lost so many good players he was busy in the transfer market filling in the gaps, and apart from the capture of Van Nistelrooy, he helped to bring in Brazilian Jorginho Paulista from Palmeiras; defender Yuri Nikiforov from Sporting Gijón; left-back Davy Oyen from Genk; goalkeeper Patrick Lodewijks from Groningen; right winger Joonas Kolkka from Willem II; Theo Lucius from Den Bosch; Brazilian centre-forward Manoel from Internacional and Abel Xavier from Real Oviedo. In total the club spent £15.89 million for 17 players, with 18 departing for a grand total of £35.55 million. It was like a market place with Robson and his team pulling in the profits.

Needless to say, with so many comings and goings it was something of an unsettled team, but with Van Nistelrooy and Luc Nilis scoring goals all over the place they still managed to finish third behind Feyenoord and Willem II.

Bobby loved a good centre-forward and he had the privilege of working with some of the best in the world over his years in the game, but he also had an eye for a good centre-half, and in rugged Dutch international Stan Valckx he had his version of Terry Butcher in both Holland and Portugal.

Valckx was one of his favourite and most trusted players. He had inherited him at his first spell at PSV before taking him to FC Porto, and upon his return to the Netherlands he was there again. He grew under Bobby's encouragement and went on to win 20 international caps, playing for the Dutch at the 1994 World Cup.

You came away from watching him thinking the guy was a giant because of his sheer physical presence, but when you stood beside him you realised he was almost a broad as he was tall, standing a touch under six feet. He also had good feet, like many of the Dutch defenders of the time, but what Bobby loved about him most was his heart and his courage.

The love was reciprocated and on a visit to Newcastle in 2008 for a game between Newcastle and PSV Eindhoven in aid of Bobby's own Cancer Charity, he said: 'To be honest, he had no real interest in tactics. Some people think tactics win games, but the point about Bobby was he was such an admired manager that every player was prepared to go the extra mile for him.

'That was the difference between him and other coaches. The most important thing for him was that we didn't let the team down, which meant running, fighting, giving everything.

'And I don't think he had any enemies, which is very rare in this crazy world of football.'

The only words Robson would have disputed were the ones about his lack of interest in tactics. He would spend hours talking to the likes of Don Howe and Dave Sexton, dissecting the games and its nuances. If he couldn't find a fellow coach or manager to discuss the value of a sweeper against a back four, he would pick on me or some other equally less educated audience.

A year later Valckx was back for Bobby's moving and touching memorial service, and again he was eloquent about a man he rightly called his friend, adding: 'There was no one more passionate about the game than Bobby. To have him as my manager was inspirational but to have him as a friend for so many years was a privilege.

'I flew all over the world with Bobby and everywhere we went there was always a unique respect. Everywhere he went he made a difference. Football was not just a business for him, and it was so much more than that. He treated everyone the same, whether they were a taxi driver or a member of royalty; he was the same to everyone. Because he was this way and the effect he had, people liked and loved him the world over.'

Stan had flown from Shanghai to be at the celebration of Bobby's life at Durham Cathedral to join the rest of us who loved the man so much.

Bobby enjoyed his return to the Dutch city, but he was ready to return to England. Despite reaching pensionable age he was eager to work again on the training pitches of England. He would have gone back to the national team like a shot, for whatever they would like to pay him, or, alternatively, back to his home town and home club of Newcastle United.

Sometimes the good are rewarded and get what they wish, and it would have been an injustice if he had never managed his beloved club in the North East.

20

'And when the day arrives I'll become the sky and I'll become the sea and the sea will come to kiss me for I am going home. Nothing can stop me now.'

Trent Reznor, American singer, songwriter, musician, record producer and film score composer.

FOR ONLY THE SECOND TIME IN HIS FOOTBALL career Bobby Robson found himself out of work when he returned to England from his second spell at PSV Eindhoven. Any normal man would have picked up his pension, doffed his hat and said goodbye to football and followed England's cricket team abroad, especially as the invasive cancer was now a black cloud hovering above him.

A recurrence of the disease came in August 1995 and it was only the persistence of Elsie which eventually persuaded him to see consultant surgeon Mr Huw Davies. Within days he was under the expert knife of Mr Dan Archer at the Royal Marsden Hospital in London.

It was the great escape as far as his life was concerned, and Mr

Archer was adamant that he should quit work altogether, telling him: 'Simply, people do not go back to work after this particular operation.'

It came as a shock to everyone and they would have been even more stunned had they known that three years earlier he was successfully operated on at St. Anne's Hospital in Geldrop, Holland, having a cancerous tumour removed from his Colon

In Bobby's autobiography, *An Englishman Abroad,* which I co-wrote with him, he revealed that even his closest friends were ignorant of the true facts, believing that he had three months off from his job at Eindhoven to undergo stomach surgery.

He was lucky then, too, ignoring the early signs, convincing himself that the blood he was passing was a result of piles and it was only when he mentioned the facts to the club's medical consultant, Mr Artur Woolf, that he was examined and the true extent of the problem was found. The club successfully concealed the truth, backing up the story that it was a medical problem which required surgery.

It was a warning, and almost minor compared to his next brush with cancer when he suffered a sharp pain between his nose and his left eye, believing it was a nasal problem until Elsie persuaded him to see his specialist before he returned from the close season break for his defence of the Portuguese title with Porto.

Bobby was prepared to write it off as he had been suffering from pains and problems in that area since his first week as Ipswich manager, when he took a blow on the nose during training. This sort of injury was an almost every day occurrence, although it left him with a seriously impaired sense of smell and nasal problems which would be exacerbated in the cold weather or on long flights.

His remedy was a quick sniff of his Vicks inhaler, and it would have certainly carried on that way but for Elsie's insistence that he saw his local GP in Ipswich, Dr Keeble, who referred him to ear, nose and throat specialist Ian Lord. Mr Lord gave him a scan and detected a blockage which needed clearing out.

But, even then, it needed a stroke of luck to push Bobby into action when Porto travelled to England for a testimonial for Paul Elliot in the summer of 1995. When his team flew back Bobby stayed on, taking the opportunity to have the minor surgery in Ipswich. It was all done in a day by Mr Lord who, as a precaution, sent off a sample of the mucus for a biopsy just to be certain.

Bobby asked the doctor if it could be rushed as he was needed back in Portugal to conduct important pre-season training, and after a night in the hospital he went home to relax and recover from the effects of the anaesthetic.

He was literally packing for his departure the next day when the surgeon made a dramatic call. He told him to stay where he was and that he was on his way round to the house. He arrived within ten minutes. It was then revealed that the biopsy had exposed a malignant melanoma in his face and that an appointment had been arranged the very next morning with a consultant surgeon.

That was when he met his hero Dr Huw Davies for the first time. Any argument about returning to Portugal was cut short when the Welshman told him he could go back by all means, but that he wouldn't see the season out if he did. The rare form of cancer, Davies explained, would spread into the eye and the brain.

It stopped Bobby in his tracks: although he was 62 years of age, he had rarely felt fitter. He trained every day with the players and lived on an athlete's diet. He rarely felt any pain.

'You need an operation and you need it now if your life is to be saved,' Robson was bluntly told. Davies, who was to become a family friend – he and his wife would holiday with the Robsons in Spain – went with him to London the next day where they met with Scouser and football fan, surgeon Mr Dan Archer.

Robson put his total trust in the two men and immediately contacted his assistant José Mourinho, club president Jorge Nuno Pinto Da Costa and club physician Dr Gomez. He had the operation within 48 hours of the consultation with both Messrs Archer and Davies. Delighted with their handiwork, they promptly told him he had nothing left to prove in the game and that he should ride gently into the sunset, leaving the pressures of the business behind.

His handsome face was a mess. To reach the cancer they had to extract his top teeth, cut the bone in his left nostril and go through the roof of his mouth. He was told the scars would heal and he would soon feel and look a lot better.

That was the spur he needed. Ignoring the advice from the doctors as well as his family and friends to quit he was, incredibly, back in work by November, less than six months since the first diagnosis. He admitted to me later that it was probably a couple of months too early. He went to watch Porto play Nantes in the Champions League and reintroduced himself to his players and staff, who were clearly shocked by his appearance.

He not only returned to action that season but went on to win his second Portuguese league title in a row, and also committed himself to joining the fight against cancer, linking up with Huw Davies to persuade people all over the country to attend free examinations. The appeal worked, with 800 people turning up for free examinations and eight lives saved. He then went on to prove everyone wrong by then taking the Barcelona job, clearly one of the most stressful in the world game. Retirement was not in his vocabulary.

He felt just the same way in 1999 as he had done in 1995. Retire? You must be joking. Not only did he want another job in football – preferably Newcastle United, where Ruud Gullit was in residence – but if he couldn't find one, he was not going to put his feet up, learn to smoke a pipe and talk about football over his garden wall to an unsuspecting next-door neighbour. Nor was he going to take up the modern option of getting behind a mic for either radio or television.

He couldn't keep still. It wasn't just our forenames, Robert William, that we had in common, we were both rather keen on sunshine and on travelling to the various corners of the globe. Neither of us fancied a laid-back retirement.

I had been covering sports across the globe for years – including ten Olympic Games, football at every level from World Cups through the European competitions, tennis, boxing cricket and a host of track and field and other international competitions – and had largely satisfied my travel lust as a sports writer. Bobby had matched me easily, especially in that year he spent as the most expensive, widely travelled scout in world football, touching just about every continent and setting up coaching networks that were to serve Barcelona for many years, and probably still are, supplying them with players from all corners. We also enjoyed a little travel on our own outside the usual work that had originally brought us, the rather odd couple, together.

It has always been an argument whether my second home was the Caribbean or that beautiful island in the Indian Ocean, Mauritius. I had talked about them enough to Bobby and I was able to fix up a visit for him to the latter, where he got so stuck into the job of teaching and encouraging the local coaches he forgot to wear a hat and suffered painful sunburn, even through that covering of distinguished white hair.

He was a little more circumspect on our visits to the Caribbean where he was overjoyed to meet the legendary Sir Vivian Richards, though it was hard to decide who was the most awestruck out of the pair. Bobby was a keen and rather good cricketer, while Sir Viv had played World Cup football for his native Antigua and held Bobby in high regard. Needless to say, they got on famously.

Bobby was fascinated with a cricket ground I had helped set up with Club Antigua, which was good enough to stage games against visiting touring sides and especially good for helping bring back the local youth into the game from basketball and even football, perish the thought.

We also looked in on Club St. Lucia, where Bobby again took it upon himself to coach both players and coaches, while he also mixed happily with the holiday makers on both islands by the pool, in the restaurants or in the bars. You have never seen anyone made more welcome who, in turn, modestly accepted the adulation of men, women and children.

We also had a couple of flights out with our mutual friend Joe Sanchez on his private plane, once to Joe's native Basque country where we strolled in the early spring sunshine, ate the local fish and, of course, met the local people. Wherever we went in the world, everyone knew Bobby Robson and treated him with more than just due respect.

But happy as he was at the end of the season in waiting at PSV, he was fidgety and always wanting to know what was happening in football back home, what jobs were available and especially what was happening at St. James' Park, Newcastle.

The 1999/2000 season was about to kick off and as much as he enjoyed the rum – he actually preferred the sparkling white wine – and the company, he wanted to be back on the training ground and he had a brief black mood when a job became available and was told he was too old, especially as we'd let it be known that he would be interested if they approached him.

What made it worse was that Newcastle, under Gullit, were awful and quickly slipped to second from bottom of the table with just Sheffield Wednesday propping them up. Then, in September 1999, the great Dutch footballer was gone and the chair at Newcastle United was vacant. There was just one stumbling block, Freddy Shepherd, who made it widely known that he no longer wanted Robson at Newcastle. Fortunately for everyone his voice was the loudest but not the most important. The key figure was actually Sir John Hall, who had spent the previous two years trying to bring Bobby back home and he wasn't going to miss out this time, instructing his senior board members to go and get him whatever the price, whatever the effort required.

It didn't need any effort and it didn't even need to break the bank. Bobby couldn't wait to go home and told me he would have packed his bag at his home in Ipswich and walked north to take the job. He was finally going back to where he belonged.

The disagreeable Shepherd had given him a few nerves and doubts, especially as the first game arrived so quickly after his appointment. He found himself with little time to prepare his side to face a talented Chelsea side on 11 September 1999, though he needn't have had worried. His reception that day brought a tear to my eye and I am sure to his as well. The game wasn't even being held at St James' Park, but at Stamford Bridge. Everyone knew he would be good for the English game.

They couldn't hope for too much right away. Newcastle were weighed down with a huge staff of 39 professionals and had endured a nightmare beginning to the campaign, losing five and drawing one of their six league outings. As ever with Newcastle fans, they had expected the earth but were soon brought crashing down to it. They began with a home defeat to Aston Villa; were thrashed 3-1 at Spurs; fell 4-2 at Southampton; could only draw 3-3 with little Wimbledon; lost at home to, of all clubs, Sunderland and were then thrashed 5-1 by Manchester United. The Sunderland defeat alone was enough to turn the Geordies against manager Gullit, board, players and anyone else in earshot.

Just about the only person not to give Robson the big welcome back in that first game at Stamford Bridge was referee Graham Poll, who ruled that Celestine Babayaro had been fouled by Gary Speed and pointed to the spot. Frenchman Frank Leboeuf put the penalty past

Shay Given. Even the BBC's John Murray thought it was harsh and Bobby himself said afterwards: 'They won with a scrambled penalty.' Polite as ever.

On the same afternoon Kieron Dyer was brought down and appealed for a spot kick and he was promptly booked for dissent, one of five Newcastle players booked against zero for the home side. Bobby was upset at the decisions but delighted with the spirit his players had shown as they kept their place next to bottom of the table.

The first look the Toon Army had of their new boss was eight days later, time for him to get into his players, work on the formation and their tactics and build them up to face bottom club Sheffield Wednesday at St. James' Park. Talk about a crunch game.

The players responded to their new boss in spectacular style against Danny Wilson's side, scoring eight times without reply as national hero Alan Shearer, who had a rocky ride with Gullit, scored five times for his fellow Geordie, with Aaron Hughes, Dyer and Gary Speed adding the others. It was the first time Shearer had ever scored more than three and afterwards gave Robson full credit, saying: 'He has put in a hell of a lot of work. He understands people, he's got everyone playing with a smile on their face.'

There was still much to sort out, but Robson was back in a tracksuit, amongst the players, sifting out the wheat from the chaff and bringing back the crowd's favourites Alan Shearer and Robert Lee. The high rollers from abroad, who had little interest in the history and the place in the community the club had, were put on the backburner and told to find themselves a move back home if they couldn't step up their games.

It wasn't just on the pitch where Newcastle were suffering. The wage bill was too high. New players were needed on a slim budget and a new stand needed to be built, not to mention the fact that they had to claw their way up the table and avoid the financial penalties of relegation.

The combination of Robson and Shearer was irresistible, however, and, with Shearer scoring 28 goals in the 1999/2000 season, the team settled into a rhythm, and, after a few setbacks – like a 4-1 defeat at Coventry – they climbed the table to finish in a creditable eleventh place. They also enjoyed a little run in the UEFA Cup as they put out CSKA Sofia and FC Zürich, before being edged out on a 1-0 aggregate by Roma. In the FA Cup they went goal happy, scoring 17 times as they beat Spurs, Sheffield United, Blackburn Rovers and Tranmere Rovers, before going out in the semi-final against Chelsea at Wembley 2-1, thanks to two Gus Poyet goals.

It was the sort of season Newcastle would have killed for as time progressed but they, with their huge fan base, and Robson himself, felt there was so much more to come and everybody wondered where they would have been but for Gullit's early season eccentricities and the strange management from the top by Shepherd and Douglas Hall.

The changes were root and branch, with players coming and going through revolving turnstiles at the players' entrance of St. James' Park as Robson tried to reshape the side, not in his own image but in one that could sustain a Premier League place and challenge for the cup competitions. He wanted to give the huge home crowds goals and entertainment and he wanted a team of young players who would give as much to the club as their black and white blooded supporters did week after week.

The now revamped ground was bringing in 50,000 supporters for every home game and though the team slipped from a highest position of third to the same eleventh place they had occupied the previous season, no one could have pointed the finger and claimed that United had gone backwards or even stood still.

The subsequent season, the 2001/02 campaign, saw the young side Bobby had been putting together blend in some style and they drove to the top of the table after beating Leeds United 4-3 at Elland Road just before Christmas. It was a typical performance from a Robson side, featuring plenty of chances and goals at either end. Indeed, it was the second time they had won 4-3 that season after an earlier victory over Manchester United at St James' Park. There was so much adventure to Newcastle's play, and it meant the fans grew to love their Messiah even more. They eventually finished in a more than credible fourth place, qualifying for the lucrative and much desired Champions League the following season.

It would have been an even better campaign but for the stumbling block of London. Chelsea put them out in the fifth round of the League Cup, while Arsenal defeated them in a sixth-round replay in the FA Cup, meaning that although he was pleased with the progress his side were making, there was plenty of room for improvement.

The London ghosts were laid to rest in the next campaign when they beat both Chelsea and Tottenham within weeks of each other – in fact they did the double over both Spurs and Charlton – and they made a genuine bid for the biggest crown, keeping pace until March. It was then they fell short, with a 2-1 defeat to a Wayne-Rooney inspired Everton followed directly by a 6-2 home loss to Sir Alex Ferguson's Manchester United and a 2-1 defeat at Fulham. They regrouped to finish third – behind United and Arsenal but ahead of both Chelsea and Liverpool.

In the Champions League they came back spectacularly after losing their first three matches in the group stage to make the second group phase. They had started well enough in qualifying, brushing aside Željezničar, with a goal from Dyer in Sarajevo enough to give them a slender advantage going to St James' Park, and once back on home soil they put their opposition to the sword, ending the tie 5-0 winners on aggregate. But in the Champions League proper they had the most awful of starts, losing 2-0 against Dynamo in Kiev; 1-0 at home to

Feyenoord and 2-0 to two Alessandro del Piero goals in Turin against Juventus.

Then came a remarkable transformation, as Robson's men totally turned results on their head. At home to Juventus they won 1-0 thanks to an Andy Griffin goal, then they came from 1-0 behind against Dynamo Kyiv to win 2-1, before a last minute Craig Bellamy strike in Rotterdam in the final group game secured a 3-2 triumph over Feyenoord. Newcastle were through by the finest of margins.

Robson and the city were energised by this remarkable comeback and the excitement continued unabated into the second group phase, excitement that was quelled after just six minutes of the opening game when Bellamy saw red against Inter Milan for an off the ball incident. The Magpies lost 4-1, Bellamy was banned for three matches and the influential Shearer was also barred for two games for a similar incident.

It meant that they were both missing for the emotional return of Bobby Robson to Camp Nou, where a less than half full ground saw them lose 3-1. It was a dampener in every sense, as the game was delayed for 24 hours because of torrential rain and a waterlogged pitch. Robson was thrilled, though not surprised, at the number of Newcastle supporters who stayed on for the rearranged game and at the performance against a Barça side who were struggling under Louis van Gaal, the man who had taken over from Robson.

But once again Newcastle showed that bouncebackability under Robson as they beat Bayern Leverkusen twice, firstly away from home without their two main strikers, and then by the same scoreline, 3-1, at St James' Park, when Alan Shearer returned to the fold to score a first half hat-trick. He scored two more in the 2-2 draw against Inter at the San Siro, where they briefly led only to be denied by a display of diving and referee harassment, which infuriated the Newcastle manager. But then, with qualification to the knockout stages in view, they crashed 2-0 home to Barça and the dream was over. Van Gaal's side would not make it past the quarter-finals in what would turn out to be the Dutchman's final season at the Camp Nou.

Newcastle went out of the FA Cup to Wolves and on penalties against Everton in the League Cup after a 3-3 draw, but in the league they were never out of the top four. Despite his age, now 70, Bobby had no thought of personal glory and continued to build the club for someone else's future and, of course, for the joy of the fans, if not for the chairman Freddy Shepherd.

How he remained at the club to plague Robson and his efforts was a mystery. In March 1998 the *News of the World* exposed Shepherd and his cohort Douglas Hall through 'Fake Sheikh' Mazher Mahmood, who posed as a wealthy Arab prince willing to do business with the pair but instead caught them on tape abusing their own supporters. There was uproar. Being a Geordie, Robson was well aware of Shepherd and his reputation, and was being kept updated by his close friends in the city and at the club. However, despite being vociferous in private, he kept his counsel publicly, refusing to become involved despite disliking the man and all he stood for. There was a big movement on Tyneside for the pair to get out of the club, even backed by then Minister for Sport Tony Banks, and they both left their posts within two weeks of the scandal breaking in the Sunday tabloid.

Memories are short and the pair, as major shareholders, were able to vote themselves back on the board just ten months later, leading to the instant resignation of PLC Chairman David Cassidy, who had accepted the position only six months earlier. Shepherd reacted by taking over himself as the PLC Chairman.

Newcastle fans are notoriously hard to please because they invest so much of themselves into their club and Shepherd, not surprisingly, was not accepted into their fold any more than the controversial Mike Ashley was later. They were unhappy that the likes of Kevin Keegan, Kenny Dalglish, Ruud Gullit, Bobby Robson, Graeme Souness and

Glenn Roeder all came and went while he was a senior decision maker. Ironically, the most stable years of Shepherd's ten years as chairman were when Bobby Robson was in charge of the football team. A timeline of his reign is documented below in short:

1997: Appointed chairman.

1997: Keegan resigns. Dalglish appointed. Runners-up in the Premiership.

1998: Club floated on the London Stock Exchange. Dalglish sacked. Gullit appointed.

1998: Exposed by the Fake Sheik in the *News of the World* and steps down for 10 months.

1998: Beaten FA Cup finalists.

1999: Gullit sacked. Robson appointed. Finish eleventh after fighting off relegation.

2002: Newcastle finish fourth.

2003: Newcastle finish third.

2004: Newcastle finish fifth.

2004: Robson sacked after four games (two losses, two draws). Souness appointed.

2006: Souness sacked. Roeder appointed.

2007: Roeder sacked. Allardyce appointed.

2007: Ashley becomes major shareholder. Shepherd departs.

Not only did Shepherd deny his manager money to invest, he also made it known that it was never his choice to appoint him. The Robson response was to shut out the noise, roll up his sleeves and work with what he had to prove that he was the man for the job.

+++

FOR THE *ULTIMATE PATRIOT* THERE WAS NO GREATER honour than being knighted by the Prince of Wales at Buckingham

Palace on 21 November 2002 after the announcement in the Queen's Birthday Honours in June.

Bobby was, at the time, 69 years old and manager of his beloved Newcastle United and for him it was all his Christmases rolled into one.

Typical of Bobby was that he was told to keep the honour to himself and he did it to such an extent that he did not even tell Elsie she was about to officially become a Lady. Did he tell me? Not on your life! He had made the promise to the Queen, who he both loved and respected. She was the boss.

He proudly took his wife to the Palace for the investiture along with two of his sons, Andrew and Paul.

Robson said that Charles had told him he was thrilled that Bobby was not only still working but still enjoying the experience, adding that he hoped it was not too taxing for him and then telling him, 'Do take care'.

Robson told me later that he was overwhelmed at the experience and especially the kind words from Charles.

He was so proud of the honour which was for his services to the game and Lady Elsie said afterwards: 'It's lovely for him. It's very exciting. He's been doing the work for a long time, so he deserves it and I'm very proud.' Without a trace of ego he happily used the prefix – although to his friends he was and always would be just Bobby.

+++

AT ST JAMES' PARK HIS PLAYERS, THOSE NOT IN THE treatment room, continued to back him to the hilt and, inspired by his wisdom, continued to perform excellently. In the 2003/04 campaign they once again found themselves near the top of the table around the Christmas period, putting four past a well beaten Spurs side in

December, Alan Shearer and Laurent Robert scoring two goals apiece. The two goals the diminutive Frenchman scored were typical of his power from distance and were described by many as amongst the best he scored.

Robert was a left-winger born in the Indian Ocean island of Réunion, a short flight from Mauritius, and earned nine full French caps. Robson liked a good winger and, at the time, had Robert on the left and adopted Geordie Nolberto Solano on the right. Robert chalked up 129 Premier League appearances and, with his ability from distance and from dead ball situations, should have had far more than his 22 goals. Had his temperament been better he would have been a real local hero. As it was he was considered as something of naughty boy and was later shipped out to Portsmouth after a public bust up with Robson's successor Graeme Souness, criticising him and the entire squad before throwing his kit into the Gallowgate End.

Solano, meanwhile, was adored by both his manager Robson and the fans in his two spells with the club, making 314 appearances and scoring 48 goals. He was an all rounder, accomplished in midfield and at right-back as well as on the wing. His versatility did not end there: he was also a talented musician, played the trumpet like a pro, formed his own salsa band and even had a Peruvian restaurant on Tyneside named after him. A legend and a bargain at £2.5 million.

The team badly needed reinforcements in the mid-season window of that 2003/04 campaign to keep them in the hunt after a steady run of form before Christmas, but Shepherd had pulled the rug from under Robson's feet after Newcastle surprisingly lost their third round Champions League qualifying tie to Partizan Belgrade at the start of the campaign, despite the fact they had won the first leg 1-0 in Serbia. The defeat had come during an early season malaise, and it adversely affected everyone, especially those players in the dressing room who had loved Robson leading them into battle in Europe the previous season, but also in the boardroom. They saw the rich prizes on offer vanish before their eyes, leading to a season of backbiting and moaning, showing a complete lack of understanding of the way the game works.

It meant Newcastle found themselves in the UEFA Cup for the season, and they made the most of being one of the stronger teams in the competition, reaching the semi-finals, the furthest any English team reached in Europe in that campaign. On the way they crushed Mallorca 7-1 on aggregate and then put out Robson's old club PSV Eindhoven 3-2 in the quarter-finals before losing to Marseille in the last four thanks to two goals from Didier Drogba, who produced one of many outstanding individual displays.

Without Champions League football Robson was refused the cash he needed and Newcastle suffered, ending the season in fifth, ironically one place outside those coveted Champions League spots. The UEFA Cup would have to do again.

In 2004 Robson's contract was extended by a further year, granting him a last, season-long lap of honour on his home ground before finally hanging up whatever a retiring manager hangs up. Despite being now into his 72nd year, he wanted to carry on and his record at St. James' Park stacked up against most of his predecessors, and, indeed, those who followed him.

However, the toxic atmosphere continued into the start of the 2004/05 campaign, and with Newcastle picking up just two points from their first four games, the background noise was cacophonous. Given the cheque book had been effectively closed to Bobby and transfer decisions placed in the hands of the chairman the chances of Newcastle competing in the top half of the table again seemed remote, and the writing was on the wall.

Robson had been in the job just a couple of days short of five years and the season was four games old when he was unceremoniously fired by Shepherd after the 4-2 defeat by Aston Villa. The PLC chairman had already told the world that the contract would not be extended, and Robson had confided in me that he would be quitting at the end of the season, but there was an agreement that he would not be sacked before then.

Bobby was left shocked when his classy but injury prone central defender Jonathan Woodgate was sold to Real Madrid in August 2004, while he also had fall outs with both Kieron Dyer and Alan Shearer, who he had left on the bench for that 4-2 defeat. Shearer was pictured on the bench looking more than a little disgruntled at being dropped.

I personally spoke to Bobby on the Friday from the team hotel before the game against Aston Villa. I was in Athens, covering the Olympic Games, and had heard whispers that his job was in jeopardy just a couple of short weeks into a new season. He told me of his plans to rest Shearer who, at 34, was in his final season before deciding whether to move into management or to pursue his career as a television pundit.

Robson told me then that he felt three games in eight days was too much to ask of his skipper and resting Shearer gave him the opportunity of having a close look at his new signing, the Dutchman Patrick Kluivert, and the exciting young prospect Shola Ameobi. Shearer, it should be pointed out, had not scored an away goal from open play since the previous November and with his job on the line, Robson knew he had to find some punch from somewhere and superstar Kluivert looked to be that man.

It was just like his unfortunate fall out with another of his heroes Kevin Keegan, who he had dropped from his England team without telling him when he first took the reins in 1982. It was much the same story with Shearer, another player he more than just admired and who he readily accepted had been at the forefront of his relative successes since his arrival at Newcastle.

Shearer had been dropped by Gullit before Robson arrived and the club, a decision that did not do the Dutchman any favours, no matter how brave it might have been, and he had soon disappeared from Tyneside. Robson, had he given the situation more thought, would have concluded he would be in a similar position of peril if he made the same move as his predecessor, especially as Shearer had earlier expressed his desire to play every minute of every game in this, his last season.

There were faults on both sides, but had Shearer stopped to think what Robson had done for him he would surely have hesitated in showing his displeasure both during the Villa game and on the day when Robson was summarily dismissed. He offered little or no support to the man who had helped extend his Newcastle career by five years after Gullit had wanted him out.

Nevertheless his praise of his former manager and fellow Geordie as the end neared, and particularly at the Memorial Service, showed his true feelings for the man. After all, no professional likes being dropped, no matter who the man is swinging the axe.

Shepherd then swung that same axe at Robson, claiming it was his hardest decision in football, adding that he didn't want to be known as the man who shot Bambi, a comment that didn't go down at all well with Robson and his army of fans, ex-players and fellow managers.

There was already considerable ill will towards Shepherd and though he hung around long enough to see off both Graeme Souness and Glenn Roeder after Robson, in May 2007 he found himself all alone as billionaire businessman Mike Ashley purchased the Hall family's 41.6% stake in the club. After a brief fight, Shepherd agreed to sell his remaining shares to Ashley and stepped down in July of the same year. Rumours had it that he twice tried to buy the club back in subsequent years before he died in September 2017, aged 76.

Bobby was well aware that Shepherd was the enemy in the camp when he accepted the job, and right from the moment Sir John Hall railroaded the appointment through, he complained that the new manager was too old for the job but in much coarser language.

It should be remembered that when Robson took charge Newcastle United were in plenty of financial strife with a group of players seemingly indifferent to the club's history and its status in the very heart of the local community.

He brought in young, enthusiastic players who responded to his personalised touch and the crowds soon rolled back to the renovated St. James' Park in their thousands. Unselfishly he brought in young players who were going to reach their best after his departure. The likes of Olivier Bernard, Craig Bellamy, Shola Ameobi, Aaron Hughes, Darren Ambrose, James Milner, Andy O'Brien, Jermaine Jenas and Titus Bramble brought a febrile energy to the squad and supported more established players such as Nicky Butt, Stephen Carr, Laurent Robert, Robbie Elliott, Lee Bowyer and Patrick Kluivert.

'I have put together the best squad this club has had for many years and while I would like to continue for another thirty years I know that is not possible, and I just want to leave the club in the best possible shape,' is how he described his unselfish blueprint to me.

It is a great pity others did not share his desire and hope for the club both in the dressing room and in the boardroom. Inwardly he felt hugely betrayed at his dismissal, but in public he was his usual dignified self, saying: 'It has been a phenomenal experience. It [the sack] has naturally stopped me from finishing the job I would have wanted to have done.

'I have had a marvellous time and I would like to wish the club every success in the world.' They were not shallow words, he meant it.

Privately he was sickened, and I cannot imagine he was great company for Elsie as they packed and set off for a break in Faro in Portugal. I know because I had been in his company the last time he been fired.

The 2004/05 season was only in its early stages when he was dismissed, but it had already thrown up obstacles, particularly an outbreak of conjunctivitis that forced the club to close down its training ground at the critical start of serious competition in August. This was no regular outbreak of flu, this was either a viral or a bacterial infection, affecting the thin transparent layer of tissue that lines the inner surface of the eyelid and covers the white part of the eye. It was not something to be dismissed or treated with an aspirin and an early night.

The dressing room atmosphere was not good anyway, with the cocky young Kieron Dyer refusing to play out wide on the right. He was promptly dropped by Robson and jeered by his own fans. The manager was also bypassed in the sale of Jonathan Woodgate to Real Madrid for £13.5 million, while his bid to sign Wayne Rooney from Everton led to rumours that Craig Bellamy would quit if the young-ster arrived on Tyneside as it would threaten his place in the team.

Alan Shearer dismissed stories of a player revolt as 'absolute rubbish', but the pictures of him scowling from the substitute's bench as he was rested for new boy Patrick Kluivert to play against Aston Villa had all sorts of rumours swirling around St. James' Park. Bobby was uncom-fortable, even talking privately about the interference of the board in his transfer dealings, and it was made obvious to me that he did not want to lose Gary Speed to Bolton Wanderers, who he replaced with Manchester United's Nicky Butt for £2.5 million in July 2004.

As ever Robson continued to back his players, even though a number of them let him down behind his back and caused unrest in the dressing room, the sort of mutiny the popular manager had not had to deal with since his early days at Ipswich Town.

Newcastle was a party town and a number of the younger squad members were drawn into that atmosphere and in November 2001 four of them – Carl Cort, Andy Griffin Keiron Dyer and Craig Bellamy – had to be sent home from a training camp in Malaga after snubbing a dinner in honour of Sir

John Hall. Instead of attending they had gone out on the razz, embarking on a bar crawl, resulting in their early flight back to Newcastle.

It all came to a head in September 2004 when a couple of the senior players went to see Freddy Shepherd in private, telling him that the manager had lost the dressing room. Shepherd was then shown a photograph taken by one of the local photographers of a senior player putting two fingers up behind Robson's back, and he was so concerned about the picture reaching the press that he paid around £10,000 to make sure it never did. The entire set up was poison and within weeks Sir Bobby Robson had been fired. The dream was over.

In truth Bobby could have immediately returned to work. No sooner had Shepherd sacked him than a club chairman, knowing my relationship with him, telephoned to say they would love to sign him up straight away. I passed the message straight to Robson but, at the same time, I promised the chairman I would keep the confidence, something I have done ever since. To this day I do not know why the marriage did not take place.

At least Shepherd never recanted on his opinion that they should never have appointed Robson, whereas others have spent the ensuing years telling everyone what a great and loved man he was without revealing their part in his demise. It was significant that when Sir Bobby was feted by the City of Newcastle at the conclusion of The Match, a pro-celebrity football show filmed at St. James' Park and screened by Sky, both Shepherd and Shearer disappeared from the Director's Box before the on-field ceremony, which saw the former manager being presented with a commemorative sword. They probably had very good reasons to so do.

There must be many regrets on every side that, sadly, can never be completely erased.

21

'The harder you work, the harder it is to surrender.'
Vince Lombardi, New York born American Football player, coach
and executive and probably the most quotable man in sporting history.

WHEN BOBBY FINALLY CAME TO TERMS WITH HIS
crude dismissal he refused to bow to the inevitable. Why should he?
After all, he had battled invasive cancer since 1995, and there was no
way he was going to hide away. He did as he should, held his head up
high and continued to inspire those around him with his manners, his
deportment and his unquenchable love for the game.

Make no mistake he was ready to carry on at another club, but
Freddy Shepherd had cast one final spell on the man he sacked. He
refused to settle the remainder of his contract with a lump sum, instead
paying him a monthly instalment until the end of that campaign.
Should Robson have accepted another job in the meantime those

payments would have ceased or reduced, depending on the differential between his former pay and any new salary.

Robson was caught between a rock and a hard place and at his advanced age he knew full well that he wasn't going to be offered a bumper pay deal, especially considering his ill health, which by now was virtually ruling him out of any full-time managerial job.

Instead he maintained his private box at St. James' Park, where he could watch Newcastle's games in the company of family and friends, showing he was still a supporter even if he did not work for them anymore. He also became a regular at The Stadium of Light just down the road, where he was made as welcome as he was by the fans at his own club.

However, he still wanted some personal involvement in the game that was his very heartbeat, and having waited in vain for the Football Association to offer him an honorary role, in 2006 he accepted an invitation from the Football Association of Ireland to help their youthful boss Steve Staunton, who had only retired from playing in 2005 and had never been a manager before.

Only Lady Robson truly knew just how difficult it was to prise her husband away from the game he held so dear. Bobby wisely kept Elsie away from the media and protected his family from our vagaries with a fierce determination, though she did offer a rare interview to Newcastle's *Evening Chronicle* sometime after his death, giving an insight into the private man very few saw, talking about his struggle to give up the game when others would have retired many years earlier.

'Bob was not a slipper sort of man.' Elsie admitted. 'He was very positive about his career and wasn't a person who relaxed a lot as his head was always working and he was always thinking about his next team and tactics.

'He wasn't the sort of person who would fall onto a couch at the end of the day and relax. He was very, very driven in the work that he did. He was very positive about his work and career as it was important to him.

'Bob didn't have many hobbies outside football, but he liked to read when he got the chance and he did like to watch comedies. His great love was Morecambe and Wise and he loved Westerns. He also loved golf and he wanted to play golf every day of his retirement, which never happened because he didn't retire.

'He had lots of books lined up on the shelves, but he just did not get round to reading very much because he ran out of time to do so.'

Most poignant was her reflections on his later life in football, revealing how difficult it was for him to step away because it had dominated his life: 'His life had been football and I don't think he would ever have come to terms with no longer working in the sport.

'It was difficult for me to see how it affected him. I always had visions of what we were going to do when we retired as I thought we'd get on buses and go to markets, but we never did because he never did retire.

'There was never a point when I told him to step back because I didn't think there was any point going down that route.'

To me, that was the most significant comment.

I am certain one of those occasions was when he decided to accept that job with the FAI so late in his life when he was battling a losing fight with cancer. He didn't need the money, and because of ill health he was unable to do what he did best – getting his training gear on, grabbing a ball and telling young players what he wanted and expected from them.

If Elsie had suggested he should pass this one by, I would have backed her up totally. It was simply a job he did not need and one that could only possibly end in tears – Staunton had no managerial experience and only turned 37 in the week he was appointed, while the Irish team were not the same force as they had been under Robson's old mate Jack Charlton in the 90s. The new boss didn't even know whether Robson would be joining him in the dugout for matches, something he admitted at the inaugural press conference.

Staunton was hoping that the partnership could work the way Kenny Dalglish had used the shrewd old Bob Paisley – another Geordie with wisdom beyond his vocabulary – when he took over at Anfield in the 1980s at the age of just 34, and there is no doubt that he had the greatest of respect for his far more experienced colleague, but it never worked out.

Bobby told me that he had been actively encouraged by Charlton to take the job, which offered a two-year contract at a healthy £171,000 a year, and swore that he was not going to be a nodding dog, but would make his contribution as best as he could without interfering too much. The fans and the media hesitantly welcomed his arrival and involvement but without really thinking it through, much the same as Bobby himself.

The simple truth is that he was not well enough to give what he wanted to give, and when results went against Staunton he refused to criticise the youngster, and defended him even more stoutly when his father fell seriously ill. It took its toll.

Not everyone gave Robson the same consideration, and he was even asked by the FAI to go on a notorious Irish radio show called *Liveline* following a narrow, unconvincing victory over the minnows of San Marino in February of 2007. The show was not known for pulling its punches or asking easy questions of its guests, and Robson was appearing at a particularly difficult moment.

He defended Staunton to the hilt on air, describing him as a fine young man and revealing how they were regularly in telephone contact, even during games. He suffered on behalf of Staunton and the FAI for 75 minutes, an ordeal for a young, fit man never mind someone not in the best of health. Clearly the plug should have been pulled much earlier and Joe Duffy, the hard-nosed presenter, was apparently a little remorseful at the end of the ordeal and said, 'I apologise if I have been rude.' Bobby's response was typical of the man, simply telling his interviewer not to worry about it.

But the days of Bobby Robson being the main enemy in the eyes of the public had long gone and while Staunton was the real target on the radio show, it was the FAI who suffered further opprobrium, while Robson himself retained his cool, his dignity and his reputation as a gentleman.

When he wasn't fighting the FAI's battles for them, Bobby filled his time watching cricket in the summer, attending dinners and celebrations – which were often held in his honour to sell out audiences – and working for charity.

In the end he bowed out of the Irish job when his illness started to restrict him even further. I don't think there was a single one of his friends who wasn't happy when that unforgiving job finally ended.

He also watched as the club he loved, Newcastle United descended into turmoil again. Graeme Souness, the man who had replaced Robson at the helm, was far too impatient to cope with the nonsenses he found at the club, with senior players acting above their station. The club's hierarchy had also displayed remarkable vanity in signing Michael Owen from Real Madrid for an amazing £16.5 million, when all the forward really wanted was to be back at Anfield. He signed in August of 2005, and Souness was gone by February of 2006.

The Owen transfer highlighted the mess Newcastle had plunged themselves into by sacking the one man likely to keep a firm hand on the tiller, and they sailed into increasingly choppy waters. Owen had enjoyed his best years at Liverpool between 1996 and 2004, scoring 118 goals in 216 league appearances. It was that form that convinced Real Madrid to part with £8 million to take him to the Bernabéu, but he spent most of his time in the Spanish capital on the bench.

Though he scored at a good rate when he did play, it was staggering when Newcastle stumped up over double fee Madrid had just paid a year before in order to bring him back home. While he did manage to score 26 league goals in 71 games across four seasons in which he was plagued by injuries, he was never close to justifying the fee paid. He was top scorer in the disastrous 2008/09 campaign with ten league goals, but he was also the man in possession of the captaincy as Newcastle were relegated to the second tier, and that summer he left to join Manchester United on a free transfer.

Between Robson's sacking in August 2004 and Chris Hughton's second interim spell in charge, beginning on 7 February 2009, the Newcastle hierarchy had appointed five permanent managers: Souness, Glenn Roeder, Sam Allardyce, Kevin Keegan and Joe Kinnear. None had come close to replicating Robson's success or consistency, and with the club in dire straits with eight games left to go of the 08/09 campaign, they turned to another local hero to try and save them: Bobby's former captain Alan Shearer. Hughton had been temporarily in charge for six games, but Shearer was stepping into the breach for Joe Kinnear, who had surprisingly replaced the outgoing Keegan at the start of the season (despite having long been retired) but was now requiring a heart bypass operation after falling ill before Newcastle's clash with West Brom in February. It was the usual soap opera. As inexperienced as Staunton was when he took the Ireland job, Shearer could only guide Newcastle to one win in those eight games, and a final day defeat at Aston Villa saw them demoted for the first time in 20 years.

+++

AMIDST ALL THESE COMINGS AND GOINGS IN THE manager's office, Newcastle had moved from one disastrous chairman to another when Mike Ashley replaced Freddy Shepherd in 2007. Desperate to impress his new fans, Ashley often framed himself as the common man, pictured drinking pints in amongst the supporters in a replica shirt, but any popularity he did have simply by replacing a disliked regime was soon on the wane, especially after Keegan's departure as manager in September 2008, closely linked to the appointment of Dennis Wise as a director of football.

By this time Robson was far from well, but we maintained contact by telephone to swap the gossip and he was genuinely baffled by the appointment of Wise in this role. This diminutive, tough-tackling Londoner had stamped his game all over England in a career of twenty years which included spells at Wimbledon, Chelsea, Leicester, Millwall, Southampton and Coventry. He had enjoyed his best times at Stamford Bridge with Chelsea, where he won two FA Cups, a League Cup and the UEFA Cup Winners' Cup, and during that period he was capped by his country 21 times.

In 2004 he had led second tier Millwall to the FA Cup final as a player-manager, a sign that he might have a bright future as a boss. It was therefore a surprise to everyone when it was announced at the end of January 2009 that he was quitting his role as Leeds United manager, just as he looked on track to take them back to the Championship at the first time of asking, to take up a senior executive role at Newcastle United.

He was designated with travelling around the world to identify new talent and with developing the academy. It was similar to the role Bobby had held at Barcelona, only Wise did not have the knowledge that Robson had of the European or South American game, nor had the respect that Robson commanded from peers across the globe.

He joined in January 2008 and was gone, suitably some said, on April Fools' Day 2009, seeing off Keegan – who never did approve of his presence or the role in general – in the process. Bobby never could get to grips with the appointment and he watched in amazement as the club went through a series of seismic changes.

Relegation left Robson grieving at the fate of 'his' club, and when they went down on the final day of the season, he admitted over the telephone to me that it was no more than the club deserved for the way it had been run and managed, adding: 'It is all very sad and we need a new, committed owner, a change of players and a new attitude.'

He did, however, express the wish that Alan Shearer be retained as manager. He wasn't, but that was typical of the big-hearted, forgiving Bobby Robson, who always strived to see the best in people.

It was a great pity he did not live to see the appointment of former Liverpool boss Rafa Benítez as manager, which for a time provided some much-needed stability. Like Bobby, Rafa is a man who has completely immersed himself in the game he loves, and holds much the same values both on and off the pitch. Many would have walked away long before Rafa did, but just like Bobby he was captivated by the club, its support and its place in the city life. He could always see a great future, but he just needed some help from those who controlled the purse strings. Bobby always said that with what was on offer, Newcastle United should have been one of Europe's leading sides, not just one of England's.

Sadly, Bobby only survived for a few weeks after Shearer himself departed the club. I was fortunate to visit him on 9 June 2009, just a short time before he passed away, making a stopover at his castle like home in County Durham with an old friend, Paul Clark, who knew Bobby from his Caribbean visits. It was a lovely summer's day and we arrived with a wicker picnic hamper and shared one last lunch with Sir Bobby and, to my delight, Lady Elsie in the comfy confines of her kitchen.

It was a meeting, of course, laced with nostalgia and the talk was not about Newcastle's inauspicious end to the season but about the joy he had from his life in football and his love for his wife and their three sons. We looked at framed photographs of the greats he had rubbed shoulders with and who were, more often than not, more in awe of him than he of them. He knew then that he was on borrowed time after his five debilitating bouts of cancer, but he never stopped fighting.

The cancer had returned in 2006 when doctors discovered the disease in his right lung after he'd been X-rayed following a skiing accident, and later that year he collapsed with a brain tumour, and the resultant surgery had left him partially paralysed. Within a year the cancer had returned to his lungs and this time the doctors had to break the news that it was terminal.

What energy he had left was channelled into his cancer charity, the Bobby Robson Foundation, and how thrilled he was at the way the public of Newcastle, and elsewhere, had responded to his plea to set up a cancer research centre for the disease in Newcastle. The initial aim was to raise half a million pounds but that was passed in the wink of an eye. Ordinary people had responded to one of their own.

He told me that he had two important promises to fulfil to help keep the flow of money to his revered doctors and surgeons in the North East, so that they could carry on their good work and extend their research on the disease.

The first of his final appointments was for his celebrity golf tournament held in the Algarve in Portugal, where he had long enjoyed improving his game. That final visit looked increasingly unlikely for a time as his doctors advised against it, and even he doubted the wisdom after his previous visit had given him so much pain and discomfort. He told me then he didn't think he would be able to go again but, knowing his time was draining away he defied everyone including, it must be said, Lady Elsie. He made the final visit to Portugal just before he died, having to pay out a £2,000 insurance cover. In characteristic fashion from someone who had long since learned the value of a pound, he stayed on for an extra few days to make full use of his insurance policy.

Literally as I was penning this paragraph on his golf tournament I learned from David Pleat that the popular resort was planning to name one of their major thoroughfares in the name of the great man.

However, by far and away the most important date in his diary was a last visit to St. James' Park. He had helped to arrange a charity game in his name between ex-England and German international players, and the response from those players, as well as celebrities and fans, was as you would have expected, with nigh on 35,000 tickets sold and players arriving from all over the globe.

The game was played on Sunday 26 July and I have no doubt that it took a supreme effort from this arch competitor to ensure that he was around to put his blessing on what was, after all, the Sir Bobby Robson Trophy match, featuring players from that semi-final at Italia '90 between the two great rivals, with the England team featuring six of the original starters.

John Barnes, Peter Beardsley, Dave Beasant, Paul Gascoigne, Steve Hodge, David Platt, Peter Shilton, Trevor Steven, Des Walker and Mark Wright were all members of that England squad who went out to the Germans that night and all turned up gladly on this special day, while three German players who ended up with winners medals at the end of that tournament also made the same trip to St James' Park: Guido Buchwald, Lothar Matthäus – captain on both occasions – and Hans Pflügler.

Terry Butcher was present despite having operations on both worn out knees and he did the commentary, though unfortunately Stuart Pearce was away with his England's Under-23s side. He had been desperate to make the occasion, but his old boss soon put him in his place and told him what was more important.

Notable absentees were Newcastle owner Mike Ashley and club managing director Derek Llambias, displaying the disquiet within the portals of this great club, with all its attendant problems.

No one missed them, for the only person who really counted on that summer day was the man himself, Sir Bobby Robson. He was confined to a wheelchair, with his once lustrous, now thinning white hair, covered by a hat, but was his usual defiant self, going away from the carefully choreographed pre-match plan so that he could shake hands with each and every one of the two teams. He was then presented with a Lifetime Achievement Award, the Emerald UEFA Order of Merit, as Tenors Unlimited performed a rendition of 'Nessun Dorma', the theme music for the BBC's coverage of the 1990 World Cup that struck such a chord with the television watching public and was forever twinned with the England manager of the time.

The irony, of course, was that those of us in Italy, including the manager, were unaware of the impact the music of the Three Tenors had back home, even though we were fortunate to hear their historic pre-tournament concert at the Baths of Caracalia on 7 July 1990 in Rome. Luciano Pavarotti, José Carreras and Plácido Domingo, charmed Bobby Robson and a global audience and the recording of the concert, the first of a number they performed, produced the bestselling classical album of all time.

Never one to forget or ignore the Toon Army, he insisted on being pushed right around the ground to a chorus of 'Walking in a Robson Wonderland', a terrace song adopted when he managed Newcastle. He took his place in the directors' box to a standing and very emotional ovation.

It was fitting that not only did England come back from a two-goal deficit to win 3-2, but that Alan Shearer should score the winning goal from the penalty spot ten minutes from time, leaving Peter Beardsley and Paul Gascoigne to lift the Bobby Robson Trophy.

Bobby was taken home to his 'little castle' in the Durham country-side and, on the morning of 31 July 2009, quietly passed away at the age of 76 and into the ranks of the beautiful game's legends. Few were more loved than this man, who spent a lifetime overcoming overwhelming odds to emerge an adored icon.

He would have been embarrassed at the genuine outpouring of grief which followed his death but eased by the knowledge that, according to his son Andrew, he was at peace and without pain. Between the announcement of his passing on the Friday and the following Monday morning, over £1.6 million – mainly in small donations – flowed into the Sir Bobby Robson Foundation.

The grief was felt nationwide and throughout the football family at home and abroad. Flags at football stadiums were lowered to half mast, as were the flags at both Newcastle and Ipswich's civic centres. At St. James' Park hundreds of fans from the main North East clubs, Newcastle, Sunderland and Middlesbrough, gathered to pay their respects with shirts, flowers and scarves at the Leazes End.

The Newcastle squad held a minute's silence when the news broke while they were at their training ground and then again at St. James' Park, with Steve Harper, Stephen Taylor and Shola Ameobi – three players who had all played under him during his time as manager – laying a wreath in the centre circle where he had been just five days earlier, accepting the tribute of fans and players alike. There was a similar story at Portman Road, where Ipswich manager Roy Keane laid a wreath at Sir Bobby's statue outside the stadium.

The memorial service in Durham Cathedral was also a national event, broadcast live on Sky News and on giant screens at both St. James' Park and in Ipswich's town centre, while 1,000 invited guests packed the beautiful 1093 Romanesque and Norman built edifice. Rarely could so many well-known personalities have packed its pews and so many ordinary folk lined the rain-soaked road leading up to the Cathedral. The journey from his birthplace in Sacriston to the Cathedral doors was a mere ten minutes away. Though he had spent a lifetime travelling the globe, this was home.

Football folk came from all over to attend, with names like Terry Venables, Paul Gascoigne, Bryan Robson and Harry Redknapp joining celebrities such as singer Katherine Jenkins and local showbiz pair Anthony McPartlin and Declan Donnelly. Former England managers Fabio Capello, Sven-Göran Eriksson and Steve McClaren were present to pay their respects, as were representatives from his clubs around Europe.

So too was Sir Alex Ferguson, a man who was more than just a fellow manager. The pair were close friends, and I am sure Sir Alex wouldn't mind me revealing that it was Bobby who persuaded him not to retire when the subject first arose and the two shared a great deal in the enclosed lives of celebrity football managers.

I was, for some health reason, on sticks that day and in a bit of pain, but Fergie knew just what to do. He took the mickey out of me and I immediately felt better for the attention from the weathered old Scot, while others were avoiding contact.

'He never forgot that. He always knew his roots,' said Ferguson, addressing Robson's loyalty to the North East.

'Fantastic that he would do that, not to change his entire life. It's a great talent that, not to change, to be the same person.

'He fought his disease with incredible courage and resilience and showed you what his background was.'

Ferguson was also effusive of Robson's passion for the game: 'It has been one of the privileges of my life to have met him and to have been enthused by him. He influenced me then and he's always influenced me.

'I think I speak for almost everyone here in football terms, he influenced me but what made him so special was he influenced people who didn't know him. They admired his courage, his dignity, his enthusiasm. He never lost that enthusiasm. That enthusiasm, you can't explain it, special people have got it.'

Gary Lineker, who has brushed up nicely as an eloquent television presenter since his England days, echoed Ferguson's sentiment.

He told of how when he was first selected for England against Wales in Wrexham, he rolled up to the hotel a nervous young man to find the manager waiting for his arrival in the reception area to greet him and tell him how good he thought he was.

'Two World Cup campaigns and a European Championship over a six-year period was easily enough time for me to realise that Sir Bobby was indeed not just a brilliant leader of men, who brought the absolute best out of his players, but also without question the single most enthusiastic and passionate man I've ever met in football,' said the former forward.

'From Ronaldo to Robson, from Gascoigne to Given, from Shilton to Shearer and from Wark to Waddle, the gaffer was hugely supportive and fiercely loyal. In return the players loved him and respected him. He was everything that was good about the game. He was a lion of a man – no, make that Three Lions.'

There were few closer over a long period than José Mourinho, who was fulsome about the man he first met in Lisbon when acting as his interpreter at Sporting: 'It is difficult to except such a person is no longer with us – but he is immortal because he leaves in everybody who knows him a mark of his personality – great coach but, more than that, a great person.

'I hadn't spoken to him in the last two months because it was hard for me. It was me who found it hard because I didn't want to think that he was dying, that wasn't the image that I wanted to keep with me forever of Bobby Robson, that wasn't the voice I wanted to hear.

'I wanted to and I will keep with me always the Bobby Robson of every day, a person who had extraordinary passion for life and football, with an extraordinary enthusiasm.

'Bobby Robson is one of those people who will never die, not so much for what he did in his career, for one victory more or less, but for what he knew to give to those who, like me, were lucky to know him and walk by his side.'

His great, great friend Tom Wilson – roommate in digs, teammate at Fulham and his best man at his wedding – who knew him as well as anyone, added: 'He had innate charm and a ready smile, but was modest all his life, even somewhat shy – though he had largely overcome that in later life.

'He was always passionate about football, had a deep love of his family and great loyalty to his old friends, with a touching and justifiable pride in his beautiful home up here in his beloved North East. Friends have said to me you should never finish a eulogy with a cliché, such as we will never see his like again. But we won't.'

Those who followed England were well reminded of Gazza's tears when the thought struck him that if England reached the final he would have no part to play in it after his second yellow card of the tournament. His tears this time were again for himself and the deep grief he felt at the loss of a man he described as a father to him, saying: 'I can't describe how much he meant to me. I loved him.'

The tears flowed again when Tenors Unlimited brought the service to an end with their rendition of 'Nessun Dorma', but this time it was not only Gazza, but most of us who knew and loved Sir Bobby Robson.

Then, at the beginning of the 2009/10 season, all English football league matches held a one minute's applause in his memory, while the Football League gave both Newcastle and Ipswich special dispensation to wear unique commemorative kits when they met in a Championship match on 26 September 2009 at Portman Road in aid of the Sir Bobby Robson Foundation. At half-time, the North Stand at Portman

Road was renamed the Sir Bobby Robson Stand. In December 2009 he was posthumously awarded the FIFA Fair Play Award for the 'gentlemanly' qualities he showed throughout his career, as a player and a coach.

The first anniversary of his death on 31 July 2010 was marked by a pre-season friendly between two of his former clubs Newcastle United and PSV Eindhoven at St. James' Park, with his former captain and right-hand man Stan Valckx presenting his own PSV shirt to Newcastle to be displayed at the ground.

Even Newcastle City Council became involved in evoking his memory when they unveiled plans for a memorial garden in Gallowgate Street, close to the stadium. The garden covers 400 square metres and was finished in the spring of 2011, featuring a tiered seating area and sculptures reflecting aspects of his life.

Bobby's love of cricket was to have been honoured by him replacing former England captain and selector Mike Gatting as president of the Lord's Taveners charity and cricket club in 2007, but sadly ill health halted him taking up a position he would have cherished. After his death the Taveners held a dinner in his honour as 'The Best President We Never Had.'

In March 2011, Lady Elsie and Alan Shearer unveiled a Class 91 electric locomotive named after him at Newcastle station, while in December of the same year, the Port of Tyne Authority named its new workboat the Sir Bobby Robson.

The bronze statue of Sir Bobby, which stands three metres tall on the southwest corner of St James' Park, was created by local sculptor Tom Maley, who also had works with two other legendary local footballers, Wor Jackie Milburn and Wilf Mannion, and was unveiled at the ground on 6 May 2012 before a Premier League game against the eventual champions Manchester City. Sadly, City did not play the game that day and won 2-0 on their way to the title.

And so it continued, when on 16 July 2013, marking the 150th anniversary celebrations of the Football Association, the 10 August was designated as the Sir Bobby Robson National Football Day, a day to celebrate the national game.

Then, in 2018, a feature length British film, Sir *Bobby Robson: More Than A Manager*, was released to critical acclaim. The journey was complete.

SIR BOBBY ROBSON TIMELINE

1933: Born in Sacriston on 18 February, the fourth of Lillian and Philip Robson's five sons.

1950: Gives up work as a colliery electricians' apprentice to sign for Fulham, making 152 appearances and scoring 69 goals.

1956: Signs for West Bromwich Albion for a club record £25,000 and is made club captain.

1957: Makes his debut for England in November, scoring twice in a 4-0 win over France.

1958: Plays in the World Cup Finals in Sweden.

1962: International career ends after an injury before the World Cup in Chile. He made 20 appearances for his country.

1962: Returns to Fulham after a dispute with West Brom over his salary.

1968 Becomes Fulham manager after a short, disastrous spell as player-manager of the Vancouver Royals. Takes over at Craven Cottage in January but fails to steer his side clear of relegation and is sacked.

1969: Becomes Ipswich Town boss.

1973: Leads Ipswich to fourth place in the old First Division.

1978 Wins the FA Cup with Ipswich, his first major trophy as manager, beating hot favourites Arsenal 1-0 in the final.

1981: Wins the UEFA Cup with a 5-4 aggregate victory over AZ Alkmaar in his penultimate season at Portman Road.

1982: Appointed as England manager in July, beating favourite Brian Clough to the appointment.

1986: Reaches the quarter-finals of the World Cup, only to be knocked out by Diego Maradona's 'Hand of God' goal and a spectacular solo effort from the same player, goals which inspired Argentina to victory.

1988: Eliminated in the group stages of Euro '88 after defeats to Republic of Ireland, Holland and the USSR.

1990: Reaches the semi-finals of the 1990 World Cup, going out on penalties to West Germany.

1990: Awarded a CBE by the Queen for his services to English football.

1990: Leaves England to take over at PSV Eindhoven, his first job European job outside of the United Kingdom.

1991: Won first of back-to-back Eredivisie tiles with PSV.

1992: Diagnosed with cancer of the bowel, taking three months out of the game to receive treatment.

1992: After failing to make an impression in the European Cup, contract not renewed by PSV.

1992: Becomes manager of Sporting Lisbon, with José Mourinho as his interpreter.

1993: Finishes third in his first season in Portugal, after finding the club in 'a terrible state'.

1993: Fired in December due to an early UEFA Cup exit.

1994: Appointed manager of FC Porto in January.

1995: Diagnosed with a malignant melanoma. To remove it, surgeons take out his teeth and go through the roof of his mouth, fitting a partially prosthetic jaw.

1995: Despite his cancer trauma, Robson takes Porto to the league and cup double, beating his old team, Sporting, in the final of the Portuguese cup.

1996: After lifting his second league title in a row with Porto, Robson is appointed coach of FC Barcelona. Wins the Spanish Cup, Spanish Super Cup and the European Cup Winners' Cup in his only year as coach, after signing Ronaldo from his old club, PSV.

1997: Voted European Manager of the Year for the 1996/97 season.

1997: Travels the world setting up a scouting network for Barcelona after Louis van Gaal takes over as manager.

1998: Returns to PSV for one season, keeping the seat warm for his former captain Eric Gerets. In the 1998/99 campaign PSV finish third and qualify for the Champions League.

1999: Fulfils a lifetime ambition as he becomes Newcastle manager in September, with Newcastle bottom of the Premier League.

2000: Guides Newcastle away from the threat of relegation and steers them to eleventh place.

2002: Receives a knighthood from the Queen for his services to football.

2003: Finishes third with Newcastle in the 2002/03 season, and they also progress to the second stage of the Champions League.

2003: Becomes part of the England Hall of Fame due to his managerial successes.

2004: Dismissed in August by Newcastle chairman Freddy Shepherd after just four games of the new season.

2005: Becomes an honorary freeman of the city of Newcastle in March, declaring the award as 'the proudest moment' of his life.

2006: Accepts a post as assistant to new Ireland coach Steve Staunton, but steps down after Ireland fail to qualify for Euro 2008.

2006: In May he has an operation to remove a tumour from his lungs after doctors' spot a shadow following a skiing accident.

2006: Robson undergoes another operation to remove a brain tumour after collapsing at Portman Road. The operation was a success but left him with partial paralysis on the left side.

2007: Routine check-up reveals he has cancer for the fifth time, this time to the lungs. Doctors reveal it is terminal.

2007: Awarded the Lifetime Achievement Award at the BBC's Sports Personality of the Year ceremony.

2008: Launches the Sir Bobby Robson Foundation, a charitable organisation to help cancer prevention in the North East.

2009 Awarded UEFA's *Ordre de Mérite*, the Emerald award for Lifetime Achievement in Football.

2009: Dies peacefully aged 76 on 31 July at home in Durham with his family.

FACT FILE
Player
1950-56: Fulham 152 appearances (69 goals)
1956-62: West Brom 239 (56)
1962-67: Fulham 192 (9)
1957-1962: England 20 (4)

Manager
1968: Fulham
1969-82: Ipswich Town
1982-90: England

1990-92: PSV Eindhoven
1992-94: Sporting Lisbon
1994-96: FC Porto
1996-97: FC Barcelona
1998-99: PSV Eindhoven
1999-2004: Newcastle United

HONOURS

Ipswich Town
FA Cup: 1977/78
Texaco Cup: 1972/73
UEFA Cup: 1980/81

PSV Eindhoven
Eredivisie: 1990/91, 1991/92
Johan Cruyff Shield: 1998

Porto
Primeira Liga: 1994/95, 1995/96
Taça de Portugal: 1993/94
Supertaça Cândido de Oliveira: 1993, 1994

Barcelona
Copa del Rey: 1996/97
Supercopa de España: 1996
European Cup Winners' Cup: 1996/97

ACKNOWLEDGEMENTS

I AM NOT, I GUESS, THE FAVOURITE PERSON FOR THE
Robson family as I took so much of Sir Bobby's time away from them.
But I have nothing but respect for wife Lady Elsie and the three boys,
Andrew, Paul and Mark, who helped shape and form him into the
super person he was inside and outside football.

Football, however, was his life, his be all and end all and if I went
through the names of the people within the game who I met through
Bobby and who offered their help and friendship, from famous managers like Sir Alex Ferguson and Jose Mourinho through the coaches
and backroom boys and girls at his various clubs around the world,
it would fill another book. There are far too many to mention and it
would be invidious to select just one or two.

Managing England and working for the Football Association was his joy, made even better by the likes of his long term friends Don Howe and Dave Sexton. Like Bobby, two of the nicest blokes you could ever wish to meet and always such a help to me.

I would also like to acknowledge the publishers of my previous books with the legend, all of which helped in the compilation of this latest tome through my notes and recorded interviews allied to personal memories.

Mutual friends David Pleat and Mike Shapow were always there for Bobby and remain there for me now. True friends.

Then there is the man behind this latest effort, publisher James Corbett, a source of inspiration and an easy man to work with, a lot easier than some I could mention!

Finally to my old mate Gary Lineker, like me a fan of the great man, and the perfect choice to write the foreword, not for the first time for one of my books. Who better after the part he played in Italia 90. Thanks as ever.

Finally to Sir Bobby Robson fans and followers around the globe. To you, all I can say is, what bloody good taste you have.

Bob Harris, May 2020

INDEX

www.decoubertin.co.uk